Full Moon over Noah's Ark

"Antonson shows an indefatigable and intrepid spirit in this swift account of his ascent of Mount Ararat and his travels through some of the most dangerous territory in the Middle East, including Iraq and Iran . . . A book filled with the enthusiasm of discovery, the delight in accomplishment, and the relief of return."

—*Kirkus Reviews*

"Antonson's absorbing narrative combines the mystery and intrigue that shrouds the historical Ark story with all the color and drama of this swirling, turbulent region. Packed with historical facts and anecdotes, enhanced by excellent maps and photos, this is a fascinating travel adventure to one of the most ancient areas of the world . . . A reader's feast that is not to be missed."

—John A Cherrington, author of *Walking to Camelot*

"Sharing a treasure trove of compelling and beautifully observed stories, Antonson draws us along on a remarkable, yet deeply personal odyssey through near-mythic lands. This is one of those rare books, full of emotion and insight, the work of a true traveler."

—Dina Bennett, author of *Peking to Paris*

"An educational, amusing and inspiring tale told by an experienced and worldly traveler . . . a fabulous weaving of adventure and research."

—Shannon Stowell, President, Adventure Travel Trade Association

"An adventure story for adults."

—from the foreword by Garry Marchant, author of *The Peace Correspondent*

"Rick Antonson radiates the curiosity and vigor of an explorer and an intrepid traveler. His writing captures the essence of the spirit of adventure and trust in fellow human beings."

—Mandip Singh Soin, mountaineer and explorer,
founder, Ibex Expeditions India

To Timbuktu for a Haircut

"Anyone planning a trip to Africa should put Antonson's book on their packing list right after malaria tablets."

—*National Post*

"*To Timbuktu for a Haircut* is a great read—a little bit of Bill Bryson, a little bit of Michael Palin, and quite a lot of Bob Hope on the road to Timbuktu."

—Professor Geoffrey Lipman, former assistant secretary-general of the United Nations World Tourism Organization

Route 66 Still Kicks

"One of the best books of the bunch."

—2012 round up of holiday travel books by *The New York Times*

"A must for Route 66 aficionados."

—*Chicago Tribune*

"The most impressive account of a road trip I have ever read."

—Paul Taylor, publisher of *Route 66 Magazine*

"A middle-age Woodstock in motion, an encounter with an America that isn't as lost as we think . . . in the end Antonson proves that Route 66 indeed still kicks—as does America."

—Keith Bellows, editor in chief, *National Geographic Traveler*

FULL MOON
over
NOAH'S ARK

FULL MOON

over

NOAH'S ARK

*An Odyssey to Mount Ararat
and Beyond*

RICK ANTONSON

Skyhorse Publishing

Skyhorse Publishing books may be purchased in bulk at special discounts for sales promotion, corporate gifts, fund-raising, or educational purposes. Special editions can also be created to specifications. For details, contact the Special Sales Department, Skyhorse Publishing, 307 West 36th Street, 11th Floor, New York, NY 10018 or info@skyhorsepublishing.com.

Skyhorse® and Skyhorse Publishing® are registered trademarks of Skyhorse Publishing, Inc. ®, a Delaware corporation.

Visit our website at www.skyhorsepublishing.com.

10 9 8 7 6 5 4 3 2 1

Library of Congress Cataloging-in-Publication Data is available on file.

Print ISBN: 978-1-51070-0565-4
Ebook ISBN: 978-1-51070-0567-8

Cover design by Jane Sheppard

Printed in the United States of America

A donation from the royalties earned by this book will be directed to assist refugees in Iraq.

To Mom and Dad, Elsie and Al Antonson, upon whose knees I first heard the tale of Noah's Ark, and from whom I got the nudge to question everything, to explore.

To editor John Eerkes-Medrano (1950–2015), a collaborator and elder to many and a friend to all.

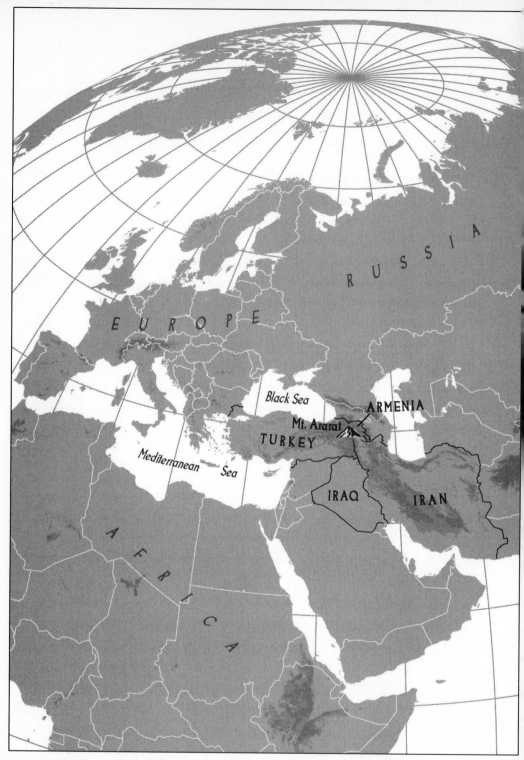

A portion of the always fascinating and complicated Middle East/ Western Asia, showing the countries of the author's travels.

CONTENTS

The "Ark Tablet" (front view, shown at actual size: 4.5 inches [11.5 cm] tall by 2.3 inches [6 cm] wide). The story within these 600 cuneiform characters revamped our thinking about The Flood. They were pressed into clay in Babylon around 1900–1700 BCE, predating the written Hebrew texts and the Biblical Noah's Ark story by over 1,000 years, and describe a round ark. (Associated Press/Sang Tan)

FOREWORD

Some travel books are the result of intense academic research of previous publications, of early journals, official reports, historic texts and autobiographies. Others are first-person narratives of private journeys.

In *Full Moon Over Noah's Ark: An Odyssey to Mount Ararat and Beyond*, Rick Antonson skillfully combines both methods to provide a compelling book—part travel, part adventure, with history, social commentary, and contemporary politics integrated into the entertaining text.

In two of his previous books, *To Timbuktu for a Haircut* and *Route 66 Still Kicks*, Antonson perfected the technique, the academic and the experiential, providing significant background information, but always keeping the story rolling along.

Once more he has managed this with his immensely enjoyable *Full Moon*.

If there is any downside to this life-long travel writer, it is a slight twinge of envy. Why didn't I think of that?

Getting there is half the fun, as the old Cunard Line's slogan goes, but reading about Antonson's odyssey offers a great deal of pleasure.

The author is as much at home scrambling over an ice field in crampons as he is sipping sherry in an exclusive London club, wearing his "post-explorer," early 1900s retro tweed suit.

Antonson is not a typical traveler. He does not seek out the obvious destinations, no matter how attractive, romantic, or popular. He admits he has never been to Rome.

Yet he has been to North Korea, Mali, and Belarus, among many other remote destinations. Few contemporary travelers, not even professional travel writers, can make that claim.

In this work, he takes us from Canada to Turkey, Iraq, Iran, and Armenia, and finally to the British Museum in London.

Antonson was inspired to make this challenging journey as a young boy when he read *The Forbidden Mountain* by French explorer Fernand Navarra. The thought of climbing Mount Ararat lay buried in his mind for decades, until he came across the book again—and he was off on his quest.

This is partly an adventure story for adults. I know many people (myself included) who have climbed Japan's Mount Fuji, Africa's Mount Kilimanjaro, and Malaysian Borneo's Mount Kinabalu. Antonson is the only one I know who has tackled this much more difficult ascent, which requires some mountaineering expertise. "The climb was for the 'professional or amateur mountaineer,'" he notes early on, with some trepidation.

Despite the title, this wide-ranging book takes us far beyond the mountain, and the mythical ark. The author says he would "venture among the oft-contested boundaries where Greater Ararat and Lesser Ararat sit, traveling to seldom-visited places."

When he gets there, Antonson notes, "I had landed at the crossroads of history, ambition, conflict, and enterprise."

On the way, Antonson has many adventures, on the mountain itself, and misadventures—getting his eardrums torched in a Turkish barbershop, dancing with Persian ladies on a train to Tehran, missing ferries, inadvertently crossing borders with cigarette smugglers, and much more.

FOREWORD

This story, both scholarly and adventurous, is more than just a tale of a fabled ark on an awe-inspiring mountain. It deals with the whole exotic, tumultuous, and increasingly dangerous region. Here he delves into the complex politics and turmoil of the area, including Kurdistan and Armenia.

"Despite Halim's warnings, I felt the desire to be where I should not go," he says. Fortunately, he takes us with him.

—Garry Marchant
Author, *The Peace Correspondent*

MOUNT ARARAT.

A nineteenth-century line drawing of Mount Ararat and Lesser Ararat (on the left), taking a south easterly view, from Armenia. From the 1893 book *The Land of Ararat; or, Up the Roof of the World* by Alexander MacDonald. Courtesy of the British Library.

Before 2000 BCE, traditional oral histories told of a long-ago Great Flood, a boat, and survivors. With the invention of writing, the story began to be recorded in various forms.

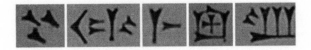

On Mount Nimush the ship ran aground,
The mountain held it and would not release it.
—Epic of Gilgamesh, Tablet XI, written down c. 2000 BCE

וַתָּנַח הַתֵּבָה בַּחֹדֶשׁ הַשְּׁבִיעִי בְּשִׁבְעָה־עָשָׂר יוֹם לַחֹדֶשׁ עַל הָרֵי אֲרָרָט

And the ark rested in the seventh month, on the seventeenth day of the month, upon the mountains of Ararat.
—Torah, Bible, Book of Genesis 8:4, written down c. 538 BCE

وَغِيضَ ٱلْمَاءُ وَقُضِيَ ٱلْأَمْرُ وَٱسْتَوَتْ عَلَى ٱلْجُودِيِّ

And the water abated, and the matter was ended.
The Ark rested on Mount Judi.
—Qur'an 11:44, written down c. 630 CE

We need not try to make history out of legend, but we ought to assume that beneath much that is artificial or incredible there lurks something of fact.

—Charles Leonard Woolley, *The Royal Cemetery: Excavations at Ur*,
1922 CE

Overlooking Khor Virap monastery (from the fifth century, CE) and citadel, near Yerevan, Armenia. The chapel, originally built in 642 CE and rebuilt in 1662, is still in use today. The view is toward the north face of Mount Ararat, a volcano whose last activity, in 1840, coincided with an earthquake and landslide. Photo © Andrew S. Behesnilian.

ONE

THE FORBIDDEN MOUNTAIN

*"Here was a mountain with character and variety to match its size!
The challenge of the peak filled us with quick, suffocating eagerness."*
—Oliver S. Crosby, *The American Alpine Journal*, 1954

When I was twelve years old, an extraordinary book sat on the shelf in the bedroom I shared with my older brother. Next to volumes of the *Junior Classics*, *The Jungle Book*, and *Scouting for Boys* was a lesser-known title: *The Forbidden Mountain*. Written by French explorer Fernand Navarra, it recounted Navarra's 1952 climb to the top of Mount Ararat in eastern Turkey, in hopes of finding Noah's Ark. The book's flyleaf claimed that "the Mountain of the Flood is the highest mountain in the world *from base to summit.*"

Paging through this book for the first time one evening as I lay on the lower bunk-bed, I was struck by the near inaccessibility of a place where border guards were grumpy and entry was frequently refused. And yet, what a fascinating place *Forbidden Mountain* depicted: the interior had captivating pictures of nomad camps on the mountain, and women wearing festive costumes while standing in pastures. But what enticed me most were photographs of the jagged terrain on the steep and permanently ice-capped Mount Ararat.

No legend was needed to lend this mountain an air of mystique in my eyes. Although the twelve-year-old me knew little about this region of the world halfway around the globe, it was tantalizing to read that the "forbidden" massif towered alongside countries with names like Turkey and Iran, and that the USSR (Union of Soviet Socialist Republics, as the Russian bear was then known) had its arms around Armenian lands adjacent to the mountain. And the book referenced "the Kurdish," a people I was to learn later held a national wish but lacked their own actual country. Lying there excited by this faraway mystery and wanting to know more, I said to my brother—who was on the top bunk listening through earphones to his Rocket-Radio (an early transistor radio of the day)—"One day, I'm going to climb Mount Ararat." He was tuned in to the Top-Ten songs countdown on the radio and did not reply. I was not discouraged.

As best I can track it, that book (along with a boyhood of hiking and wilderness camping) inspired an adulthood of roaming oft-forgotten places living in the shadows of past glories, and my own personal pursuit of a life less ordinary. I've traveled to Timbuktu, taken a meandering road trip down dilapidated sections of the old historical Route 66, and slept in a yurt in Mongolia. As a husband and father, I've benefitted from a rare individual freedom adjacent to family obligations. You're more likely to find me in North Korea than in Rome (where I've never been), or in Belarus rather than Belgium (where I've also never been). However, in spite of the many places I've journeyed, over the years the imperative of climbing Ararat drifted away from me.

That changed nearly two decades later, as I was clearing boxes of memorabilia and stumbled across my old copy of *Forbidden Mountain*; the red and brown cover art of a jeep in the foreground of a mountain was beguiling. It brought a flood of memories, and my childhood dream. I reminded myself: "I'm going to climb Mount Ararat." But things were not as simple as they might have appeared when I was young. Despite the immediacy of the temptation, I had a job that kept my life at a hectic pace, built on the precept that I must work until the work is done. Much as I wanted to go, I told myself, "I just can't," and continued to squander time on what now, having retired from the business world to become a full-time author, seems like a comparatively irrelevant task—career building. The trade-off was that it brought business travel, often in the field of tourism and frequently with side jaunts.

So *The Forbidden Mountain* moved homes with me for another twenty years, earning a respected if ignored place amid a growing spread of bookshelves. I came to an age when I couldn't wait to go to bed at night because I so much liked waking up in the morning. Still, something was unfulfilled.

One evening, as I was looking at a map of the Middle East, Mount Ararat drew my eyes to the cartography's upper right hand corner. I remember thinking, *What might come from a journey in eastern Turkey?* Reminded of my adolescent commitment-to-self, I sought out *The Forbidden Mountain* from its place on the shelf. Rereading portions of it revived that longing I feel after hearing the whistle of a train—that tomorrow might find me somewhere completely different. I set my intentions, now much more determined, to see the mountain that had motivated a life of travels and have a walkabout on its slopes. Afterward I might

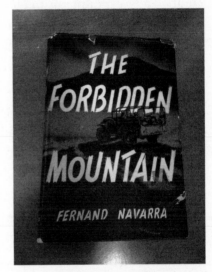

The author's tattered copy of Fernand Navarra's 1956 book, *The Forbidden Mountain.*

venture among the oft-contested boundaries where Greater Ararat and Lesser Ararat sit, searching out the sources of both the truths and the fictions I had come to believe.

I began to do some research. I found a guidebook to Turkey, which mentioned that trekking on Ararat offered an experienced hiker the opportunity to summit the mountain. *Summit!* Stand on top of! A fit outdoorsperson, the handbook assured—armed with determination, practicing proper field craft, and led by a knowledgeable local guide—could ascend the peak.

In less time than it took to finish my glass of wine, I'd made up my mind; I would join an expedition attempt to summit Mount Ararat the coming August. *Summit.* I clutched the word in my hand, opening and closing my fist around it as one would a stress ball.

Naturally, the uncertainty of success when it came to summiting a 16,854-foot (5,137-meter) Mountain (with a capital "M") tempered my talk as departure neared. I'd trekked in the foothills of the Annapurna range in Nepal, hiked the Bandiagara Escarpment in West Africa, and climbed a few mountains in North America, all under 8,000 feet (2,500 meters), but I would in no way consider myself a seasoned climber. Just looking at pictures of Ararat was enough to convince me that I would have to take preparations and training for my climb very seriously (and even then, nothing was guaranteed). "I'm going to hike on Mount Ararat," was all I would tell family and friends about the pending journey. Travels in far-off lands frequently bring unexpected difficulties, and I have a tendency to drift into awkward situations. When in the company of mischievous people, I'm easily led. I'm also no stranger to aborted intentions; I've taken plenty of trips where the feasibility of half-baked schemes quickly turned sour once I found myself on the ground. So, I did not mention my private plans to reach the mountaintop of Ararat. Such a statement seemed presumptuous to announce until the feat was accomplished, if it was.

I found several reputable mountain guiding services in eastern Turkey and, as is common elsewhere, just as many "chancers." I homed in on one in particular, mainly because I liked the website's confidence—when traveling to remote locations often overlooked by popular tourist guides, there sometimes isn't much more information to go on. When this outfit's guides did attempt to reach Ararat's summit, their website implied, they were often successful. I also noticed that Zafer, a leader with the company, lived not far from Mount Ararat, in the Turkish city of Van.

Zafer's email response to my inquiry confirmed that it could take two or more months to secure a Turkish permit to trek on Mount Ararat. He could help arrange that. "I will have your permit here when you arrive in Van." It was spring when we first connected and he had not yet firmed up a climb date for mid-August. "I would try for us to begin the mountain on a Friday morning, if the weather is good. There can be thunder. Rain. Maybe rainbow."

He set out his intentions. "First climb day leaves Doğubeyazit in morning. Truck will bounce you to between six and seven thousand-foot levels on mountain. There, physical trek begins." The day would be a long climb, with packhorses carrying our provisions. "Aim for Base Camp around 10,000 feet. Next day climb to Camp II near 14,000 foot level." The summit would be approached from there. "If people have difficulty with altitude, we use day to acclimatize." From Camp II, one night—weather, conditioning, and health on our side—we would attempt the summit, leaving camp at 1:30 a.m., headlamps fastened. "Starting in the middle of the night, we climb mile and a half toward sunrise," Zafer noted, saying we'd take at least five hours to make a gain of three thousand feet in altitude. August showed nighttime temperatures at this altitude to range from −4°F to 23°F (−20°C to −5°C). "The final thirteen hundred feet is over snow and ice and will be difficult. The summit wind can be forty to fifty miles an hour at the top."

Zafer advised: "Bring an ice axe to Ararat. You won't likely need it for the climb. But if you fall you may need one to keep from sliding off the mountain."

Zafer's colleague at the time, Dr. Amy Beam, an American educator living in Barbados, owned a company that provided logistics for climbers heading to Ararat, and she took over my booking. "Yes, I've been to Ararat," she informed me via email, "while working with another guide."

She confirmed that August was the most favorable month to attempt an ascent, but stressed that at any time of the year, unpredictable weather made a big difference between successful and unsuccessful summits. "You may not reach the peak. Extra days are needed if the weather turns. Go only if you have patience."

"How many other trekkers will be coming along?" I asked, hoping to hear "None."

"We like small groups, perhaps six or eight at the most," she replied. "There will be other groups from other nations on the mountain at the same time. Usually they are also small in size. Some trek only partway. It is a lot of work to summit." She said that the plan was to depart Doğubeyazit and be on the mountain the morning of Friday, August 23rd.

That worked for me. It allowed time to apply for the permit as well as make air and train arrangements. A few days later, I was looking around online and realized that the August full moon would occur one day after we completed our ascent. The possibility of seeing a full moon over Mount Ararat took hold of me. I phoned Amy.

"Amy, can you imagine summiting Mount Ararat at night under a full moon?"

"That," she said, "would be awesome."

"Can we shift our mountain arrival date?" I begged. "Or spend a day trekking around?"

It sounded like she smiled over the phone. "Yes, we will delay your on-mountain start-off," she said. "This will be a special journey. There is only one other person going right now anyway—a Welshman from China, or maybe a Chinese man from Wales, Ian. You'll be in good company. He's a climber; he's been to the summit of Mount Kenya and to Everest Base Camp, and both are over seventeen thousand feet. I'll email him the change."

She added what I wanted to hear: "If the weather holds, you'll leave Camp II at 1:30 a.m.—it will be dark! But you'll climb Ararat under the light of a full moon."

Before the trek could be confirmed, it needed a few more participants to make the trip financially worth the company's while. Amy sent a note one day saying she'd had an inquiry from a "New York fellow. Architect. Sounds fit for the climb. Name's Goran." I received another email four days later, saying that "Charles of Ireland" had signed on. Then, to complete the team, "Patricia from Canada and the Dutchman Nicholas. They are coming together. He lives in Toronto."

Our expedition was beginning to gel.

We are told that those who live at the foot of great mountains are often the last to climb them. Mount Ararat reinforces that idea. Although ancient oral and written accounts tell of Noah's Ark landing there after navigating a flood-ravaged Earth, there is no record of anyone ever having climbed to the top of this dormant volcano before the nineteenth century. For millennia, the people living in Ararat's shadow believed the mountain was un-climbable. Its year-round cap of snow and glaciers protected it, dissuading even those who gazed upon its heights on a daily basis.

For many centuries, locals believed that their gods would not let the mountain be climbed to the top—ever. (This didn't mean that the mountain was never climbed, however; historical documents do reveal that its slopes[1] were walked on.) Religious edicts from local Christian or Islamic authorities forbade approaching the sacred summit until the mid-1800s. Eventually, attitudes changed. Aided by monks and Kurdish shepherds, locals began welcoming visitors seeking to unravel the mystery of Ararat.

The early explorers of Ararat were therefore of two kinds: mountaineers, anxious for an exceptional climbing experience, and searchers, hoping to find evidence of Noah's Ark.

There are many notable ascents of Mount Ararat. In 1829, the German scientist Friedrich Parrot led the earliest expedition to successfully ascend the craggy slopes. Russian Colonel Iosif Khodzko reached the top in 1850, as did an 1856 British expedition led by Major Robert Stuart.

---

1 In 275 BCE, the Babylonian historian Berossos wrote of the Ark that it was "still seen in Kurdish Mountains of Armenia," bolstering his claim by noting, "The people scrape off the bitumen (from the ark), carry it away and make use of it."

The Americans arrived with Oliver Crosby in 1951, but were forced to abandon their mission 150 feet (50 meters) from the summit as daylight faded and Crosby determined, "We had to get ourselves off of three thousand feet of snow and ice before dark."

The Frenchman Fernand Navarra's summiting of Ararat in the middle of the last century became ensnared in controversy around a relic he claimed to be from Noah's Ark. Treks in search of the Ark in the 1970s and 1980s were also made by US astronaut James Irwin, whose trips attracted the thrust and parry of both religious traditionalists and non-believers, scientists siding with each. In contemporary claims, a Sino–Turkish team announced in 2010 that carbon dating of a wooden construction they found on the mountain confirmed it to be a part of the biblical Ark. That team's ongoing pronouncements have been greeted by insatiable public curiosity.

Along with these more well-known ascents, numerous documentarians, geologists, searchers dubbed as "*Ark*eaologists," and self-promoting fabricators have all taken to Ararat's slopes, with varying degrees of success. Whether they are credible explorers or fact-distorting charlatans, their stories are primers for those either seduced by Mount Ararat's fabled history or seeking an exhilarating experience in mountaineering.

If Ararat itself has gained celebrity status over the decades, it's undoubtedly because of its connection to Noah, whose story of surviving a global flood plays a significant role in Abrahamic religions. Here's one translation of Hebrew text, from the Book of Genesis:

> *God paid mind to Noah and all living-things, all the animals that were with him in the Ark, and God brought a rushing-wind across the earth, so that the waters abated.*
>
> *The well-springs of Ocean and the sluices of the heavens were dammed up, and the torrent from the heavens was held back.*

The waters returned from upon the earth, continually advancing and returning, and the waters diminished at the end of a hundred and fifty days.

And the Ark came to rest in the seventh New-Moon, on the seventeenth day after the New-Moon, upon the mountains of Ararat.

The *"mountains of Ararat"* refers to a range, located in the eastern end of Anatolia, not just the region's namesake edifice. Yet Mount Ararat gets all the attention as the presumed landing site of Noah's Ark, gaining prominence through mistranslation and interpretations. It has been nicknamed in a dozen different ways, including the Mountain of the Deluge or the Mountain of the Flood, the Mother Mountain, or even the Mother of Mountains. In Turkey, "The Holy Mountain" has been known

Looking northward to the Ararat mountains' southern approach, the access route taken by the author's expedition. Mount Ararat at 16,854 feet (5,137 m) and Lesser Ararat at 12,782 feet (3,896 m) are the heights referenced herein (although also widely used are 16,945 feet [5,165 m] and 12,877 feet [3,925 m], respectively). All measurements include the thick, snow-covered ice cap.

as *Ağrı Dağı*, translated as "Steep Mountain," or as "Mountain of Pain," as well as *Agri Dagh*, "Mountain of the Ark." In Arabic it is Nûh's Mountain, or *Kuh-e-Nûh*, while in Armenian it is *Masis*. Kurdish designates it the Fiery Mountain: Çiyayê Agirî.

"Ararat" itself is a version of *Urartu*, the earlier kingdom name. Both labels can be taken to mean Armenia. But no matter what name is used; in the minds of many, Ararat itself remains The Forbidden Mountain.

It quickly became clear during my research and preparations for this trip that traveling beyond Ararat would be complicated, as many of the border crossings were less than friendly and safe passage was far from guaranteed. From the peak of Mount Ararat, one can look on Armenia and Iran as well as the mountain's current host country, Turkey. Visiting all three countries was necessary to my understanding the region. Iraq was not that far south either, and that intrigued me as well.

But traveling between these four countries is not just a matter of geographical logistics; it also involves staying on the right side of strained political relationships. Borders can lead to uneasy encounters. Prominent among these tensions is that between Turkey and Armenia. Their unresolved disputes can be traced back to what many now refer to as the Armenian Genocide, beginning during World War I, when over one million Armenians were killed or displaced in a single year. Sources vary, but many agree the Turkish government exterminated approximately 1.5 million Armenians in a seven-year period, starting as the Ottoman Empire fought through the war in cohesion with Germany, and continuing as the new Turkey evolved in the aftermath of World War I.

The Turkish-Armenians were Christian, while Turkey's larger population was Muslim; established religious tolerance became strained. Along with that, land ownership and power over minorities were central to the conflict, as were neighboring geopolitical factors. Parts of the Armenian homeland were within the sphere of the Ottoman Empire. The Ottomans cast the Armenians as potential traitors who would side with the Allies to achieve independence after the war was won. In part, that was based on worry about Russian geopolitical expansion, including the courting of restless Armenians to fight the Ottomans against whom they'd protested throughout the latter half of the nineteenth century into the early years of the twentieth century.

Fearmongering about organized retaliation by the Armenians was used to justify preemptive action by the Ottoman forces. Now known as Red Sunday, in early 1915 numerous Armenian community leaders, academics, and elders were arrested and deported, many eventually killed, to prevent the remaining population from organizing to defend themselves. Many young Armenian males were sentenced to forced labor. Others were deported on mass marches into the Syrian Desert, in which the elderly and women and children were doomed to slow death by dehydration.

The abduction of Armenians was wide-ranging, systematic, and often brutal. Ottoman officials expropriated abandoned properties. The directing minds behind this effort had significant resources; the world's press was manipulated, reportage was stifled, and swift retribution was meted out to any journalist who stepped out of line. The decimation of the Armenian population in Ottoman territory was thorough and devastating.

Henry Morgenthau, the American ambassador to Turkey in 1915, characterized the Ottoman government's actions as a "campaign of race extermination."[2] In his memoir, *Ambassador Morgenthau's Story*, Morgenthau wrote, "When the Turkish authorities gave the orders for these deportations, they were merely giving the death warrant to a whole race;

---

2 The word *genocide* did not exist until World War II. Learning of the Holocaust, Winston Churchill said, "We are in the presence of a crime without a name." In August 1939, Adolph Hitler had asked, "Who, after all, speaks today of the annihilation of the Armenians?" Polish lawyer Raphael Lemkin's research into the 1915 Armenian Massacre was about to give that crime a name. He conflated a Greek term for "birth" with one for "massacre," creating the term "genocide." The 1948 Convention on the Prevention and Punishment of the Crime of Genocide entrenched its use for "acts committed with intent to destroy, in whole or in part, a national, ethnical, racial or religious group."

they understood this well, and in their conversations with me, they made no particular attempt to conceal the fact."

In 1918, the war's victorious combatants were anxious for spoils as they negotiated settlement. Boundaries from prewar times were often ignored, and nations were reconfigured after the conflict. One Axis government petitioning for peace did so while flexing its muscles strategically: Germany's ally, Turkey.

In the vast lands where Armenia and Turkey had lived amalgamated at the start of World War I, citizenry and ethnicities overlapped. In the cosmopolitan Ottoman Empire, identities blurred; absent single nationalistic terms, one might, for instance, be an Armenian Kurdish Jew. While disputes had erupted both in towns and in the countryside, peaceful coexistence was also prevalent.

At the war's end, during the reassessment of borders, many provinces initially proposed as part of the country Armenia were reconfigured amid jurisdictional decisions that ignored history in favor of expediency. Among the geographical assets removed from within the new Armenian borders was Mount Ararat. That Mount Ararat, a long-time symbol in Armenian culture, is no longer a part of Armenia looms heavily over strained relationships between the two countries, even today.

This was the cultural and political climate I would be entering.

For three months, my pre-trip regimen was one of securing climbing gear, undertaking a fitness routine, and conducting as much research as I could about the area where I hoped to travel. I began packing for a long journey in various climates, getting good medical advice, and procuring supplies for safety and comfort. My immediate focus needed to remain on being physically fit, well organized, and mentally prepared to ascend what William Bueler's *Mountains of the World* calls "one of the most impressive volcanoes on earth."

I read of climbers who arrived ill equipped for the rigors of Ararat, and was determined not to be among them. The mountain demanded to be taken seriously, and its weather could be harsh, surprising, and unforgiving. Ararat was said to "defend itself" against climbers. You had to be able to adapt, or you could suffer defeat. A repeated inference I read from various websites was that the climb was for the "professional or amateur mountaineer," with the emphasis on "mountaineer."

Acquiring the necessary equipment was straightforward, including getting the ice axe Zafer advised. I had a large backpack that could accommodate the various clothing as well as camping paraphernalia, and it could be pulled on wheels through railway stations and airports or saddled onto a horse when on Ararat. Added was a lightweight daypack with cushioned air vents where it would rest against my back. New hiking boots were purchased, which I broke in by wearing every other day on steep hill climbs and forest walks. Alternate days were for a three-mile run. An hour twice a week at a fitness center concentrated on building core strength and encouraged a mindset that sorted out a better diet and dashed alcohol intake. I woke each day and checked the computer screen's photograph of Mount Ararat, its summit looking both intimidating and achievable. As the trip neared I could see myself standing in that photo, at the top.

When my travel plan came up in conversation, I heard the same question over and over again: "Are you going to look for Noah's Ark?" Maybe this shouldn't have surprised me, but it did. At first I responded with a smile and shouldered the question away with a "You can't be serious" shrug, but frequently this was met with a sincere follow up query: "So, really, are you going to look for it?"

The well-known story of the Ark is a fundamental piece of early history for Judaism, Christianity, and Islam. What I knew about it was either from childhood or from Navarra's book, which had been written over fifty years before, and is clearly an exaggerator's account. As I delved into the backstory for Noah's Ark and the flood, I was surprised by much of what I found. I could not at the time imagine the context this would provide for my entire journey.

First among my surprises: the commonly referenced account of Noah's Ark was not the first flood story of its kind. Interestingly, the oldest written testimony yet discovered regarding a "Great Flood" recounts similar details: the sparing of a chosen man and his family, the collection of a necessary range of animals and food stocks, and a deluge that destroys all other living things. This first report comes from the Sumerians, a society with shared settlements around Mesopotamia. The Sumerian account, finally written down around 2000 BCE[3], tells an age-old oral history about a massive flood that would have occurred prior (perhaps well prior) to 2700 BCE. The ancient Sumerian account offers an intriguing provenance to Noah's subsequent appearance in Hebrew written records as chronicled in the Book of Genesis, which many scholars say was redacted and prepared between 538 and 332 BCE. Additionally, a corresponding story of Nûh, his boat, a flood, and the saving of his associates, appears in the Qur'an (Koran) as transcribed between 609 and 632 CE. Might it be possible that all of these stories share an origin?

In addition to their common narrative themes, all of these Great Deluge narratives from this part of the world share a similar ending— the massive vessel that survives the flood, and whose occupants allow life to continue on land after the flood waters recede, eventually comes to rest on a mountain.

Where do these flood stories[4] and their various iterations come from? It is not just the religious connotations that are confounding. There is a

---

3   BCE = Before Common Era, CE = Common Era, secular terms replacing the Gregorian Calendar's BC (Before Christ) and AD (Anno Domini—In the Year of Our Lord).

4   At the core of any flood hypothesis is the provocative question: Did a devastating, wide-ranging deluge ever occur in or near the Mesopotamia region, inundating the land and killing inhabitants? Geological surveys say that isolated and localized floods occurred—although such studies clarify the comparatively

(Footnote continued on next page)

14

huge mystery here, one not easily explainable, and it is tethered to the mountain I had decided to climb. So of course that sent me in search of more massive flood suppositions from the region.

Although enchanted by mythology and legends, I would not classify myself as religious. I would not consider many of the stories and history as told in the Torah, the Bible, or the Qur'an to be taken literally. But notwithstanding the circumstantial improbabilities, the story of Noah and his ark has captivated many people for a very long time, and the more I looked into the history of Ararat and the search for the Ark, the more intrigued I became.

For centuries, many who climbed on Mount Ararat were driven by the search for Noah's Ark, in the firm belief it lay waiting for discovery. Consider the dictates of seventeenth-century Irish bishop Rev. James Ussher. Ussher's 1650 book, *Annals of the Old Testament, Deduced from the First Origins of the World*, determined beyond a reasonable doubt (for the bishop's era, and followers, done mathematically and relatively rationally based on the "begat" generations provided) that Earth was created on a Sunday—October 22, to be precise—in 4004 BCE. Ussher's work-up, which in many ways simply reinforced common belief at the time, was that the Earth was no more than 6,000 years old. From that weekend in 4004 BCE to the Great Flood of Noah was, by Ussher's reckoning, 1,656 years, and further, Noah's craft came to land on Ararat on Wednesday, May 5, 2348 BCE. When the term "dinosaur" was first coined in the early 1840s, a popular theological explanation emerged

---

modest scope and scale of such events. On the matter of an enormous flood, if one did occur, speculation regarding its cause abounds. Included is a chaos of swelling waters brought about by another planet passing too near the earth with a gravitational pull influencing giant tides; a massive asteroid or comet with an Earth-altering slam that tilted the water flow of oceans; or the intense ice age melt inducing the Tigris and Euphrates rivers to back up, overflow, and overwhelm both the landscape and collective memory.

of "age built in"[5] to the earth at creation, furthering fanciful notions of dinosaurs and man coexisting, as though "God put bones in stones" to be found later by geologists.

Over the centuries, there have been numerous announcements claiming to have found remnants of the Ark on Mount Ararat. Archbishop and encyclopedist Isidore of Seville, back in the seventh century, stated, "Even to this day wood remains of it are to be seen." The fact is that none of the numerous sightings or findings have ever been substantiated through the scientific method or corroborated by independent specialists. This, however, has done nothing to stifle a common acceptance that these stories or relics are actual proof of the Ark's existence.

I emailed Amy, asking whether she knew an Ararat mountain guide named Paraşut whom I'd seen mentioned over the course of my research. "A website claims that he's found an ice cave with frozen wood and other relics," I explained. "That interests me. Do you think I might ramble around a couple of days with him?" The chance to climb in an ice cave, even if the alleged wooden contents were dubious, was alluring.

Her reply was circumspect. "He is . . . yes, a guide. The finding of beams . . . hmmm . . . in a cave at thirteen thousand feet on Mount Ararat . . . however . . . " She stopped there. "I will give you an email address. You can ask for his phone number."

The doubter's direction of my mind was reinforced, although having myself replaced rotting wood beams in a log cabin, I relished the

---

5 Contemporary Orthodox creationist beliefs are a product of the Protestant Reformation, emerging long after the advent of Christianity. Journalist Douglas Todd, writing in October 2014, quotes that "43 percent of Americans (16 percent of Britons, 24 percent of Canadians, by way of further examples) accept the creationist teaching that the earth is less than 10,000 years old, which means they reject the established scientific view the universe began roughly 13.82 billion years ago." He references that "roughly 60 percent of the world's Muslims are creationists." Pope Francis, at the Pontifical Academy of Sciences in 2014, cautioned, "When we read about Creation in Genesis, we run the risk of imagining God was a magician, with a magic wand able to do everything."

possibility of confronting that skepticism directly, to stand in an ice cave and ask the guide about the doubtful durability of a wet, wooden structure surviving thousands of years.

Riffling through research books in search of the earlier flood accounts, oral and written, I found more details about one that had an immediate impact on my travel plans. It related the aforementioned

Cuneiform is an alphabet with hundreds of consonants, a syllabic system with shapes such as this tablet's information on apportioning a supply of beer. Without punctuation, paragraph breaks, or sentence structure as we know it, words simply follow one another. This form of writing was invented in Sumeria between 3300 and 3100 BCE. It is thought to have begun with symbols impressed on clay, denoting livestock and numbers for inventory. It was never a spoken language. Photo © The Trustees of the British Museum. All rights reserved.

older-than-Noah story recounted in the Mesopotamian narrative from what is colloquially known as the "Flood Tablet": the eleventh chapter from the *Epic of Gilgamesh*. Onto this tablet the story was pressed into clay with cuneiform characters around 2000 BCE. This powerful account continued to be retold over time and engraved onto newly shaped clay tablets, keeping the story alive in written form, though with inevitable variations during the copying process. A vast collection of these tablets was stored in the ancient Library of Nineveh, near present-day Mosul in Iraq. But with Nineveh's destruction by the Medes in 612 BCE, and the later arrival of Babylonians, thousands of intact tablets were shattered into tens of thousands of fragments and buried for centuries. Some were carted off.

The Flood Tablet is thought to have been among the archaeological treasures discovered by an Englishman, Austen Henry Layard, in the 1840s during excavations alongside the man who has been called "the first archaeologist born and raised in the Middle East," Hormuzd Rassam. Layard and Rassam appear to have transferred that tablet, not knowing what exactly it was or the secret it held, along with other holdings from the ancient library's ruins, to the British Museum in London. And given the difficulty of deciphering cuneiform, it was over twenty-five years before anyone was able to find out what it said.

It was in 1872 that Assyriologist George Smith—"an intellectual pick-lock," according to his friend Archibald Sayce—deciphered that particular tablet at the museum, with striking results. The story he discovered shocked the British public: an ark and flood narrative that antedated the timelines of the Biblical account. Smith was cast as both scholarly and blasphemous for revealing a story about a world-drowning outburst, a survivor's boatload of migrating family and animals, all with a protagonist *not* named Noah, but, instead, Utnapishtim.

Could I possibly visit Nineveh where this work of literature had been rediscovered, and learn more about the tablet? I contacted the British

The "Flood Tablet" (shown front view, at full size: 5.5 inches tall [15 cm] by 5 inches [13 cm] wide). The language used in ancient Assyria and Babylonia was Akkadian, and from it comes the *Epic of Gilgamesh*. The epic's eleventh chapter was discovered during explorations in the mid-1800s undertaken in the ruins of the library of King Ashurbanipal, at Nineveh. Later deciphered at the British Museum, the tablet tells a flood story similar to that of Noah's Ark in the Hebrew texts and Christian Bible, although written earlier and with a hero named Utnapishtim.

Museum, seeking information on their current archeological activities in the vicinity. A brusque reply: "We'd not be permitted to travel there, even under military protection. Obviously, neither should you put yourself in harm's way." The ruins of the Library of Nineveh are across the Tigris River from the city of Mosul, a no-go area in northern Iraq at the time and, sadly, in the foreseeable future.

While strife with ISIS in Syria and Iraq had not begun at the time of my travels, I nevertheless found an instructive caution about travel in Iraq on the Lonely Planet website, from a writer who had crossed into Iraq from Turkey. After getting an entry visa at the border near Dohuk and staying one night, he advised: "Just don't tell your relatives in advance if you're going to try this." Never one to be dissuaded so easily, I connived to get into Iraq and updated the roughed-out itinerary of my trip to Mount Ararat, hoping that after my climb on the mountain I could make my way to Turkey's border with Iraq. And possibly cross over.

Seeing an image of the Flood Tablet with its, to me, indecipherable cuneiform characters piqued my inquisitiveness. I'd recently encountered instant eye fatigue brought on by pondering those angled symbols at length. The characters form one of the first writing structures, initiated between 3300 and 3100 BCE. These slanted and tilted figures developed as the Sumerian script. Earlier in this same year I was a delegate to an international summit concerning sport and tourism and peace. There were forty people from around the world attending the daylong gathering and I was seated next to an Olympian from Iran. He had with him a replica of the Cyrus Cylinder, an ancient clay piece about nine inches (23 centimeters) long and four inches (10 centimeters) wide. He spoke about it with pride and vision, calling it "the first declaration of human rights," and told the assembly it was written in 539 BCE.

British Museum archeologists discovered the Cyrus Cylinder in 1879, during excavations in what was then the Ottoman Empire. Cyrus appears in the Hebrew Bible. He was a Zoroastrian, a member of the first monotheistic religion, established in Iran 3,500 years ago by the Prophet Zoroaster. Under Cyrus the Great, Persia became "tolerant of all faiths."

The Olympian told us that Cyrus was the founder of Persia, today's Iran, and that his "message of religious tolerance is needed today." After the assembly adjourned the Olympian gifted the cylinder to me. I have it in my home. It is a quality reproduction and the complexity of its marks is mesmerizing. I planned to visit the British Museum and see the original of the Cyrus Cylinder—and the original of the Flood Tablet—on my return route from Mount Ararat.

A few days before leaving for Turkey, I visited my neighborhood pharmacy for medicine that would prevent mountain sickness. To avoid altitude illness, I had been told to begin taking it four days before my ascent, and to continue throughout the entire climb, finishing two days after I was off the mountain.

"Where are you going with this?" the pharmacist asked me as he rang up my purchase.

"Mount Ararat. Eastern Turkey," I replied, embarrassingly pleased that he'd asked.

What would turn out to be a pivotal part of my journey wasn't the pharmacist's response, but the reply I heard behind me, from another customer in line: "You'll love it there. It's beautiful."

I turned around to see a young man smiling. "Really, beautiful."

"You've been there?" I said. "To Ararat?"

"Not there," he said, "but close. My family is from northern Iraq. Kurdistan. Erbil. My dad was home to visit his brothers and parents four months ago."

"Iraq?" I felt the universe colluding in my favor. "Mind if I wait while you finish up here and ask you some questions?"

He nodded happily and introduced himself. "My name is Andam."

I paid for my prescription and waited near the door while he made his purchase. A wash of ideas came over me. We left the store and walked away together as I peppered him with questions.

"Erbil is safe," he said. "It's where my uncles, my cousins live. My grandfather too."

"Do you think I could get there?" I asked.

"You should phone my dad," he offered.

The next morning I phoned Taha, Andam's father, who was expecting my call. He suggested that, since I was about to leave town, we meet that evening. So it was that, two nights before departing, I met Taha Jabbar at his favorite coffee shop. He was quick to smile and captivated me with his storytelling, accented with a raspy voice.

"I think you'll be safe," he said. "Stay near Erbil. Do not go to Mosul. Do not go to Kirkuk. Not secure. Erbil, now, is calm. It is Kurdish land. We are Kurds," he informed me, seeming unsure that I understood his meaning.

The broader concept of Kurdistan as its own country flows together with the mountain I was going to climb. Mount Ararat, formally on the border of Turkey and Armenia, is also considered the northern corner of a country that does not technically exist, of what some believe should be a united Kurdistan nation, expanding out of Iraq to include a touch of Syria's northeast, a long, narrow portion of Iran, and an eastern section of Turkey. Together, many Kurds hope, this area would one day form a sovereign nation, along the lines once envisioned by the Western forces. The United States and others encouraged the concept of an autonomous Kurdistan after World War I, through the Treaty of Sèvres in 1920. But Turkey outmaneuvered those plans at the time (abetted by certain Western powers[6]), and the result has been ongoing insurgent fighting, where contested realms are seldom safe.

---

6   With high concentrations of Kurds in the newly established (1920) mandates (French over Syria and British over Iraq), the French and British also declined to cede territory to the Kurds. In 1923 the earlier pledge to grant Kurds their own country was annulled by the Treaty of Lausanne, wherein the modern borders

(Footnote continued on next page)

Because of this, I wondered about Erbil and the long-fought-over northern reaches of Iraq actually being secure. Taha cautioned me not to travel overland through disputed territory in far eastern Turkey, which I had looked into as a possible bus route from Van to Iraq. But he did not discourage me from finding another way to get to Iraq. After half an hour, our cups were empty and our conversation finished. We shook hands and said our farewells. I left with a safe fear.

As I walked home through dark streets, I knew late night would bring the closing sliver of the old moon. Soon I would begin two weeks of travel toward my hoped-for sight of a full moon over Mount Ararat.

I reached our townhouse and fifteen minutes later the phone rang.

"Rick, it's Taha. I've been thinking. I trust you. I will give you a letter to introduce you to my family in Iraq. On the envelope I will write a note with their phone numbers. If you can get into Iraq, show the envelope to a taxi driver. He will phone them. They will meet you and help you find a hotel. Probably they will take you for a meal."

I didn't know what to say.

"Rick? Is it OK?"

"Taha," I said, overwhelmed by his generosity, "I've no idea if I can get into Iraq. If I do, I'll owe the experience to you."

We met again the following morning, the day before I was to leave, at a schoolyard up the street from where I live. Taha's wife, Gulie, was with him; Sean, my youngest son, was with me. It occurred to me that this might be a final character check by each of us.

"Can you read this?" Taha asked, handing me an envelope with a beautiful—and, to me, incomprehensible—style of cursive Arabic or Persian script, written from right to left, flowing as smooth as a horizon of sand dunes. I thought it was written in Farsi at first, which it was not; I am habitually travel-hampered by early assumptions, and this would prove to be another mistake. Among all the conjoined words, the only

---

of Turkey, Syria, Iraq, Greece, Bulgaria, Egypt, and Sudan were established and a Kurdistan was not. Oil was "officially" discovered in the Kurdish portions of the new Iraq later in 1923.

Taha Jabbar at 19 years old in 1974 as a member of the Peshmerga, who battle to this day for Kurdish independence. After fighting Saddam Hussein's forces decades ago, he led his pregnant wife Gulie and their two year-old Andam (whom I'd meet as an adult at a pharmacy 72 hours before my departure) on a rugged mountain escape. They hid by day and climbed by night, ever so dangerously traveling from Iraq to Iran and eventually out of the Middle East to a new life in North America. This photograph conveys a man characterized by resilience, tenacity, and confidence and, I believe, integrity. His was a handshake I needed to trust.

characters I recognized were those I took to be the promised telephone numbers. The envelope was sealed.

Taha and Gulie laughed at something she'd said in a language I'd never heard before. He explained: "In Kurdish, she says that you will love our family. You must go."

"I do hope to see Iraq," I said, reaching for his hand.

"Say hello to my father for me," he said, a tear cornering his eye.

"And to my sister," said Gulie.

"And to my brother," Taha added. "He's married to her sister."

A chance encounter in a pharmacy had opened up a new path for me. Would I ever be able to make it into Iraq to take them up on their offer?

From my own family, the reactions to my desire to visit Iraq were slightly less enthusiastic.

Sean: "Get me a message if you're going in. I'll alert an embassy. Just in case."

My oldest son, Brent, thinking one of us would find a way to decipher the information within the envelope, or at the least that those words should be kept on record, emailed: "I've steamed open the envelope, pdf'd the two-page letter and pdf'd the note on the front. I emailed you and Sean and Janice copies." His actions eased my guilty conscience. Under the reasonable guise of safety and despite my inclination to trust this person I had only recently met, I wanted to know what the letter said. But Taha's private message to his family remained respectfully hidden behind a script unreadable to us.

My wife, Janice: "You're what? You're going into Iraq carrying a letter that you can't read, from someone you don't know, and showing it to border guards and taxi drivers?"

Me: "Right, OK. I won't show it to the border guards. And before I get there I'll find someone to tell me what it says."

Though I was leaving behind my cell phone, I promised to try and send an email to the three of them if I thought I might get into Iraq. It would say, "I'm going south." At least, that was the plan.

So it was that I embarked on an odyssey to Mount Ararat with hopes for travels not only in Turkey but possibly Iraq and Iran or Armenia, as well as to return home via the British Museum in London. After decades of procrastination, I was finally on my way to the forbidden mountain, and beyond.

Map of the region highlighted on this book's introductory Locator Map
(page viii), featuring Turkey, Iraq, Iran, and Armenia, the countries
within which the author traveled. This map also forms the reference
base of subsequent maps in the book.

TWO

THE BOSPORUS STRAIT

"The question is, was there a mother of all floods? . . . We went in there [the Black Sea] to look for the flood . . . Not just a slow moving, advancing rise of sea level, but a really big flood that then stayed . . . The land that went under stayed under."
—Robert Ballard, Institute for Exploration, Sea Research Foundation, Inc.

I arrived late in the night, and Istanbul's Atatürk Airport greeted me with a cavernous yawn. The airport hotel was more welcoming: the front desk clerk poured his newly registered guest a glass of wine before locking up the liquor cabinet for the night.

I awoke in the morning impatient; there was much to do. Janice would arrive that evening on a flight from London. Together we'd take a connecting flight to Cappadocia to have a few vacation days before I left alone by train, eastbound toward Mount Ararat, and she returned to work in England. I skipped breakfast and ran out of the hotel to hail a taxi. Hopping in the back seat, I started instructing the driver in rapid English. He calmed me: "Slowly. Slowly. Please."

"I need to buy a train ticket," I explained—more slowly, I hoped.

"Sirkeci Istasyonu," he said. "Train station," he interpreted.

As we walked up the station stairs, the striking oriental rotunda, contrasting with the long reach of the functional terminal's expanse, gave the impression that competing architects had had a hand in designing it, which I later found out was not the case. The imposing building certainly deserved a look-round; it was, after all, until 1977, the terminus for the Orient Express. But the taxi driver hustled me into a ticket line and waited until the agent nodded in our direction.

The driver's request in Turkish was clear even to me, beginning with, "He wishes to board a train from . . ." He halted and looked at me. We'd not talked about where I was going, but his presumption hung in the air; I was a westerner and heading further into Europe.

"Cappadocia to Lake Van," I said.

I felt his immediate hesitation. Looking at the agent and at the national map, this clearly meant a train service called the Van Gölü Express, which ran from Ankara to the city of Tatvan on Lake Van, far in the east of the country, where it connected with a ferry service that carries the train's passengers across the lake to the city of Van, on the opposite shore.

Hearing the agent's reply, the driver turned to me. "Yes, he says, there is no train."

"Well, there is a train," I said. "*I know that.*"

"Yes, it is true," he revised. "There is a train. But not from here."

"I don't want it from here. I would like to board near Cappadocia, perhaps Kayseri, and have my ticket through to Van."

The taxi driver again turned to the clerk, who had gone back to looking down at the counter, wishing we had left. From their exchange I was told: "Yes, you can do that, but not buy ticket here. Must go to station different—*Haydarpaşa* railway station. I will drive us there. It is across the strait, on Asia side of Istanbul. You are heading from Europe Turkey into Asia Turkey, across bridge."

Back in the taxi, we began to talk. I told him it was my first visit to Istanbul and that I was here for only one day. He asked, "You go back to hotel later?"

"Yes, eventually."

"Then we go by ferry boat. It is a prettier way. You see Istanbul better." I soon realized he'd just booked himself a return fare. As we drove the streets, the driver encouraged me to visit the Blue Mosque, built in the early 1600s and identified by the colored tiles lining the walls of its interior, which he pointed out as we passed. He was adamant that his home city compelled a visit of at least several days, which would include tours of the Tokapi Palace and the Grand Bazaar. He steered toward the E-5 Karayolu, which would take us over the bridge across the strait and eventually to Istanbul's other major train station.

The driver's name was Toygar, and he asked about my plans for traveling in eastern Turkey. Hearing my reply that I would spend time in Van, he became a travel adviser. "They are Kurds there, too. Different. Language, food, all is different. As if other country. But it is ours, still. All Turkey."

"You should today take boat tour on Bosporus." This was something I could not do as part of my limited stay in Istanbul. Toygar knew that so he encouraged a return visit, implying that all *real* travelers visiting Turkey stuck to Istanbul, and insinuated that I was lacking as an adventurer because I was skipping it. "There is much less in east. Your stay here would be superior."

As we crossed a long bridge, Toygar shifted his tour guide persona to that of a history buff. "This is the Istanbul Strait. Very famous. Also called Bosporus Strait. One side, us now when going onto bridge, is Europe. In moment, on other side of bridge we will be in Asia. Marvel place, this." I passed over the threshold.

He asked specifically where my travels would take me. On hearing "Mount Ararat," he used instead its Turkish name. "*Agri Dagh*? No train to there."

"Yes, but a train will get me near there. To Tatvan," I replied, sensing a chance to nudge him into conversation about Agri Dagh's legend. He stepped into it, though it took a minute.

Raising an eyebrow to his rearview mirror, he asked, "Noah's flood?"

Toygar offered a narrative twist on the mountain and myth. "The great flood came through here," he said, motioning to the waters below the bridge. "Through Bosporus. You know?"

I *knew*, but not much. There is a hypothesis[7] that around 5600 BCE, the force of the waters of the Bosporus, then an inlet restrained by an isthmus of bedrock at its northern reach, burst the natural dam, cascading a flood of Mediterranean saltwater (its waters becoming the Aegean Sea and moving through the Dardanelles Strait into the Sea of Marmara) through the Bosporus Strait into the then existing body of freshwater and creating what is today's Black Sea. Such a catastrophe would have generated a flood of Biblical proportions.

Soon Toygar's taxi neared the double-spire-fronted terminal of Haydarpaşa Station[8] and we parked. Haydarpaşa has graced Istanbul's Kadiköy neighborhood since 1872, though the neoclassical building we approached came from expansion and replacement in the early 1900s. Toygar accompanied me to the terminal, not waiting to be asked for his help. A more amenable commercial agent nodded as I spoke in English while Toygar hastened to explain the ticket requirement in Turkish. I stopped speaking; neither of them were listening to me.

"Yes, you can get ticket on Van Gölü Express, but not all the way to Tatvan," said Toygar.

"But I want a ticket all the way!" I protested.

"Then no ticket."

I was close to a train journey I'd scouted online before leaving home, had read was reliable, and was much looking forward to taking, for I'd heard it covered beautiful country. I pleaded with my eyes, but it was not to be.

---

7   The hypothesis was put forward in the *New York Times* and in an article in the scientific journal *Marine Biology*: "An Abrupt Drowning of the Black Sea Shell," by William Ryan and Walter Pitman, in 1997. In the *Quaternary Science Reviews* in 2009, marine geologist Liviu Giosan proposed that the Black Sea had risen more modestly.

8   A fire heavily damaged the historic Haydarpaşa Station in 2010. While restoration was undertaken, the building's role as a busy transportation center was suspended in June of 2013 due to construction and refurbishment of the commuter rail system and the related rapid rail service between Istanbul and Ankara. Sirkeci station also closed to be adapted for the new commuter line known as Marmaray.

"Repairs," said Toygar. "The train ran yesterday, it will tomorrow. Other days, it runs too. But date you want, it is not. It has repairs that day." I watched him argue with the clerk, hoping that he was advocating for my travel preferences, although he might have been arguing local politics or ordering lunch, for all I knew. Whatever the case, the two men were not agreeing. Neither one liked the other very much.

"You will get to Tatvan," Toygar said with more confidence than I felt after hearing their terse words. "Possibly over switched transportation, to bus." I passed the money to the clerk. He handed me a train ticket.

My ordeal wasn't over. "Toygar, there is also the Trans-Asia Express. I need a ticket to take me from Van, a month from now, to Tehran."

The man behind the counter smiled for the first time. "*Trans-Asya Ekspresi*," he uttered. I think his enjoyment came from making a full interpretation of the request.

I was sure he said "*güvenilmez*." It was a word I'd concentrated on during my drives between work and home, listening to Turkish language lessons in my car. It meant "unreliable." Along with greetings and place names, *güvenilmez* was a word I had prepared myself to encounter in eastern Turkey.

Toygar confirmed. "He can sell you ticket for Iran. But the Trans-Asya Ekspresi he says is unreliable."

"I'll take the chance."

Having the two different train tickets in hand, I could sense my journey before me. I would make my way by the Van Gölü Express as far as allowed, ride the bus to Tatvan, and take a ferry from there further into eastern Turkey. Arriving in Van, I would attempt to summit Mount Ararat out of nearby Doğubeyazit, then fill an uncommitted two weeks with spur-of-the-moment travels in Kurdish lands. I would make every effort to spend time in Iraq if possible, later returning to the city of Van, and board the Trans Asya Ekspresi into Iran. This plan offered me ample unstructured time. If Iraq failed to come about, Armenia was the fallback. Eventually, I'd fly out of Tehran to London and keep an appointment with Dr. Jonathan Taylor, Assistant Keeper of Cuneiform

Collections in the British Museum's Department of the Middle East, to share some of whatever I learned and, I hoped, get some answers to my evolving questions regarding early oral and written stories about massive flooding anywhere near the Ararat region.

Toygar slowed near a trinket stand at the station's exit and put his palm behind an eye symbol on a flock of key rings. "The influence of evil eye is fact," he said. "That was stated by Muhammad. Be careful. Know when it is looking at you."

His concern for my spiritual risks passed. "I will take you on the ferry boat across the river. You should touch this history water."

I boarded as a foot passenger while Toygar waited in his taxi. Looking over the railings at the docile waters of the Bosporus Strait, I thought back to what Toygar had said about the Great Flood. I tried to imagine that the flow of water below our boat into the Black Sea was, millennia ago, blocked miles north from here by a solid wall of rock and earth forming the northern end of what we might, in hindsight, name the Bosporus inlet. On the other side of that natural dam, perhaps appropriately referenced as the Bosporus isthmus, was a landlocked freshwater lake. Circa 5600 BCE, new water from melting ice at the end of the most recent ice age would have been substantial enough to raise sea levels around the world by an astonishing 300 feet (90 meters). Those rising oceans included the Mediterranean Sea, which fed into the Bosporus inlet, whose immense box canyon offered a dead end for the increasing volume of water. The strength of this blockade would eventually have proven untenable, given the buildup of pressure.

The mounting waters would have first swelled over the Bosporus's northern barrier, the isthmus, like rising water would overflow the edge of a sink. Eventually, however, the flow's unrelenting exertion would have collapsed the land obstacle and advanced over it, causing erosion of its base, and flooded into the freshwater lake. The inundated area, in effect a lesser Black Sea, would have swelled to more than seven hundred miles (1,125 kilometers) across, with a new depth of over seven thousand feet (2,130 meters), becoming what is known today as the much

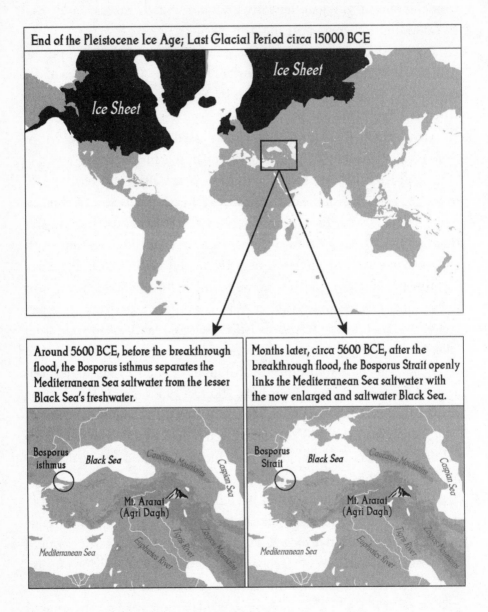

End of the Pleistocene Ice Age; Last Glacial Period circa 15000 BCE

Ice Sheet

Ice Sheet

Around 5600 BCE, before the breakthrough flood, the Bosporus isthmus separates the Mediterranean Sea saltwater from the lesser Black Sea's freshwater.

Months later, circa 5600 BCE, after the breakthrough flood, the Bosporus Strait openly links the Mediterranean Sea saltwater with the now enlarged and saltwater Black Sea.

Bosporus isthmus

Black Sea

Caucasus Mountains

Caspian Sea

Mt. Ararat (Agri Dagh)

Euphrates River

Tigris River

Zagros Mountains

Mediterranean Sea

Bosporus Strait

Black Sea

Caucasus Mountains

Caspian Sea

Mt. Ararat (Agri Dagh)

Mediterranean Sea

Euphrates River

Tigris River

Zagros Mountains

larger Black Sea. The aftermath of the surge would have left the waters of the previous Bosporus inlet flowing freely between the Mediterranean Sea and the Black Sea, having created the newly formed Bosporus Strait.

In European Istanbul late that afternoon, I visited a restaurant Toygar had recommended and ate an early dinner while overlooking the Bosporus. I wondered about his reference to the epic flood. As a Muslim, Toygar would have been familiar with the coverage of Nûh's flood, as recounted in the Qur'an:

And it moved on with them amid waves like mountains.

Or in the Hebrew texts:

then burst all the well-springs of the great Ocean
and the sluices of the heavens opened up.

Explorer/scientists and Columbia University professors William Ryan and Walter Pittman have hypothesized that the torrent over and through

(opposite page) The flooding of the Black Sea. Illustration of one flood hypothesis. Top: At the height of the most recent glaciation (15000 BCE), North America's landmass northward from today's Seattle and Vancouver was covered in ice; the sites of New York and Toronto were buried beneath half a mile of frozen water. New Guinea was land-linked to Australia, as was Japan to Asia. The Bering Sea was solid ice. A land bridge connected the British Isles to a Europe covered by an ice cap that spread over unborn cities such as Berlin and Edinburgh. As the ice sheet retreated and melted into the oceans, it is estimated that sea levels rose nearly three hundred feet by 5600 BCE. Lower left: An inlet of rising seawaters pressed against a land barrier, here called the "Bosporus isthmus," where Istanbul is located today. Lower right: Inundation by seawaters destroyed the land barrier, creating the Bosporus Strait. Floodwaters made the lesser Black Sea into the larger Black Sea.

the Bosporus isthmus would have been the equivalent volume to "two hundred times the flow of the Niagara Falls" cascading each day, for three hundred days, swelling the Black Sea (also known as the Upper Sea or Western Great Sea). In the late 1990s Ryan and Pitman furthered their research, looking for evidence that such a cataclysmic event could have occurred. It has been said that explorers need the courage to lose sight of shore if they are to see the world with new eyes. So they began oceanographic studies, eventually resulting in findings that were staggering in their implications, and far from the shore of conventional thinking. Encouraged by the Turkish government and watched over by a permitting but suspicious Russia, they drilled core samples in the Black Sea's seabed, discovering fossils of freshwater shell species—a startling indication of a onetime freshwater preserve. Further dredging and research unearthed radiocarbon-dated fossils from 7,500 to 15,500 years ago.

Then came a more astonishing find: sonar probes indicated pristine beaches at a depth of 550 feet, an anomaly that was interpreted in many different ways. An early hypothesis was that if the Black Sea had at one time been a freshwater lake, it could have been populated by settlements of croppers, herders and fishers along its shores.

Underwater archaeologist Robert Ballard, well known for discovering the wreck of the *Titanic* in 1985, explored this idea under the auspices of the National Geographic Society. His work in 1999 and 2000 found human-crafted artifacts along the sunken shoreline, and, not surprisingly, his submersible's photography found evidence of human settlement near those beaches, hundreds of feet below the surface of the Black Sea.

While the hypothesis is not irrefutable fact, here is one conclusion the evidence allows: a widespread flood occurred here thousands of years ago, one that forever changed the composition of the Black Sea's water and rapidly expanded the surrounding shoreline. At the time of the flood, not everyone in the lesser Black Sea settlements would have been able to flee the soaring rise of water around their lake. Many of those on the southern and eastern shores would have attempted an eastward getaway toward the then-unnamed mountains of Ararat and the as yet to be established Mesopotamia ("the land between two rivers"—eventually known as the Tigris and Euphrates), and would have found themselves faced with more flooding from the rising waters pushed up them from the then yet to be named Persian Gulf.

Every story of escape would have been individual, every survivor a hero. Nightmare getaways and apocalyptic scenarios would be recounted wherever refuge was found, told by the lucky ones. Stories would emerge wherever they finally rested in communities, untold numbers settling in Mesopotamia, which rose to prominence between 5000 and 3500 BCE.

The many survivor stories would be verbally anthologized, distilled to a few apocryphal, epiphany-laden examples and carrying themes of despairing gods, warning, punishment, and sole survivors. Successive generations might learn of this spectacular incident through accounts now known as "Babylonian (or Assyrian or Mesopotamian or Sumerian) flood stories," shown to exist at least by 3100 BCE. These oral testimonies would first be formally recorded when writing was invented, 2600 years after the Bosporus breakthrough and the flooding of the Black Sea.

Might the resulting ancient cuneiform texts have eventually carried versions of the same flood story forward? Might the Jewish people have become conversant with this storyline of devastation and retribution when they were in Babylonia during the Jewish Exile, beginning in 579 BCE? Could not it have morphed, starting in 537 BCE, when they were freed to return to Judah by Cyrus the Great, as Hebrew texts turned into the Jewish Torah, and then into the Christian Bible's Old Testament, and eventually, as the story of Prophet Nûh, into Islam's Qur'an?

Frankly, I'd never taken the time to ponder this storyline, and I wondered where exploring it would lead me. At the least, it would be thought provoking. William Ryan responded to news of Ballard's discoveries with a message: "It's going to rewrite the history of ancient civilizations because it shows unequivocally that the Black Sea Flood took place and that the ancient shores of the Black Sea were occupied by humans."

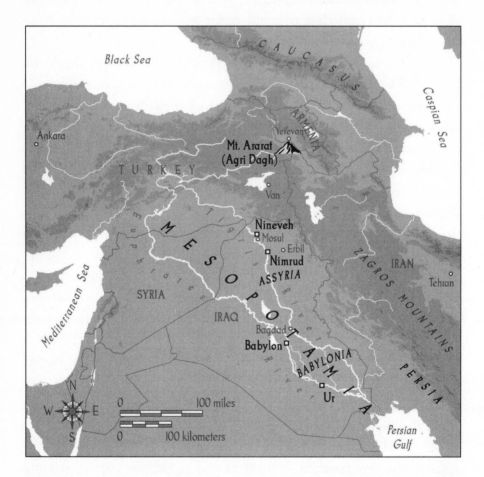

5000 to 3500 BCE: The origins of ancient Mesopotamia, Greek for "land between two rivers," the Tigris and Euphrates. Known as "the Cradle of Civilization" and "the Fertile Crescent," home to Sumerians and Babylonians, among others, it emerged as an active civilization from 3100 to circa 1000 BCE, followed by Assyrian and Persian dominance.

*   *   *

Getting up from my table at the Istanbul restaurant, I settled the tab and returned to the hotel to pick up my luggage. I was ready to go to the airport to meet my wife and travel on, very much looking forward to the days ahead with Janice in Cappadocia before I embarked on a month of solo roving. Years earlier, on a trip to Timbuktu in West Africa, I'd left her out of the trip entirely and later regretted it. Perhaps she'd found me a better person when I returned from that journey, but damage of a sort was done by my selfishness. We wanted to do this jaunt differently.

Cappadocia is dotted with dwellings carved out from huge rock formations by locals thousands of years ago, quite literally caves. Now those homes are either deserted and damaged, or refurbished and rented. Given my willingness to stay in any old place, I had found one that seemed modest but had been de-cluttered by district entrepreneurs, and I showed Janice for her approval.

As is her inclination, she did some independent research and in no time found a different cave that offered more comfortable, one might say luxe, surroundings. It was tastefully spacious and appointed with exotic curios. Its restaurant's cuisine was of a high order. We took long walks, found hiking trails, discovered new wines, and were introduced to the resident connoisseurs' slow cooking of fresh ingredients. We were taught to convey our one pecuniary food aversion in Turkish: "*Hayir soğan lüt-fen.*" No onions, please.

The letter I carried, the one written by Taha, came up over dinner one night. I promised her that if the chance to head to Iraq actually arose, I would find someone trustworthy who could read it for me before I ventured in, just to ease her mind.

For several wonderful nights, a nascent crescent moon accented our evenings. And when Janice left for home, I moved to a different cave.

THREE

WHIRLING DERVISH

"Whoever you may be, come. Even though you may be an infidel, a pagan,
or a fire-worshipper, come. Our brotherhood is not one of despair."
—Mevlâna Jelaleddin Rumî, Islamic poet, Sufi mystic

I awoke to an eerie sound coming from outside my cave, a labored wheeze followed by a commanding silence. It was like hearing God breathe.

I pulled on my shorts, stuck my feet into sandals, slipped a T-shirt over my sunburn, and left in search of the haunting sound. Across the dirt road was a hillside of abandoned caves—the color of apricot in the early morning. I climbed rocks that crumbled beneath me as I pushed hard up the hill. A trail emerged between boulders, leading to a rock-strewn staircase. I slipped through a stone arch, and the trail continued along flat rocks until I reached a plateau two hundred feet above the road.

Peering over the cliff edge, I looked out on a sky of hot air balloons. One blasted its furnace, then another. The gods breathed. Ten balloons jostled for position; those lower down provided their baskets of passengers with a view of a village, while those higher up rewarded with a vista of the horizon a hundred miles away.

Opposite me was a hilltop I'd been on the night before. When I'd moved into the Çavuşin cave, I'd met Halim, the lanky owner of the refurbished lava rock abode's six rooms. "My grandfather's father was here," he said; Halim runs the Village Cave Hotel with his wife, Serife, who had settled me in with a glass of local red wine and a bowl of Anatolian soup. Suitably primed, I had been invited by Halim to come check on his olive trees. He was intent on inspecting each and every tree, not just a sample. He assured me (and perhaps himself as well) that the recent lack of rain had not harmed his crop.

In another direction I could see a trail leading to the end of the village. Eight hundred people call Çavuşin home, though daily tour buses will artificially swell that number during the summer. The locals welcome visitors as a stimulant for their stuttering economy. But it was still too early for the buses to begin arriving, and the townsfolk were asleep. I descended a trail to the village and spent an hour strolling empty streets. Wandering among yards filled with scraps of uncompleted carpentry work and piles of split and spoiling squash, I saw a young boy perched atop a brick wall.

"*Gunaydin effendim*," he said as an offhanded good morning.

"*Merhaba*," I replied, happy to be able to communicate at all.

Cappadocia is Turkey's land of "fairy chimneys," hollowed caves and hallowed sites.

A tractor and cart passed me and stopped beside a field. Two young men filled the cart with squash, the vegetable's pale yellow color at one with the land. The driver yelled "*Merhaba!*"

I strolled up a short hill, where the trail entered a valley in which abandoned hill homes perched on the irregular mountainside, and found myself alone in a large garden of healthy-looking squash. While I was admiring the vegetation, my reverie was broken by a crackling call from the speakers of the local mosque. It was *ezan*, the call to prayer. The scratchy recorded message broadcast the call around the amphitheater of vacant caves pockmarking the rock face. In the fourth century CE, this valley alone had hummed with the activities of a thousand people. Now the muezzin's strained voice echoed among empty buildings, abandoned for more modern homes.

A widening in the town's main street made the current road broad enough to once have been a small square for inhabitants to gather. Now a dozen chairs sat there, nearly empty, and a gray-bearded man in the one occupied seat waved to greet me.

"*Salam,*" he said, "*Bonjour, salute,*" bantering to break down this visitor's defenses, if not my nationality.

"Hi," I replied. Thinking this might be too brief a reply or mean something different in his language, I added, "Hello."

He willingly shared his place in the shade, pointing to one of the empty chairs beside him beneath two trees that wound around one another in the way strings make a rope. One, a pine, seemed half dead at its base, yet its needles were a healthy green; the other had leaves that looked like limp lettuce. Removing his fez, the man continued in Turkish, adding English words for clarity at first, but after "visitor" he forgot and reverted to French. "*Chef,*" he said, pointing to a restaurant and mimicking eating; "*carte*" when gesturing toward a water cooler that looked like it would be more at home in a modern office than bolted to this village sidewalk. He motioned to me to take advantage of this and fill my water bottle. I obeyed.

Whenever he spoke, he gestured with both hands before the left one landed on the nook of his cane. The other clutched his bracelet of prayer beads.

A moped went by, driven by a young male with a pretty girl on the seat behind him. She smiled at the old man, and he grinned in return. She waved. He waved. He nodded approvingly about the girl's allure, giving a thumb-up before letting his right hand again tend his prayer beads.

"*Fraulein,*" he said, adding to this German overture a phrase in Turkish that I took to confirm he found her attractive. "*Fraulein,*" he repeated. He pointed to himself to signify he knew he was mingling languages. "*Bonjour,*" he said by way of extension.

"*Fraulein,*" I parroted back, and paused before adding, "*Bonjour.*"

As we chatted with few common words, three men emerged from around a corner and walked out into our street, more trailing behind. Soon there were twenty of them approaching us.

"Walk after prayers," my companion observed, stroking his beard. Thousands of such strokes over time had flattened the beard and shaped its downward wave into a metronome that kept time as his head swayed while talking.

As the men approached us, I considered that I might be occupying someone's seat—but whose? As each one arrived, I rose from my seat to let its presumed owner take his rightful place. Each time, my gray-bearded friend motioned me to sit back down. Eventually another elderly fellow stood beside me. The other men had taken their seats and all the chairs were occupied. This time, Graybeard stood up, propped on his cane, and offered his seat to the last arrival. He walked away without another word, as though he'd had sufficient time with me. I did not see him again.

Enjoying a mid-morning coffee with Halim on the patch of grass outside his collection of caves, I asked him about the practice of prayer. He said that the drumming that wakes the day was *Davul*, and the morning and evening prayers were short because "the world goes on." The night's last prayer was the longest. About the divine scheduling for this, Halim said, "None of us knows the time, just the caller."

Halim gave me a map and drew lines over it to show the way to the Göreme Open Air Museum, a World Heritage Site. From there I could work my way up a long road, to the Rose Valley path, which led into the hills and eventually curved back to Çavuşin. If all went well, I'd return before dark. "Once you leave that hub of tourism activity," Halim promised, "you'll not see another soul until near the end of your hike."

My water bottle was again empty by the time I'd kicked dust on a sparsely peopled path and reached the museum. This fourth-century campus has seen years of adaptive reuse, refurbishment, and, after neglect, restoration. A repository of frescoes and icons within the monasteries, its stone-cut layout was fascinating for the acreage it covered, its hint of hidden tunnels, and the above-ground erosion of carved architecture. In the gift shop I was delighted to come across an edition of the *Epic of Gilgamesh*. It seemed just the right kind of reading to be doing here. I didn't know then just how useful this Stephen Mitchell translation would become to me.

Outside the museum, on seeing the lineup waiting for transportation back to town and the crowd taking the narrow sidewalk in the same direction, I headed up the hill, looking for the quiet I'd hoped to find. Halim's hand-drawn map showed the path, which he said "was not actively used." I checked my directions with a man at the roadside.

"Yes, you are here," he said. "Yes, I have heard of that—what you call 'offshoot'? Map might be okay. Might not be. Take the first turn you think it is."

Emboldened, I was fifteen minutes along before I determined I was in the wrong place. I retraced my steps to the paved roadway and walked down another dusty road to a left fork, wondering if the right hand one was instead the offshoot I wanted. After ten minutes I was again sure I'd misread directions when two young women wearing skirts, tank tops, and runners emerged from a gully. Definitely not locals. They climbed up the dirt embankment to where I stood, looking perplexed.

"Are you lost?" one of them asked.

"Because we think we are," the other added. "If you're lost, then we're in the wrong place together."

They had walked the same ambling route as I was attempting. One of them explained, "We saw two paths and have been many minutes on this wrong one from here, but it deads-in-the-end." She added as an after-thought, "I am Lana."

"Rick," I said. We shook hands and I turned to the other woman.

Out came her reluctant hand, with a nervous hesitation as she searched for words. "I'm Suncica. Croatian." Having successfully completed her introduction in an unfamiliar language, she gave a brilliant smile.

We decided to walk back to the fork in the dirt road and go along the other path. The trail dipped in places, sometimes steeply, as it rounded the cliff. Half an hour in, the path had found its level beside a running stream, but we still hadn't come across anyone else.

"We are from university," Lana said at last. "We arrived yesterday. Tired this morning. Need this walk for energy."

"Long walk, we wish," added Suncica. Her face, out of the sunlight, gleamed, her skin akin to bronze. "At home, we are both much sports. Sitting on planes not good for people who are much sports."

"Well," I replied, "if we find our way out of here, it will only be after a long walk. You have your wish coming true."

When we were an hour in, having come onto a path with many foot-prints, something ahead of us on the trail moved, and then quickly dis-appeared. I had been bringing up the rear of our little troupe but now moved to the front. Soon a man appeared on the trail, but when he saw we were coming his way he moved on. Odd.

At the next bend a canteen had been set up, and there the strangely behaving man waited with a friend. They'd constructed an awning near the rock wall and stacked cushions under it on low-rise seats. It turned out they were merchants; their wares included canned cold drinks, grilled chicken, packets of crisps, and fresh-squeezed orange juice.

We rested there for a while, and given the attractiveness of the young women, I could not help but feel the two shopkeepers resented my presence. Suncica sprawled out as though ready for a nap. Lana initially maintained her decorum, her posture straight and legs neatly folded. Then she too fell asleep, losing her decorum.

Later we took a few side hikes, detours off the trail, talking of our families and journeys. When I mentioned Mount Ararat, Lana asked, "Will you look for Noah's Ark? That is where it is, is not?"

"In the minds of some," I replied, adding a doubtful "yes."

"If it is not true," she asked, "how come everyone knows about it?"

That evening the town was quiet. My table was the only one set on the grass outside my cave. Halim came by to ensure I'd enjoyed his wife's specialty, *kiremite tavuk*, chicken marinated in tomatoes, peppers, and garlic, cooked in a clay pot in a stone oven. It became clear that I was eating a serving from their family dinner. I omitted mention of my aversion to onions, of which there were plenty present. Pleased with my glowing review, he asked, "Have you spent time with whirling dervish? It is important part of our heritage. You will not see it eastward. It is about love for humankind."

"It's a little late," I said lamely. "I leave tomorrow."

"Tonight. I can arrange. I will drive you to the place." Agitated, he looked at his watch. "There are seven parts to the ceremony. You may miss the first, the respect for Mohammed. We should hurry."

Soon I found myself in a dark theater, shuffling toward the third and last row of seats around a circular stage. The chamber was hushed. I sensed without being told that using a flash camera would be poor form. On stage, several men in full black cloaks stood still, their robes draped over what showed as white skirts flowing to their feet. Each wore a conical headdress symbolizing his "ego's tombstone."

I'd missed the first part of the service, as Halim had anticipated. The kettledrum beating commenced the *Kudum*, the second part. A flute evoked calmness and contemplation. This was followed by greetings

46

among the men on stage, setting a distinctive role for each as they exchanged acknowledgements. These are said to portray one's secret soul meeting the actual soul. The room went into silence.

A solitary figure, the spiritual leader, was in the midst of the men. Then came the demonstration we were all waiting for—the dervishes dancing in a rapid flow of attire and attitude. First they flung off their black capes to expose white under-robes. The act is said to "cast off falsehoods" and to be a "revelation of truth." In synchrony, the dervishes clasped their arms to their torso in tribute to the "oneness of God." In turn, each kissed the hand of the spiritual leader to seek entrance to the *sema* (or *sama*), the service and the "mystic cycle to perfection."

Then the whirling began, setting off with the dancers' right arms unfurling heavenward, a gesture to channel blessings down through the heart to their left hand, pointed toward the earth. As the spinning intensified, the audience's mood became upbeat, yet still respectful, with commensurate foot shuffling in the bleachers. The music clinched the audience's attention, slowed, and abruptly rose once again. The dervishes whirled with mind and heart and feet. At intervals they rested, though they didn't make eye contact with any onlookers. All the while, the men's skirts billowed, the ends tailored with rims that circled the dancers' feet. They heeled, turned, toed, and repeated the footwork, dancing around the floor's circumference. Near the end of the frenzy, the master joined in, his moves measured at a different pace.

This meditation flows from the writings of Mevlâna Jelaleddin Rumî. The twirling has an unlikely origin: Mevlâna, which in Persian means "our guide," was a thirteenth-century mystic renowned for his poems and philosophical musings. It is said that his excitement with his own words often sparked him to whirl in public, even on the streets of his adopted town of Kona, in the Turkish Sultanate of Rum.

The ritual is a religious testament. Readings from the Qur'an are a necessary part of it, delivered in the context of a prayer. Halim had emphasized the importance of the recitation of the *Fatiha*. The end of the dancing must not be seen as the completion of the event; only the

A whirling dervish ceremony. The swirling, twirling dance is a tribute to God by believers (the dervishes) for whom this Sema ritual is part of an individual spiritual journey.

Fatiha could conclude the service—which, Halim had explained in our drive here, "should not be mistaken for a performance." This part recognizes the memory of all believers, religious martyrs, and prophets from the time before Mohammed.

When the *Fatiha* concluded, the lights were turned on. Although some visitors had unpacked their cameras, nothing of the whirling remained to be photographed. Halim had returned and met me outside. We drove away under dark skies lit only by the maturing arc of the moon. Our conversation during the drive turned to talk of the guests he'd hosted in his cave rooms over the course of a year and how they differed. He frowned on those he suspected only visited Cappadocia to cross off their accomplishment as though they were working through a prescribed grocery list of life-things to do. The triteness of their motivation bemused him, and he admonished me to remember the Seventh Advice of Mevlâna: "Either exist as you are or be as you look."

48

FOUR

THE VAN GÖLÜ EXPRESS

"For it is commonplace that every voyage is an exploration
and every journey a discovery of the true self."
—Kildare Dobbs, *Away from Home*

Encountering Mount Ararat on his way to Asia in the latter part of the thirteenth century, Marco Polo wrote: "In the heart of Greater Armenia is a very high mountain, shaped cube-like . . . It is so broad and long that it takes more than two days to go round it. On the summit the snow lies so deep all the year round that no one can ever climb it." Others before me had proved Marco Polo wrong on the latter point, and I hoped to join their ranks. But first I had to extract myself from my lodgings.

Halim had promised to drive me to Kayseri, an hour away, where I could catch the overnight train to Tatvan. While squaring up the bill for lodging, I noticed an entry for "transfer."

"What is this?" I asked.

"It is for the taxi," Halim replied. "You have the train station to get to."

"Yesterday you said you'd drive me," I reminded him. Prompted by his blank stare, I added, "All the way."

"Did I?" His eyes peeped inward as though ogling his mind to find a posted note. Then: "I did." He handled a cup of coffee, which looked very small in his large hands. He made as if to sip it, but set it down. "Let's go now."

He scrunched my oversize pack into the back seat of the compact car and sprang into a conversation about politics as we drove off. "These are better times in Turkey, but the outside world does not see. You are going where it is unsettled. You should stay here. The Kurdish part, it has terrible fighting near where you head. Think about this. Climb your mountain but don't stay longer. Return to Cappadocia."

I took it as a warning as much as an invitation. The day before, I'd had a brief look online to check the latest travel advisories. One US advisory stressed that "travelers should avoid public transportation in eastern Turkey, particularly on inter-city routes." That made me wonder about how best to handle the ten days that were open to me once I was off the mountain. Should I travel north to Armenia rather than attempt southeast Turkey and its possible access to Iraq? Despite Halim's warnings, I felt the desire to be where I should not go.

"That," said Halim, waving his hand in front of my face as we drove along, three fingers pointing as one to the south, "is Turkey's second-highest mountain. "We call it Erciyes Dağı. You will attempt to climb the highest at Ararat. This is more beautiful."

"It looks stunning," I said. "And that makes it all the more intimidating."

"Mount Erciyes is the backdrop to Kayseri, which is city I will show you. First go to train station in the town center. Check for sure we have time."

The train station was set back from the street to create a stately arrival point. Large letters designated it TCDD, the Turkish railway. We entered the station, encountering more noise than people, a testament to the level of Turkish conversation. An old woman sat on a bench, slouched over, her neck perched on the crook of a cane. I wondered if she was here to greet someone or to bid farewell, or if she was on a lonely tour of her own. At the other end of the long pew was an aged man with a sad disposition. A gentleman, I thought. Noticing his clothing, I reconsidered:

a farmer. At the base of his forehead was a unibrow, once undoubtedly dark but now a single stitch of gray. By the looks of his shoulders, his was a life spent working the land.

Halim took my ticket and led me to the ticket booth. He spoke directly to the agent on my behalf. What might otherwise have been a prolonged discussion on my own became a blunt, "Train's late."

"How late?" I asked, concern slowly rising in my throat.

"Not much. Only four hours."

"Ask him please if I'm booked all the way to Tatvan on the train."

"Yes, of course," he said. "That's where the train goes." I took his assurance; it backed up my suspicion that the Istanbul rail agent had been wrong. As a traveler I tend to seek information that reinforces what I want to believe, correct or not. According to Halim, the train on this day was running freely all the way. I asked no further questions. Why would I, having heard the answer I had wanted?

Hesitant, Halim turned to the agent. When their banter had ended, Halim faced me, saying, "Maybe they will stop train in Elazig. It seems uncertain. If you get off, be careful there. They will smile while shitting you." It was a phrase I didn't understand, yet its caution was implicit.

Turning to more positive considerations, he smiled. "You must now have the best sausage there is. In the world. It is here in Kayseri. Special. I will take you." I'd expected him to disappear after depositing me at the station. "Leave your big bag here. Check it. Then we drive. You can walk back here. Time is your friend."

Our car argued for its right of passage in traffic around a large square, circling twice so that Halim could orient me. "The market. That you do. After I leave. It is right there." His hand flashed in front of my face. "But first we find sausage." His nudging of the car into a parallel parking spot was a feat accomplished by near misses but done with finesse.

"There," he said. I followed his stare toward a storefront window displaying stubby links of meat, none of them looking obviously special to a visitor like me. Inside, a horizontal case held a sequenced exhibit of black to increasingly lighter colored tubes of foodstuff.

51

The butcher smiled at a compliment from Halim—there was humor in the air. Within a minute, four different types of cooked sausage, each shortened by previous slicing, were pulled from the display. With his knife he slivered pieces from three of them and a much thicker ration from the fourth. Halim popped two into his mouth; chomping away quickly while advising me, "Go slow. Taste."

By the time the fourth slice was in my mouth, I was wishing for bigger bites of the spicy lamb and herb-imbedded beef. I could imagine the sizzling smell of it over a grill. It was enough to make me believe this actually was the best sausage in Kayseri, maybe the best in the world.

"Goodbye, Rick," Halim said as I was buying supplies for the train trip. "You can get bread around the corner." He was getting ready to leave. "Walk. You have to walk. But first get the bread. Then walk. Take extra for the train." He then forgot to leave, instead taking me to find cheese to go with the bread I was yet to find and the two days' worth of sausage varieties I'd purchased. Soon my daypack was stuffed with provisions.

"Sweets." Halim pointed me to another storefront. "Go there." Gripping my hand in a farewell shake, he was gone. He pulled his car out of the cramped parking spot with one sweep of the steering wheel. Three fingers waved goodbye. Now I was truly on my own.

Arriving at the sweet shop, I took two bite-size chunks of what is internationally dubbed "Turkish delight" but in Kayseri is Locum, a solid-if-jellied inside of corn flour and sucrose dusted with icing sugar. While I was strolling to the market eating one of them, I heard a voice behind me: "Where are you from?" It was a youngster's come-on, a greeting as bright as it was disingenuous. Before I could answer, the boy said, "I will show you around. It is best that way. Come with me."

I demurred: "I'm fine. Thank you, no."

He would not let go of the verbal chain, ignoring my continued refusals, that I soon realized were hurting my case, as they kept him tied to the conversation. Even after I said, "I'm walking away now, so you go too," he stayed in my field of vision. Although it is rude to say, "Go away," to someone who is saying, "Welcome to my country," I sensed that the boy's offer of help would only lead me to trouble, or at the very least a lightening of my wallet. The duel became a matter of which one of us could maintain polite rudeness the longest. When the crowd movement was favorable, I darted inside the market, around two quick left bends and as many to the right. I turned into an alcove, and he was nowhere to be seen.

One problem solved. But now I was lost.

My dawdling since arriving in Kayseri had only taken an hour or so. A stall near me offered a diversion, an array of colors for *nazars*, the talisman worn to stave off the curse of the evil eye—an antidote to the various ills my Istanbul taxi driver had warned me about. The malicious stare from an amulet can bring on a variety of maladies, inflicting jealousy and sickness. Counteraction is required. Wearing a cross is said to work, as might carrying incense, a nail, or other distractions that convey strength. In some countries it is socially acceptable to thwart this superstition's damage by a pinch on the endangered person's bum. That seemed to me an imprudent gesture from a visitor. The symbol hanging on the post before me, looking near exactly as the threatening one I'd seen in Istanbul, was correspondingly called an evil eye. The necklaces and earrings were pretty. I left without one, relying instead on the invisible travel gods that look after ne'er-do-well rovers like myself.

Halim had left me with a general sense of direction to get back to the train station. Making my way out of the market, I wound along a street, cornered into the main plaza, and saw my erstwhile "like to be your guide" youngster charming a middle-aged pair. I had to admit that he certainly worked for his money. With time still on my side, I succumbed to the lure of nearby side streets. That's when I saw the barbershop.

I find barbershops irresistible (this is not as hyperbolic as you might think; I once journeyed days through West Africa en route to Timbuktu in Mali, all ostensibly so I could get a haircut there). There are few more honest places to hang out than where one's hair is cut. Prices are usually set and posted, so tricky wording does not enter into the encounter. You want a cut; you get a cut. Deal. In barbershops, the music is what the owner wants to hear, and usually the music is local. It is also here that televisions are frequently on, giving you an indication of life in the surrounds. Mostly, though, it's the other patrons who set the scene with their clipper-and-clippee repartee. Once, in another country, I'd sat in stunned silence as two barbers argued over my head as to what haircut I should be given. One grabbed the scissors away from the other and began hacking away at the hair on my uncut left side to demonstrate why the already-cut right side had been clipped in the wrong style. As they yelled at one another, there was a push and a shove. A razorblade whooshed in front of my eyes. To demonstrate how he felt, the knuckle of the man holding the razor hit the side of my head to punctuate his yelps at the other guy.

As I entered this Kayseri shop, the barber was busy with a balding man who was having his sideburns trimmed. Keeping his head down, the barber said "*Buyurun*" in greeting. His eyes glanced up, shifting to indicate another patron ahead of me seated on a side bench. The waiting man smiled his indifference and pointed me to the empty barber's chair, then waved to indicate I'd jumped the queue with everyone's consent.

Barbershops are like theater stages. People walk on in brief cameo appearances, then exit. The next act appears on the same stage in a peaceful, orderly sequence. I was on.

The barber clipped me up nicely and massaged my shoulders. Nearly done, he casually bowed over the glass countertop, reaching for a tumbler with a narrow mouth filled with some unknown liquid. Beside the tumbler was a stack of cotton swabs and a cigarette lighter.

Into this calm came fire. The barber was a self-assured craftsman, not one to give short shrift to an out-of-town customer. He would provide the Turkish finish for a haircut. He picked up the cotton swab, dipped it in the liquid, and let it drip—most of it evaporated as I watched. He took the lighter and lit the end of the swab, which then passed in what seemed slow motion in front of my eyelashes. The barber's flame moved beyond my peripheral vision, but I had the mirror in front of me and could see him bring the burning stick close to my right ear. My startled eyes tracked his action. He blew the flame into the hollow of my ear and quickly clapped his hand in a slap over it to extinguish the fire, blocking my eardrum just as the heat reached it. The wax had melted, presumably expunged. Unwanted ear hairs had burned away. The barber took a wet cloth, wrapped it around my ear and poked inside with his little finger, removing the wax and gliding away burnt hair. That task completed, my fear abating that I might claim an eyebrow or two as barbershop casualties, he singed the other ear.

Done, I stood with a slight imbalance. His goodbye, more felt by my ears than heard, was warm. I had a train to catch.

"*Vangölü Ekspresi*," the public address system blared as the train neared, followed by, "Van Gölü Express," for those of us who were linguistically challenged. It was dusk. The announcement raised my hopes of reaching Tatvan. I went in search of a bathroom, walking by the same weary farmer I'd noticed here earlier in the day. His face was lined with stories but not worries, or so I thought when he looked my way. Unfamiliar, contradictory smells came from the bag he held on his knee. The smells intrigued and repelled, and I ultimately was glad to gain distance from them.

Freshly arrived from Ankara into Kayseri, the Van Gölü Express was a smooth-looking train, white with striking red doors. The coach livery was striped low down, with a narrow red and slightly wider blue line running the length of the consist (as the train set of railway coaches is known). Attached to each coach, rather than painted on, was a metal sign proclaiming, "Vangölü Ekspresi." Turkish Railways call this their "classic train," to differentiate it from the high-speed trains that link Turkey's major centers.

Train arrivals often spark a flutter among people suddenly repacking luggage that has sat dormant for hours. An older couple hugged an also-weeping younger pair as though they'd never see one another again. A strapping man rushed to the station's food counter to buy packets of food, preferring what he could see in front of him to the mystery of what he might find on board. One family of five swapped emotional hugs, seemingly engaged in the saddest goodbye—and then all of them boarded the train together. None of them got off before the train left Kayseri.

Turkey's cross-country, eastbound train, in English the "Van Gölü Express," promises the eventual destination of Tatvan, on the western shores of Lake Van.

The bustle organized itself as everyone moved to the coaches. The lone platform agent glanced at their tickets and answered their questions. He gestured toward sleeper cars as if to indicate, "Over there, silly." When he looked at my ticket, he briskly pointed down the line. Was it my imagination that I heard him say, "Over there, silly foreigner"?

My pack was laden with mountain-climbing gear as well as lighter clothing for any possible time in drier lands. I had over-packed, as is my wont, and was now predictably regretting the size of my bag. Climbing into the vestibule between two carriages, I leaned into the designated one, slunk along the aisle, and spotted my assigned quarters. Shouldering open the door, I dragged my bag in behind me, whiffing a suddenly familiar odor. And there, on *my* bed, already made down for the night, sat a sprawling man. It was the elderly farmer from the train station, his various foods arrayed. His unibrow scrunched into an arch as he watched my arrival, conveying his own disappointment at having to share space.

"Rick," is how I introduced myself, strangely feeling like I was *his* inconvenient companion.

"Ick." He smiled, offering his hand.

"Rick," I corrected, taking his grip.

He smiled. "*Ick.* I, Murat." He said this with a mouth full of cheese and held out a napkin with a chunk of it for me to sample. It was off-white and dry. Against my impulse, I accepted it, but was rewarded: a tentative nibble brought forth a gush of a lovely, salty flavor.

With night coming, Murat was at *meze*, the early stage of a meal between the appetizer and a starting point. He was well into his eighties, I thought. His clothes hung on him as if reluctant to be seen. Mine probably looked the same. His face was a gray-brown brindle with hooded, friendly eyes that conveyed understanding, though his sideways glances showed he was confused about my presence. The makings of his meal were strewn over a towel on his side of the compartment. He'd been preparing for his own on-board of privacy. The towel held slices of red pepper and bread crusts that had been pulled apart. Resting against the backboard of his (*my*) bench bed was a little cup of floating yogurt threatening to spill the moment the train lurched.

A large dish of slop sat flat on what was clearly now going to be his bed-seat. It was the source of a rich smell that permeated the room, clawing its way into the woven seatbacks—and into my clothes where I was certain it would linger for days. It looked to be part soup and part gelatin.

"Pudding?" I asked. "Noah's Pudding?"

The disheveled gentleman pounced on the words, replacing them with "*Aşure.*" He offered to share his bowl, passing it toward me and asking, "*Ick*?" It was a soup of leftovers, traditionally concocted from what Noah's family might have found on the floor of the Ark: dribbles of barley, leftover vegetables cut and dropped in a pot of other remainders, along with dried fruits mixed with assorted nuts—the earliest muesli.

I let my pack fall to the floor and folded out a bed set-up opposite him. As we were leaving the station, Murat attempted to pour some of the *Aşure* into a cup, doing so simultaneously as he rose and handed it to me. The train then unexpectedly shunted to a start, and the soup lapped over the side of Murat's bowl and into my container. Falling backward to my seat, I clutched the dish, happy to be traveling by train. Noah's Pudding spilled across my wrist.

We traded more food before Murat dozed off. My sausage was a hit, as were the breads. We exchanged cheeses, and between the two of us there were six or more varieties. We lapsed into sign language and repeating basic words to understand one another, happy in our struggle to do so.

He told me, or I took it to be, that he was traveling to Elazig.

I said about myself, for conversation's sake, "Tatvan to Van."

Murat replied, "Kurdish."

"You are Kurdish?"

He shook his head sideways—saying "Kurdish" in an unmistakably negative way—adding, about himself, "Turkish!" as though one could be either but not both.

The third and fourth seats in our couchette remained vacant. If it stayed this way, we'd not have to lower the upper bunks. I would be able to watch the moon's progress. It neared a half moon now, moving toward full in the coming week.

Murat fell asleep, his head crooked into the windowpane and cushioned with a train-issue pillow. He snored with a pleasant rhythm that aligned his breathing with the train's steady noises. Hills slipped away outside the window until we slowed to let a very long freight train take a priority whiz by us, blocking the view. When the freight finished its intrusion, the fields seemed suddenly larger, the rises of land more distant, the green landscape more brown, as though we'd let a seasonal month pass in those minutes.

*   *   *

Rifling through my pack, I found the copy of *Gilgamesh* I'd bought in Göreme. I propped myself against the train compartment's wall with its little reading light and lost myself in the book.

Out of Mesopotamia, there are three particular flood stories of old brought to light in the past 150 years by archaeologists—their possible sequence being the Sumerian flood story, which flows to the *Epic of Gilgamesh*, and the *Atrahasis Epic*, the latter oral story committed into writing mid-seventeenth century BCE or earlier. It is profound in its similarities of an impending flood and preservation of selected life from a destroyed earth. I was reading a translation of the separate though related original epic poem about Gilgamesh (or, in Sumerian poems, Bilgames), an historic king believed to have lived sometime between 2700 and 2500 BCE. It is the longest example of writing in the Akkadian language used by Babylonia and Assyria. The periodic merging of the Bilgames and Gilgamesh stories is an early example of combining oral flood histories.

To avoid direct communication between a god and a man, the *Gilgamesh* story has the flood epic's hero, Utnapishtim, overhear Ea, "the cleverest of the gods," whisper a directive not to a person but to the inanimate reed fence around Utnapishtim's house:

> *Reed fence, reed fence, listen to my words.*
> *King of Shuruppak, quickly, quickly*
> *tear down your house and build a great ship,*
> *leave your possessions, save your life.*
> *The ship must be square, so that its length*
> *equals its width. Build a roof over it,*
> *just as the Great Deep is covered by the earth.*
> *Then gather and take aboard the ship*
> *examples of every living creature.*

The design is unorthodox for a boat. It is equal sided; lending itself to a cube description. Utnapishtim relates what happened when the ship was ready and the angry gods were prepared to proceed:

At first glow of dawn, an immense black cloud
rose on the horizon and crossed the sky.
Inside it the storm god Adad was thundering,
while Shullat and Hanish, twin gods of destruction,
went first, tearing through mountains and valleys.
Nergal, the god of pestilence, ripped out
the dams of the Great Deep, Ninurta opened
the floodgates of heaven . . .

The magnitude of the resulting flood covered the land, or at least the ground within sight of the soon-to-be floating vessel:

For six days and seven nights, the storm
demolished the earth. On the seventh day,
the downpour stopped. The ocean grew calm.
No land could be seen, just water on all sides,
as flat as a roof. There was no life at all.
The human race had turned into clay.
. . .
(then) I brought out a raven and set it free.
The raven flew off, and because the water
had receded, it found a branch, it sat there,
it ate, it flew off and didn't return.
. . .
When the waters had dried up and land appeared,
I set free the animals I had taken . . .

Sitting on the Van Gölü Express and flipping through the book, I realized for the first time that all but one of the epic's twelve chapters have nothing to do with a flood story. Rather, the book's first half is about Gilgamesh and a rogue player named Enkidu with whom he has a conflict that resolves into an abiding friendship. Deeply disturbed when Enkidu is sentenced to death by the gods for an escapade they were both

60

involved in, Gilgamesh embarks on a pilgrimage of self-examination to find everlasting life. He encounters a man who has achieved exactly that. The immortal man is Utnapishtim, survivor of the "Great Flood," and the raconteur recorded in this epic's eleventh chapter (colloquially known as the Flood Tablet because it is a separately retrieved ancient cuneiform tablet discovered in library ruins near Nineveh in the mid-1800s). Utnapishtim's achievement of immortality is a post-flood gift from the god Enlil.

This drama foreshadows later written accounts of Noah and his flood adventures, with notable differences. Utnapishtim's boat is square, or likely cube, to Noah's rectangle, and has six stories to Noah's Ark's three. Each vessel has at least one window. The downpour that floated Utnapishtim's boat lasted for a week compared with Noah's forty days and forty nights. More people in addition to family are saved aboard Utnapishtim's oversized houseboat, while only immediate family members are taken aboard Noah's Ark. When it comes time to release birds in search of land, Noah has a raven and three doves in his story while Utnapishtim has a dove, a swallow, and a raven. Noah's boat comes to rest "in the mountains of Ararat." Utnapishtim lands elsewhere:

> On Mount Nimush the ship ran aground,
> The mountain held it and would not release it.

While some believe "the Mountain of the Ark" is to be found among the mountains of Ararat, the *Epic of Gilgamesh* makes it clear that Mount Nimush is also a candidate to be the Mountain of the Ark. If I could get to northern Iraq in my travels after climbing Mount Ararat, might I get near Nimush—or whatever the mountain is called today?

With the gentle rocking of the train and the darkness outside the window, I grew drowsy reading about Gilgamesh as the man who tried to escape the inevitability of death while being taunted by Utnapishtim:

. . . Who will convince them
To grant you the eternal life that you seek?
How would they know that you deserve it?
First pass this test: Just stay awake
For seven days. Prevail against sleep,
And perhaps you will prevail against death.

I held my head up and kept reading against the soothing tilt and sway of our carriage. There was an abrupt jolt as the Van Gölü Express cornered and picked up speed coming out of the curve, taking up the slack between cars. I looked across to see the jerking had not disturbed Murat, and so read more. Gilgamesh fails to "prevail" and falls into a long sleep, his later awakening bringing realization that his greater ambition will remain out of reach if he cannot even master the urge to sleep that befalls mortals.

This mortal reader nodded off as well, listening to the music of the train wheels accompanied by Murat's descant snores.

I woke with a start, my heart pounding. One week before climbing Ararat, I dreamed that someone ahead of me in our climbing queue lacked oxygen, had fainted on the steepest part of the climb, and had fallen back onto the rest of us. We collapsed, domino-like, everyone tumbling down the mountainside.

Apprehension never sleeps. I put the dream down as a check on any overconfidence, nothing more. I tramped the train end-to-end, walking off my anxiety as well as the lure of sleep by pushing through heavy metal

(opposite page) An Assyrian sculpture thought to be Gilgamesh, King of Uruk, holding (some say strangling, others say overpowering) a lion. "This was the man to whom all things were known; this was the king who knew the countries of the world." The *Epic of Gilgamesh* is considered the oldest great work of literature. This stone carved likeness of its prideful hero, from the eighth century BCE, was found in Khorsabad, Iraq, and is now in the Louvre, Paris. It stands 18 feet (5.52 m) tall. Photo © Musée du Louvre, Dist. RMN-Grand Palais / Thierry Ollivier / Art Resource, NY.

doors and into windy vestibules where the metal floorboards dueled, demanding my concentration as I stepped into another carriage. Our coach's layout of compartments soon gave way to curtain compartments of bunk beds where only random snores betrayed passengers rocked to sleep. I jostled past these bedsides, careful not to fall in.

Murat was awake when I returned, sitting upright and looking uncomfortable. There had been a train announcement while I was walking the aisles, but I hadn't understood it; nor could I hear it properly when it was repeated in English. Murat pointed at me with a confident directive. "Elazig." I did not want to know what he meant.

A porter knocked on the door, asking for tickets. His English was good, but his news was bad. "You will get off at Elazig," he said. Murat nodded. "There are track repairs," the porter explained, not sounding sincere.

"But . . . Tatvan," I said. "I want the ferry connection."

"I wish you good luck."

"I need to get to Tatvan," I continued. "And then to Van."

"Bus. You will get on a bus in Elazig. It will take you to Tatvan. No train to Tatvan. Bus." He smirked. "Don't make plans. Just live."

When we were alone, I told Murat—who could not understand my comments except the key crossover words in our respective languages—about my intentions. "I will travel from Tatvan to Van and to Doğubeyazit. Then climb Mount Ararat."

His brow furrowed. "Ararat?"

I made climbing motions, clutching at the air as if it held rock sided grips. I indicated a pinnacle by forming my fingers into a steeple. Murat shrugged his head while saying "Ararat?"

And then the light went on in my head's lexicon. "Agri Dagh," I announced.

He grinned. Mimicking my climbing pantomime, his smile faded, "*Ick*. No." He found an English crossover word that yanked my heart into my throat with his tone. "Danger."

*   *   *

Danger was not a deterrent for Friedrich Parrot. By the early 1800s, adventurers decided to contest "God's prohibition against man's ascending" Mount Ararat. At the forefront of this ambition was Parrot, an experienced mountaineer. He was in his late thirties when he achieved the first recorded summit of Mount Ararat in 1829, climbing in the full belief that he could reach the landfall site of Noah's Ark, which he believed to be "one of the most remarkable events in the history of the world."

A German doctor, Parrot was a medical officer in the Russian army. During the year he ascended Ararat, he was also a university professor of physics and pathology in the later-named country of Estonia. His patron for the expedition was the czar of Russia. In early May, Parrot's expedition traveled south from Moscow to the shores of the Caspian Sea and through the Caucasus of Georgia to Yerevan. Arriving there in September, they had missed the favorable months for climbing.

Parrot's party used St. Jacob's monastery, on the northeastern side of Ararat, as a base camp. But a near-fatal mountainside slip and resulting fever during their first attempt forced Parrot to seek medical treatment, and the climbers retreated to the village Ahora (Agori, or Aghuri),[9] just below the 4,000-foot mark of their ascent.

A second endeavor, six days later—from the northwest—also failed to summit, though they reached the 16,000 foot level, near enough to the top for Parrot to write they "set foot upon that region which certainly, since Noah's time, no human being had ever trodden."

During the third attempt, three peasant assistants in the climbing party turned back with illness. Undaunted, Parrot "pushed on unremittingly to our object, rather excited than discouraged by the difficulties in our way." Even with the most confident ascent team, anyone attempting

---

9 A decade after Parrot's visit, in 1840, a devastating earthquake along with volcanic activity and a resulting landslide destroyed the village of Ahora and the Monastery of Saint Jacob on the north side, and killed 10,000 people (also obliterating Parrot's original route).

Friedrich Parrot's account of his expedition to Ararat, translated into English and expanded by W. D. Cooley, was published in 1846, five years after the climber's death, as *Journey to Ararat*. It included five sworn affidavits Parrot had sought in support of his account—two from Russian soldiers and three from villagers who had accompanied him. Despite this, skeptics labeled him an impostor. One scholar asserted, "Ararat's icecap was too steep and too slippery for human feet." Parrot steadfastly claimed, "We stood on the top of Ararat." Portrait by Alexander Julius Klünder (1829).

to summit Ararat must face the same nagging question en route to its peak: *Will we make it?*

On October 9, 1829, "A last effort was required of us to ascend a tract of ice by means of steps, and with that accomplished, about a quarter past three . . . we stood on the top of Ararat."

"Will we make it?" is an apt refrain among those who call home the troubled lands in the shadow of Mount Ararat: Iran, Armenia, and Turkey

lie at its foothills, along with nearby Iraq, Syria, and the portentous Kurdistan. The silhouetted contours of bygone borders for Mesopotamia, Persia, Urartu, Greater Armenia, and the Ottoman Empire are as unavoidable as is the Islamic State of Iraq and Levant (ISIL).

A prudent map of this area begins with religious cartography: Judaism, Christianity, and Islam come rapidly to mind, as do their subsets, whether Shia or Sunni, Maronite or Copt, Zoroastrian, Samaritan, and Druze, Shabakism, and Yazidi—a mere sample of the potpourri of faiths hereabouts. Over five millennia of societies in movement, settlement, and conflict, religious fervor has both dictated and crossed boundaries between countries often—absorbing recalcitrant territories under the banner of conversion-or-punishment. Today's national borderlines are shifting fault lines, uneasily drawn because they are so difficult to ensure.

This part of the globe seems to satisfy a need for disorder. If you asked Mother Earth where she hurt the most, she might well point to the Middle East. Here is where many of humanity's brightest hopes have been raised and crushed often. The region is known for killing up close and for efficient retribution for infractions. Its peoples feel misunderstood, maligned, and manipulated, in the land of foredoomed peace talks. The challenge for those who seek regional stability is monumental; dialogue is unfortunately less precise than a drone strike.

The concept of "Middle East" arose during the nineteenth century, when Britain created much of the West's geographical terminology. Cartographers noted the farthest travel destination eastbound from "home" was China—the Far East. The midpoint when traveling eastward for trade was designated as the Middle East.

Clear and consistent identification of the Middle East's modern demarcation lines is not an easy task, whether one thinks in geographical terms, or political terms, or religious terms. On the latter, there are a plethora of ordained overlaps and doctrinal divisions.

To spark a discussion, one could commence with the struggle among the prophet Muhammad's followers to choose his successor subsequent to his death in 632 CE. War broke out within the span of two generations, mainly between the proponents for continuing Muhammad's family lineage, who viewed his son-in-law Ali as the necessary choice, and those who instead favored a consensus selection for the new Muslim caliph. Ali's supporters, known as Shiat Ali (contracted to Shi'ites or Shiites, often as Shia), initially won sway over those favoring selection through consensus, the Sunnis.

Ali's assassination in 661 pitted the two factions against one another in conflict that continues to this day. Clusters of believers became regional powers as populations grew and their expanding land bases consolidated.[10] The divisions intensified as Persia (today's Iran) became primarily Shia and the Ottoman Empire (including present-day Turkey, Syria, and Iraq) became preferentially Sunni. Add the Kurdish dilemma to this stew. The Kurds, mostly Sunni but also Shia, Christian, Yazidi, Jewish, and Zoroastrian, have a demonstrated tolerance for other religions. In Iraq, notably under Saddam Hussein, Sunnis—a minority of the population—held power over the majority Shia. That situation shifted with the US invasion of the country in 2003, which deposed Hussein, resulting in the rise of a Shia-controlled government and a corresponding repression of Sunni influence. The latter factor is a cautionary reminder: to explain the enmity between Sunni and Shia as an "ancient rivalry" is to absolve responsibility from the many outside forces that have also mobilized and manipulated those divisions over centuries of meddling for their own political ends.

Journalist Joe Klein noted in *Time* magazine: "There is not a politician, policymaker, or journalist who hasn't been wrong about Iraq at some point," a comment arguably applicable to the entire Middle East.

---

10 In the eyes of some (and the author treads on shifting ground here), the Sunni and Shia doctrinal and practical differences get a nodding comparison to the at times severe relationship between Catholics and Protestants; much spilled blood, yet as they've lived in the same neighborhoods, intermarried, and lived peacefully.

FIVE

WOMEN OF ARARAT

"Is it a terrorist that speaks your language?"
—Documentary, *The Women of Mount Ararat*

Murat and I, like all the passengers on the Van Gölü Express, found ourselves disembarking at Elazig early the next morning. We left our couchette feeling goodbyes could be saved for later, when we were on the platform. But the train-to-bus arrangements were not as smooth as I anticipated. Once we were on the platform, in the midst of the chaos, Murat merged into the crowd, and I found myself stranded with the other passengers.

"Where is the bus?" an Asian traveler asked me.

I couldn't help. A Turkish man, dressed in a suit as though headed to work, noticed our dilemma and motioned across the parking lot. "You will find there a station. It is down the road a walk. That is where you want."

Two dozen travelers and their gear headed out toward the destination. Once inside the cavernous depot, everyone dispersed in search of a connection.

With great expectations I approached three waiting buses, motors running in the open-air, high-roofed parking lot. None of the signs said what I hoped to see: "Tatvan." Standing alone, propped up by my orange pack, I was a beacon in search of a ride. A bus pulled in. It did not display a sign indicating any destination but already had twenty people on board. The door swung open, and a female bus driver looked down at me.

I could have asked myself why many Western politicians so often think of hijab-wearing women as hiding something. I might have asked why Westerners on the religious right so often think "Muslim = extremism." I could even have asked myself why a woman here had what is traditionally considered a man's job. I'd heard it condescendingly phrased as: "You have your fingers in dough. Why do you poke your nose in a man's job?"

But I actually thought of none of those things. What I wondered about in the seconds after she opened the door to me was if this woman seeking personal independence was also among those striving for Kurdish independence from Turkish rule. It was not an inappropriate question to ponder, so why was I surprised when she spoke to me in my own language?

"Tatvan?" I asked.

"Tatvan," she confirmed. Down she came, unlocking the luggage compartment leading to the bus's chassis holding bin and helping me slip the backpack in. "You are from where?" she asked, then answered herself: "Not from here." There was no judgment in either her timbre or her words. Why had I expected such a thing?

Eastern Turkey is an area where females are encouraged to not leave the household behind to pursue a career. Illiteracy among women is much higher than it is among men. The need for educated words is still seen as less important to women for whom men wish to speak.

I boarded. No money changed hands.

The bus was surprisingly comfortable—I had half-assumed that I would be enduring a rickety, bone-clatteringly bumpy ride. In lands that are so old, Westerners' views and expectations can quickly be proven outdated, or just flat-out wrong.

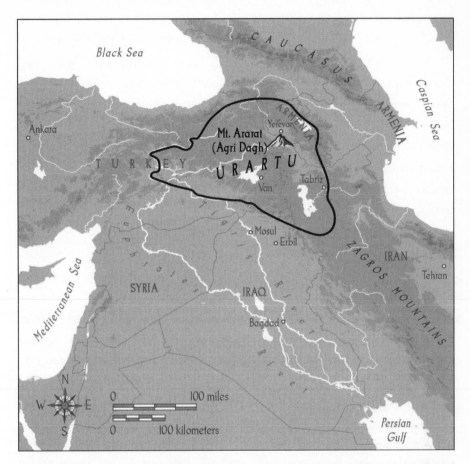

860 to 590 BCE, the Kingdom of Urartu (approximating the geographical region of Urartu). Scholars debate translations of ancient, vowelless texts showing that "the ark came to rest on the mountains of rrt," where "rrt" could be "uRaRTu" or, later, "aRaRaT." A similar geographical area referenced as "the historical Armenian kingdom" was a continuation of the Kingdom of Urartu, also known as the "Kingdom of Van."

To approach Tatvan is to traverse overlain land claims, revisionist history, and the flow of kingdoms into and out of history, all on the same footprint of ground. I found it puzzling—and like most puzzles, it can be explained only when finished, and I had just gotten on the bus. Still, I spent a good part of the trip thinking about what I already knew.

Mesopotamia (3500 to 1000 BCE) is a name many Westerners know, a region that long ago had established borders in the land I was now traveling through. Centuries later came the Kingdom of Urartu, where Lake Van and Mount Ararat were politically housed. I'd recently learned a new word: toponyms. "The toponyms Armenia and Urartu are synonyms for the same country." Yet neither ancient Urartu of 860 to circa 590 BCE or the ancient Armenian kingdom, circa 600 BCE, which evolved into Greater Armenia, 190 BCE to 428 CE, jibe closely with modern Armenia's borders. Both historic regions do, however, shelter parts of Armenia's assertion of grander borders.

As the bus arrived near Tatvan hours later, I clung to a fading hope of catching the ferry, which was scheduled to leave mid-afternoon. When I mentioned this to the bus driver, she chuckled. "Ferry leaves when ferry leaves."

Coming into the town, we had a view of the lake and I saw, a quarter mile from the dock, the ferry. It looked to be arriving according to schedule. As I watched it, however, I realized that the ferry was getting smaller as it moved into Lake Van. Outbound.

I pointed this out to the driver, who noticed my disappointment. "Next ferry," she replied.

"Today?" I asked.

"Today, yes."

Tatvan is a good-sized town, a mile of highway doubling as its main street with business and residential buildings along the way, some several stories high and others one-business tall and wide. We slowed with all the cars in our way, ones that had been absent on the open road.

The bus driver pulled over beside a line of parked cars. "There is shop. Ticket. For ferry. Or for bus to Van."

Disembarking, I nodded to her wave and walked into a near-empty store with a service counter. "A ticket please, for tonight's ferry," I said, dropping my small pack to rest on the larger bag. The clerk looked at me from where he sat at a knee-high round table with two small coffee cups on it. The top buttons of his shirt were undone, and he looked uncomfortably warm. He picked up his coffee, slurped what was left of it, and averted his eyes.

"There is no more ferry," said a short woman who'd been sitting with him when I arrived. Her eyes held the hope of a cash transaction.

"Yes, I saw it leaving," I agreed. "But for tonight's—the next one. I'd like a ticket, please."

"No more ferry," she said. "Maybe tomorrow. No train now. No freight. No ferry."

"I need to get to Van," I protested.

"Yes, you can get to Van," she assured me.

"Bus?"

"Bus for day has left. You got off it. Next is late. Tonight. Maybe tomorrow."

"How . . . ?"

"Taxi. There is a taxi. You can find around the corner. Go there."

I departed pulling my duffle bag on wheels, bumping along the uncertain sidewalk to the street corner where I turned left. There, as promised, waited a taxi with a young man leaning on the hood.

"Taxi to Van?" I asked.

"You should take the ferry," he replied.

I sighed. "How much for your taxi to Van?"

"There is a bus tomorrow."

"Do you drive a taxi?"

"It is long way for taxi. So . . ." He did not finish.

"Let's go," I said. We swung my gear into the trunk of his taxi and were off.

The drive through the rolling countryside along the southern shores of Lake Van gave me a relaxing sense of openness. If he had wanted to, Naim, my driver, could have beat the ferry's crossing time, but that was clearly not his game. Naim's afternoon had just become a day out of Tatvan's snarl of traffic, and with greater revenue. He rambled. "You are good to take time. We will stop for lunch."

We were in the Muslim calendar's ninth month, and fasting for Ramadan (in Turkey referred to as Ramazan) had begun. One hour along our route, Naim, a Muslim, suggested that it was the time of day when I should be hungry. His friends had a roadside food stand ahead. "You eat," he urged. "I will be waiting. Is Ramazan."

He spoke about the food like a hungry waiter rattling on about a menu off-limits to staff. I imagined a Western take-out kebab and wrapped *shawarma* as I knew it. Naim talked as though he had just taken a bite of it. "The rice is what people notice. The taste is mint, usually. Other spices too, like cinnamon." His words were moist with saliva.

After some thought he added, "Always, almost, *shla* is there—like stew, and if chicken is available, that and rice make a very fine soup. Soup. Always on. For Kurdish meal, always there is bread. Everywhere here you will find bread, naan, or thicker bread that is also flat, not risen. Even during Ramazan it is fresh-smelling in mornings . . . that is tough."

"You observe Ramazan?"

"Oh yes." A breeze carried away his whispered, "Usually."

We pulled onto gravel siding where a shelter offered protection from the sun. Flimsy posts held up a tarp, under which several tables waited. Behind the tarp was a dining place out of the view of anyone driving by. Naim took me inside to the owner-cook, a stocky woman with a confident smile, who took my order and asked if I'd like to sit inside. I missed her cue.

"Outside is best. Fresh air," I replied.

Diced and grilled beef was served on a plate for one, placed in front of me and slightly out of reach for Naim. The longer it sizzled, the more it made its own delicious gravy. Beside this were stuffed leaves.

"*Ekmek* it is." Naim looked at it hungrily. "And *dolmetes*."

There was plenty of food on my plate. At first bite I sensed it had been cooked to tenderness, perhaps after marinating a long time in an herb concoction. Without thinking, I instinctively moved the plate over to share.

"Is problem," Nain said.

"My apologies." How could I forget so quickly? I wondered.

"Should we go inside?" he asked.

"I'm fine here," I said, clueless to my second cue.

A car passed, leaving the roadway clear of onlookers. Naim reached across and took a piece of meat and ate it. As the savory taste settled in his mouth he grinned and suggested, "We should go inside."

Inside (and out of sight of anyone who might have given Naim a disapproving look), our meal was shared openly between the two of us, with the blessing of our host. She promptly put a place setting in front of Naim. "It is not uncommon to break with Ramazan if you think of a different world," my taxi driver said as he reached for my plate with a fork.

The woman added, "But . . . one needs to show respect."

Later, as we continued our drive alongside teal-blue Lake Van, a large island came into view. Naim said, "It is Armenian."

"Here?" I was a bit confused.

"Not from now, but from palace built by bishop. We are where Armenia was over one thousand years ago. Then Armenia included here. Now it does not. This is island with Palace of Aght'amar. Now, in ruins. Ruins but restored. Parts. It is called Akdamar Island."

He sounded proud of this fact, rather than defensive of his own country's hold on the land.

"In Armenian eyes, Greater Armenia includes Akdamar Island."

"Do you have Armenian friends?" I asked.

"I am Kurdish. We too think this land should be ours. Some Armenians are also Kurdish. Most are not. Some are Muslim, most are Christian. My friends are both."

I assumed he meant "either," not "both," but my knowing seven Turkish words was no ground for correcting his competent English.

Having heard that statement before, I asked, "What do you mean? Are you not Turkish first? Then Kurdish?"

"Both," he said. "There are maybe thirty million Kurdish people. But we have no country." He paused a bit, as though I should ask for more information before it was polite for him to provide it. "This, where we travel, it will one day maybe be part of Greater Kurdistan."

"You must all have much in common, these Kurdish ties," I said, thinking of song and language bringing the Kurdish people together.

"They are not 'ties,'" he said. "They are us. It is who we are. But in Turkey, Kurdish people cannot sing certain songs, or write names with certain letters from our own alphabet. Is prohibited. Because Turkish make rules. And Turkish are afraid of Kurdish."

My thoughts swirled. Turkey, where I knew I was, held these lands tenuously against the remembrances of a Greater Armenia that once existed, and against the vision of a Greater Kurdistan that never has.

Upon reaching the outskirts of Van, Naim overshot the entrance to the Merit Şahmaran and had to retrace the last mile more slowly. The hotel's name was on a sign tucked back a little. Naim pulled through an entranceway under a portico.

We patted one another on the shoulder in a nervous goodbye, one of acquaintances but not friends. I reached in my pocket where I'd earlier put about as much cash as he'd told me to expect for the fare. I had a bit more than the final price and, the trip having been enjoyable for both of us, I passed it all to him in a handshake. It was equivalent to the cost of a cross-town taxi in a major western city.

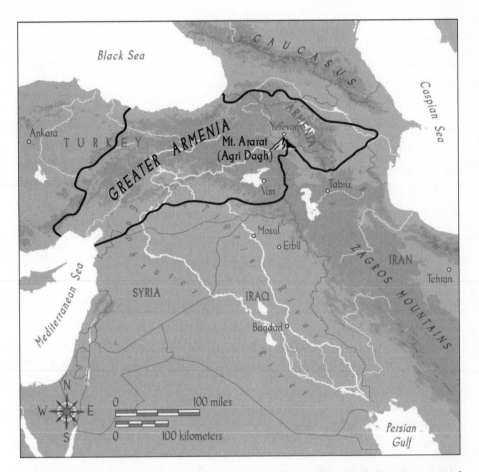

200 BCE marked the emergence of Greater Armenia (also written of as Major Armenia and the Kingdom of Armenia in various contexts), which existed in one form or another as late as the sixteenth century CE.

As he drove away I walked into the hotel's high-ceilinged, brightly-lit lobby with a balustrade swinging upward off to my right. Tall windows ahead looked onto a pool in an outdoor dining area. Beyond the tables was the shore of the mile-deep, alkaline Lake Van. The dining area was empty as staff smoothed tablecloths and placed food-warming units on a buffet table.

The cleanliness of the hotel was a stark and sudden reminder that I hadn't showered in the last two days.

In the lobby, from behind the check-in counter, a smartly dressed young woman in a pressed shirt smiled and greeted me: "*Buyurun.*"

"Hello, Emre," I said, prompted by her nametag. "I understand you've one nice room left, with a view of the lake and away from the road noise. Not too close to the kitchen air vents," I continued, hoping that perhaps she could provide an upgrade from my modest booking.

"We have only a Mr. Antonson left to check in this evening. You are him, no?"

"Yes to your no," I said, immediately feeling silly that I'd made fun of Emre's English when my Turkish fell between fumbling and nonexistent.

"Yes then, we have a room for you." In an afterthought she said, "You seem tired."

I realized that Emre was practicing her English on me. Seizing the opportunity I said, "I want to ask a favor, Emre, since you speak good English."

She smiled again, her head making a shy nod. "Depends," she said. "Depends on how I can help with favor."

"I have a map to show you. I need advice to get overland to Iraq, from here to the border."

"You cannot go there," she said, adding rather confusingly, "but I don't know how to not go there."

A young man had entered the check-in area. He also wore a pressed white shirt and carried an easy demeanor. Emre called him over. "Aysenur, he can help you. He will know what you don't know."

Aysenur adjusted his nametag, knowing I would need to see his name spelled out if there was any hope of recalling it later.

"I heard your situation," he offered. "And people from the West, it would be not good to take bus that southward in the eastern mountains. Anyway," he said as if practicing slang, "that shorter route is blocked by military. It is not actually short. There is fighting. Some die. You take long route instead. Two bus days."

I pulled my map out of the daypack and spread it across the counter before either of them could leave. The absence of other patrons meant I had their attention. My shower could wait. I pointed to my intended route.

"That road is dangerous one," confirmed Aysenur.

"Yes, that road is dangerous, Richard," added Emre, who had picked up my full name from the passport I'd placed on the counter for check-in. "Fighters, they are fierce. Fierce men. Women too."

Aysenur drew his finger along the road that ran south from Van and east into the mountains, heading south to Hakkari, then west to Sirnak, ending at the Turkish border town of Cizre. Across the boundary sat Zakho—in Iraq. Drawing his finger along the road to Hakkari, he said, "It is here that the PKK fight with the Turkish government forces. Days at a time, right now weeks, that road is not one you can passable." I liked his newly coined phrases, and tried to store them away in a mind place where I could remember them later.

The danger sparked a thought about the letter in my packet. "Do either of you read Farsi?"

They shook their heads in unison. Aysenur continued tracing the longer route, suggesting that I could leave from Van back toward Tatvan, then Bitlis to Siirt, using that route to get to the Cizre border town in a more circuitous manner. "It is this way you must go, if you go. But you cannot go. It is not to be workable. It would not come to be. You would not be let into Iraq."

Disappointment must have shown on my face, as Aysenur was quick to offer solace. "Turkey is beautiful country. I can show you elsewhere to go."

"But I don't want to go elsewhere," I said. "I want to go to Iraq."

Aysenur replied with what every stranger stuck in a strange land wishes to hear: "I think I have an idea." He hesitated. "I am not here tomorrow. My cousin is away for two days. Then I am back. You can fly. That is it, Richard! You can *fly* from here."

"Fly from Van to Iraq?"

"I am sure. My cousin works for airport. He will be more sure. We will make you sure. But not today. Today you must be unsure. Until day after next day."

"I will be gone then."

"That is too bad."

"Please find out more information," I asked. "I will come back here after Mount Ararat."

"You are climbing Mount Ararat?" Emre said, somewhat doubtfully. "Some do. Others try. Many don't make it." She hesitated. "You look tired," a repeated phrase that I thought might be code for "smell."

Now I really wanted that shower.

Aysenur spoke. "I am going. Home. I will phone cousin when he is back. See you before you leave for Ararat."

In my room I propped up pillows; sleep crawled in beside me. As I fell away, I remembered Emre's warning about the dangerous eastern Turkey region where battles regularly broke out and I should avoid: "Fighters, they are fierce. Fierce men. Women too." She spoke of those on one side of the battle: Kurds. Their ambition is for a Greater Kurdistan.

On the flight over I'd read a magazine article in an old copy of *The Economist* that provided me a little context. Simmering like a Kurdish lentil soup dish, the local broth of separatism ranked near lawlessness in Western media, but the further east one was in Turkey, the more likely such rebels were seen to be fighting for independence from tyranny. Leading this fight is the Kurdistan Workers' Party (PKK), an organization many Western governments label a terrorist group.

The insurgent PKK began battling the Turkish and Iraqi governments in 1978, over the establishment of a homeland for all Kurdish people. Its tactics may have changed over the years, but its goal of independence

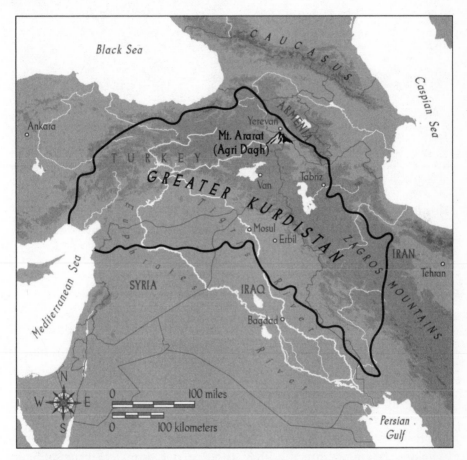

A 1918 CE petition for an independent Kurdistan delineated the nascent
Greater Kurdistan depicted here. Ambitions for reconfigured borders
are at the heart of Kurdish separatist movements.

Kurdish women fighters have been called the Women of Ararat, variously portrayed as freedom fighters or terrorists. Photo © BijiKurdistan.

has not. The role of militant women, referenced by Emre, came about in an equal mix of philosophy and strategy, backed by guns. Along with the fighting men are "The Women of Ararat," a self-styled all-female mountain guerrilla militia that operates independent of the male army, intent on a focused revolution with patient purpose. It is a female army within a hierarchy dominated by men.

The documentary *Les Femmes du Mont Ararat* (The Women of Mount Ararat) follows half a dozen women, a *magna* in the guerilla echelons. A unit within the PKK, their predecessor detachments have been around since soon after the PKK's surreptitious activities in 1995. They are members of the Movement of Free Women of Kurdistan. The fight these women take against oppression has many aims, including to forestall Turkey's assimilation of Kurds by forcing them to live in special jurisdictions, to reverse Turkey's banning of the Kurdish language, and to counter what they see as one country's indoctrination of another race. One woman soldier canvassed in the film claims, "As a Kurd, my choice

The photographer wrote of the People's Defense Units, known by their Kurdish initials YPG: "After the Kurdish YPG Forces have liberated the ISIS Stronghold Girê Spî, this Female Fighter found a weakened white dove on the battlefield and takes care of it." Photo © BijiKurdistan.

is to fight or to live as a slave." These women want their children to grow up in a Kurdistan, or at least in a Turkey where they are respected and free to be Kurdish.

As I fell asleep, I wondered: Where might Emre sit on this debate?

SIX

TURKISH HONEYCOMB

*"There must have been a heritage memory of the destructive
power of flood water, based on various terrible floods.
And the people who survived would have been people in boats."*
—Irving Finkel

Aslab of honeycomb lay on a saucer near the morning's coffee service. A waiter crushed coffee beans into my morning java and added a spoon cut of the bee's work, calling the honeycomb *balari* and smiling at my look of unfamiliarity as he handed it to me.

Emre hovered behind the desk as I reentered the lobby carrying my coffee. "Aysenur phoned for you, Richard. He said his cousin still away but airport friend says no flight from Van to Iraq. His cousin knows best. You wait two days."

Accepting this confirmation, I said, "Emre, today I would like to get into Van, find a bank, maybe have lunch. Is there a taxi?"

"Better you go out on the roadway. Stand there. When *dolmuş* comes toward you, wave. It is what you call a minibus. They will stop. Is our system."

Out on the street, I looked up to see a minibus approaching. I waved, as Emre had instructed. The kids in the back seat waved back as the vehicle passed by. Soon a passenger van slowed in front of me without my having to wave. The door popped open, the driver's beckoning hand an invitation to board.

"How much?" I asked, holding out half a dozen coins for his choosing. He picked those he wanted, put them in a pouch and shifted his vehicle into gear. I jerked toward a seat through a sea of smiles, feeling a sense of "it's nice to be a stranger in a place where no one wants to take advantage of a stranger." Three people moved their personal goods to give me room. I fell in beside an elderly woman wearing a dress printed with flowers, and I wondered if they were local flora.

In Van, I stepped out of the bus into a cacophony of stammering cars, five dangerous steps away from the curb; the sidewalk was a foot off the ground. Open boxes of fruit I thought to be cherries filled the full range of the first store width I saw. Next to it was a restaurant with its window open to the street and sweet baking on offer. Commerce happened as much in front of shops as within them. There was uninterrupted pedestrian flow; where four men sat around a square table further along the sidewalk, people streamed by them with ease. A shoeshine man polished a leather hat, bringing it a shine through quick strokes on the flimsy surface. I did not see a disgruntled face.

Emre had told me her city was "pearl of east," yet I wasn't so sure. In the heat, the streetscape shimmered. But if this was a pearl, it felt a bit like an artificial one, constructed by irritating the surrounding host lands with an intrusive commercial district.

Servicing an area population of several hundred thousand, these shopping streets had everything on display, but I was looking for an ATM that would give me the cash I needed for meeting my guide Zafer later in the day. In one of our email exchanges he'd specified, "You must provide me with cash payment, not traveler's checks." I'd left any thought of carrying cash behind—I did not want to take it on the train. Now I had to get some.

An ATM sign proclaimed "İş Bankası Van Şubesi." I inserted my credit card. As it popped out, the screen displayed words I took to mean,

"Not connecting, try again." I tried my debit card, and it showed amount options. I punched keys. It slapped me with a low daily limit on this card. That would be a problem. Just today? This week? My only chance of getting what I owed Zafer, I quickly deduced, was to dart between five bank locations before the international transaction system cut me off. First one: I entered a lesser amount. The money came out. I grabbed it and left.

A block away was an Akbank ATM. I quickly withdrew the same "limit" on the same debit card. Feeling flush, I inserted my declined credit card. The machine coughed multicolored lira bills. I hustled into the nearby Yapi Kredi Bank, hoping I might still have luck on my side.

My credit card worked (but at a reduced amount) as two armed guards inside the bank watched me hurriedly stuff money in my pocket. I hustled over to a teller for assistance, thinking a personal touch might be more successful than the electronic dispenser. But both cards failed the teller's test. The system told her I was overdrawn. She looked at me as though I was attempting fraud, handed back my cards, and glanced toward the guards. I walked over to a narrow table by the window.

Under the gaze of the bank's security, I smiled a dumb-tourist smile, and then proceeded to empty one bulging pocket at a time, counting up all the cash. I was short of what Zafer expected from me. I needed one more withdrawal, or I was hooped. I darted out of the bank, heading back to the first one, where I tried my credit card at the lowest amount needed. It was cut off. I tried my other card. Thankfully, the currency gods smiled on me.

Back at the hotel, I organized my money into an envelope that Emre had given me. I put it into the daypack and went down to the outdoor area for coffee. I thought of the next day, when I'd meet my expedition teammates and head out of Van and into the countryside.

A thirtyish-looking man wearing a sleeveless T-shirt and blue jeans approached. His open-toed, slightly torn shoes smacked to a stop beside my table. His hair was thick and curly, accompanied by long sideburns and an inch-wide soul patch. A less intense brush of black hair crept up both arms. He smiled warmly.

"I am Zafer," he said, sitting down across from me. "I am your guide to the mountaintop."

"Zafer, it is good to meet you. Would you like food?"

"I am here often. They know me. They will bring me what I like. Are we ready for payment so that we can go to Mount Ararat?"

The abruptness of it all was disarming; if my desperate search for cash had failed, would he have altered the plans?

The waiter served him coffee and a forkful of Turkish honeycomb.

"We all give you cash," I said. "You will be carrying a lot of money. Is that safe?"

He ignored my concern. "You are first here. Two more are now in hotel. This afternoon. You will meet them tomorrow morning. We four go to Çavuştepe fortress. You want to see that. Also see Necropolis. And to Iran border. Or, well . . . near Iran border, to see mountains that tell stories."

On the table, I'd set a sheet showing email exchanges with Zafer and Amy, outlining the amount already paid and leaving a fair balance owing. Nearer me was the envelope of cash that equaled that amount. I turned the printout right side up for him to see. "Is this still the amount?"

"It could be more," he said. "You wanted to be part of a small group. That will be. Only six of you. Me, I am your guide. Two cooks. Horses. Help boys to pack the horses. Tents. Food. Many expenses." It was his last minute of negotiation.

"Stop, Zafer. Are we good with the amount shown?"

"If you have that amount, we are good."

I picked up the envelope of Turkish lira as more coffee arrived. "Give it a count, please."

He sipped the coffee and, before setting it down, sipped more. Perhaps he did not want to seem eager.

"Exchange rate is *not* good," he said in a practiced voice.

The envelope showed where I'd calculated the exchange rate, so I said: "At the bank this morning, on the wall, it was close to this. Banks favor themselves. It has not changed much since our emails. We are good to go with this."

"Well . . ."

"Thank you for resolving that, Zafer. We're square. Done."

He had an immediate smile, that of a gamer who'd been called out. In America I'd have felt on the verge of being taken advantage of. Not here. This world was about slivers of money. Many slivers. Zafer's revenue was periodic and the entrepreneur in him would never leave money in someone else's pocket for lack of asking for it.

One could not but like him, even trust him. "Now let me tell you about other two climbers. First though, you should know, the weather for you is not for sure."

"Unpredictable? Or bad?"

"Ararat is always unpredictable. Bad, not bad, maybe not bad."

He scanned the bills again, stuffed them and folded the envelope. "Two climbers are at hotel today. After breakfast, tomorrow, I will meet you three here. We travel to countryside."

He stood up to pocket the money. "He is Nicholas. She is Patricia. She is pretty. Him you might miss. But not her."

Another coffee arrived for each of us. He said, "You look in shape. That's good. I had wondered. Many trekkers are not knowing Ararat's threat. Is a tough mountain and steep, and has dangers. People who like to hike only should not climb it. You need different skills to summit." He bent his head, shyly, saying, "An American climber told me it is 'attitude for the altitude.'"

"How many times have you climbed Mount Ararat?" I asked.

"I climb sometimes all the way, sometimes part the way. With you, I promised to be your guide to the summit. It will be third time this year—one time was with people who wanted to find Noah's Ark. Do you want to find Noah's Ark? It is not on Ararat. I know where it is. I can show you. After mountain climb I can take you to where is Noah's Ark."

"That would be interesting," I said. "Are you certain it is there?"

88

"Very."

"How can you be so sure?"

"What I show you, the formation is as Bible says. The measurements are truth. Height. Length. How wide it is. There is only one design for the Ark. Everyone knows that."

Irving Finkel—curator, Assyriologist, and detective, with the rare ability to "sight-read" cuneiform. The "Ark Tablet" he deciphered predates by over one thousand years the Book of Genesis written version of the "Great Flood" story found in the Hebrew Torah and Christian Bible. He revealed ancient phrasing that animals boarded the boat "two by two," something previously thought to be unique to the Hebrew telling of Noah's Ark. Portrait © Simon Carr

Not quite a truth.

When the discovery of the ancient cuneiform "Ark Tablet" became public in recent years, it described the boat that saved people and animals from the destructive flood as *round*.

The oblong floating zoo portrayed as Noah's Ark is a reflection of Hebrew texts. The "Ark Tablet," which predates Hebrew texts, describes a novel shape, a practical circular design large enough for the job. Without a rudder, it would move at the behest of winds and tides. The round design would provide for a buffered landing without breaking apart.

Dr. Irving Finkel is Assistant Keeper of Ancient Mesopotamian Script, Languages and Cultures in the Middle East Department of the British Museum, which houses 130,000 ancient clay tablets moved there from old Mesopotamia well over a hundred years ago. In 1985, an English collector of odd things, Douglas Simmonds, brought a cuneiform tablet to Finkel's attention. Simmonds's father had served with the Royal Air Force in the Near East when World War II was winding down. He'd acquired a collection of memorabilia from the area, among which was a clay tablet, which he left to Douglas. When Douglas first showed this tablet to Finkel, the expert—being among the very few able to sight-read cuneiform—recognized the piece as unusual. He attempted in vain to persuade Simmonds to leave the tablet behind for complete deciphering.

Fourteen years later, the two men met again at an exhibition and Finkel was at last loaned the treasure for in-depth review. Many clay tablets record financial transactions or marriage information or community details, and there is little marginalia. But this one told a Babylonian flood story, with a twist.

In the *Atrahasis Epic*, the god of water, Enki, informs Atrahasis the god Enlil has decided that the world will be destroyed by flood. Written earlier than the three existing tablets known to tell the *Atrahasis Epic*, Simmonds' tablet also has Atrahasis in the hero role. It proves to be an adaptable story, modified over time.

It took Finkel weeks of painstaking work, patient translation of uncertain strokes, and double-checking the wedges of cuneiform craftwork before he could be certain of what he was reading. What he read astonished him. The Simmonds tablet provided comprehensive instructions for a man to build an ark:

Draw out the boat that you will make
On a circular plan;
Let her length and breadth be equal.

This Ark was *round*. The structure was to be 220 feet wide with a height of twenty feet, and waterproofed with bitumen, a derivative extracted from prehistoric fossilization. The directions stipulate the length of rope required to help construct the unusually large coracle. Finkel shared the results of his discovery in his book *The Ark Before*

Noah, which indicated that Mesopotamians modeled this Ark after the coracles commonly used for transport in those times (actually, the practice continues today). Round and with a shallow draft, these boats were never large, nor did they carry much weight. They were capable of being navigated by an oar. For the size of Ark coracle indicated by the clay tablets, Finkel determined that the rope, uncoiled, "would have stretched from London to Edinburgh."

This time-worn tablet differs from the *Epic of Gilgamesh* in many ways, but there are similarities between the two (its opening line, for example, begins, "Wall, wall! Reed wall, reed wall!"). It then provides complete instructions for building a barge to save the life of Atrahasis and his family, along with plants and animals, from a flood caused by a disgruntled deity. The instructions for the circular boat are clear, complete, and precise.

The tablet stipulates that this ark be used to rescue "wild animals." Perhaps it was assumed that domestic animals would be an obvious

The Ark Tablet. In the hands of an Assyriologist, the 60 lines of this cell phone-size tablet convey a fascinating Ark story about a boat 220 feet (67 m) in diameter. What other ancient texts may yet be found that will alter our common assumptions about a flood and an ark?

Woven like a basket or other wicker structure, an oval boat or coracle (or gufa) is constructed by entwining branches or young trees into a stable vessel. Wrapped in waterproof skins and covered with tar or resin, they are sturdy and can bear significant weights, such as large animals or stones. For thousands of years, these have been used in shallow lake areas or rivers around the world (including Mesopotamia). Photo © Sreeraj PS.

inclusion. It specifies that the menagerie be gathered "two by two," creating a phrase that would much later become ubiquitous and synonymous with animals surviving Noah's flood.

In a dramatic conclusion, the person identified as a shipwright in the *Atrahasis Epic* is instructed:

When I shall have gone into the boat,
Caulk the frame of her door!

By examining the writing approach, colloquialisms, and style, as well as the clay construct of the actual tablet, Finkel dated it between 1900 and 1700 BCE, the Old Babylonian Period. This dating changed what had been previously believed to be the earliest known version of the Epic of Atrahasis, 1635 BCE. Thus, with the new discovery, this story's written record predates the written Biblical telling of Noah's Ark by over

Constructing a life-size replica of the round ark that Atrahasis was instructed to build, according to descriptions in the Ark Tablet, proved difficult. This "to-scale" coracle is perhaps one-fifth the size. Boat craftsmen in Kerala, India, took four months to build it. Photo © Kuni Takahashi.

a thousand years. That said, these various flood stories share the same motivation: an upset deity. They are all about epic high waters and a similar escape plan. Their individual tales about saving the world gracefully align—sequential versions working off of the same story, modified as it was retold and finally written down.

Discussing the vast flood plain that was Mesopotamia, Finkel told Tom Chivers of England's *Telegraph* newspaper: "There must have been a heritage memory of the destructive power of flood water, based on various terrible floods. And the people who survived would have been people in boats."

Finkel's assertion is that this tablet records an earlier version of a "story of the flood passed from Babylonian cuneiform to alphabetic Hebrew and [that] came to be incorporated within the text of the Book of Genesis." Given the shared source materials, the tablet would have informed later flood narratives. The British Museum designated this discovery as "The Ark Tablet," equal in stature with the "Flood Tablet" that related the *Epic of Gilgamesh*. Together, these tablets and their flood-ark-survival stories, with their respective heroes Atrahasis and Utnapishtim, give Noah and his ark story (whether in the Torah, the Bible, or the Qur'an) enlightening precursors. Finkel accentuates the lineage when he writes, "Comparison of the Hebrew text with Gilgamesh XI highlights such a close and multi-point relationship between the accounts that the dependence of one upon the other is unavoidable."

"Zafer, can you help me stay a night or two in a village near Ararat after our climb?" My thought was to have time alone with those who spoke as little of my language as I did of theirs.

"It could happen. I will speak with Ahmet."

"Who is Ahmet?"

"He is mountain guide. Like partner to me."

"I would also like to see Paraşut's ice cave." Amy's lead hadn't panned out; I hadn't received any response from Paraşut to the email I'd sent. I'd tried his phone number from the hotel but so far hadn't been able to contact him.

"Do you wish to explore rumors or do you wish to climb?" Zafer asked.

"I am here to summit," I said, as much to bolster my conviction as to answer Zafer's question.

Zafer changed the subject. "You join long list of adventurers on Ararat." He cared deeply about his mountain and all who had climbed it. "We now have third century of men to summit since first success of Parrot. Women too. I guide many, like Patricia." He steered my interest away from Paraşut. "This year Europeans . . . Americans and Chinese. Russians." Zafer paused after the last nation's reference. "That is history repeating. Early Ararat team success was Russia. Military man Khodzko."

94

*   *   *

In July 1850, topographer Iosif Khodzko, a colonel in the Russian army, reached the summit of Mount Ararat. A distinguishing feature of Khodzko's expedition was that sixty soldiers attempted the apex, emphasizing collective responsibility and teamwork, tenets of mountain trekking that remain valid for all who set an ambitious foot on the mountain.

Having begun their journey on a clear sky morning, by afternoon wind and hail slowed them and "a dense fog swallowed up the peak." That evening in base camp, at 10,580 feet, an electrical storm exploded upon them "with a blinding flash and green, red, and white side effects."

The next day, eventually compromised by exhaustion that "forbade another step," they established Camp II at 16,520 feet, where nasty weather forced the expedition to bivouac for three days in a tent village clinging to the mountainside. As the blowing snow eased, members of the outfit worked their way to the crest, where the crew set up precision equipment for use by Khodzko and his compatriot Peter Sharoyan to survey and record meteorological data. The two men stayed near the peak for five windswept days, taking shelter in a snow cave walled with carpets.

The colonel ordered the construction of a seven-foot-high snow monument with a bronze plaque recording the expedition's achievement and acknowledging the group effort. Khodzko's outfit's approach to mountaineering was the paragon of preparedness, with its focus on the teamwork required to achieve their aims. Zafer's stated philosophy was in Khodzko's lineage.

Our visit ended. As he made to leave, Zafer said, "We are level with the money, Rick. Enjoy your evening. I put note for Nicholas and Patricia about time tomorrow. They laugh easy. Him, in his sixties. Her you can't tell. I think both lift weights. They are together. They share a room, so are together in that way too. Let's do departure at eight o'clock in morning."

"And the rest of our team?"

Zafer's chest rose as his mind rattled through a list. He exhaled check marks: "You have new friends. Ian here tonight on ferry. He's first by train, from Ankara to Tatvan. He has the experience of skill. Charles, I will later become certain when his flight is tomorrow. Amy thinks he is more walker than hiker, more hiker than climber, but will have exercised legs. Tomorrow afternoon, different flight is Goran. We think he's most fit of group."

I wondered what Zafer would say about my six foot frame, disheveled hair, and non-lean body from three months ago if I weren't present: "Rick? I saw his photo and hope he arrives in better shape than he appears. His face looks lived in. Probably a salad dodger. Does he know how high this mountain is?"

I accompanied Zafer to the hotel entrance. He had conveyed the challenge that Ararat presented. He did not want to be on the mountain with anyone who felt differently, and I trusted him more as a result. Thinking of the Iraq introduction letter in my pack, I asked, "Zafer, do you read Farsi?"

"No."

After he left, I went for a workout in the hotel's little fitness room. I felt unsettled. Pre-climb misgivings. So many things could go amiss— the team was not yet assembled, the weather was iffy, my glimpsing a full moon on our ascent remained uncertain. The only thing I could ensure was my own readiness. At least I had met the man who would guide us to the summit. Now he needed to muster our expedition.

That evening, the hotel's outdoor patio was busy. I spotted the last dinner table for two near a railing overlooking Lake Van. I tipped up the chair opposite mine so that I would be left alone to make field notes. Ten minutes into the calm, a burly man walked over and pulled the leaning chair away from its perch. "Looks like you want to be left alone, too," he said and sat down. "This is only quiet-looking seat. Hope you don't mind if I be quiet with you." He set a thick book down on the table.

For half an hour he was hunched over the book wrapped in plain paper, never speaking except to respond to the hovering waiter, and then saying only that he didn't need anything. He kept his self-imposed silence as I doodled in a notebook and read.

Little bugs flew about and dotted the pool in tiny splashes, as would the occasional drizzle of rain. They smeared on my paper as I wrote. The waiter gestured like a boxer, fighting them off from around our table. They paraded on the tablecloth. I wished for a wind to scatter them.

Two tossed green salads arrived at our table, unordered. It was an indication that the hotel staff didn't set aside tables for idlers; we were expected to order or leave.

"It's wine-o'clock," smirked the man pretending to check his watch. That broke our silence. We each asked for a glass of red wine, and I added on spaghetti with meatballs as a carb-build up afterthought. He duplicated the order.

Marzban was an industrialist from Iran, in Van for two days of "trading" as he put it. His girth nearly outdid the chair. In compensation, some of his weight rested on his elbows, which were braced by the table. He ate that way, his left hand dipping his fork to the plate and raising it to his mouth, the elbow rotating but not lifting.

"What trading do you do?" I asked.

"There is much to trade. My country exports natural gas. Pipelines need parts. Turkey exports machinery we need and tobacco we don't. They make better electrical and steel things."

Why didn't I know this? I thought, thinking back to gaps in my pre-flight research.

"We have oil to share, at profit."

That I knew.

He talked about long-term business needing assurances. "Iran is not giving anyone confidence." Turkey courted its own "reputation for distrust," he said. "You have dinner tonight in a land Kurds claim is theirs. Armenians say is for them. Turkish will kill to keep. Along with deaths we have always made trade. If economy gets good, maybe people stop dreaming of borders."

Marzban sipped from his glass and tongued the drink around in his mouth, squinting as he swallowed. "Even wine here has the aftertaste of gunpowder."

As if to remedy such bitterness, the waiter brought two coffees and a serving of warm honeycomb.

SEVEN

TAKING TEA WITH VAN CATS

*"For (the expedition) team to work properly there needs to be a clear
sense of a shared goal and a willingness on the part of all members
to muck in for the common good."*
—Mick Conefrey, *The Adventurer's Handbook: Life Lessons
from History's Great Explorers*

At eight in the morning I arrived at the second-floor landing of the staircase to see a couple lock up their room. They had day-packs at the ready. The man's teeth leapt out of a narrow face made lean by age, apparent fitness, and perhaps adversity.

"Might one of you be Patricia?" I asked, looking first at this mountain man. I turned to his partner.

The woman beside him was every inch the fashion-fitness instructor that Zafer had implied her to be: arms that could lift a hefty pack onto shoulders broad enough to carry it, and calves that could power a laden body up a steep hillside. A large block of blonde hair swept away from her forehead. She poked the man's ribs, saying, "You can be Patricia if you want. But just on this trip where nobody knows you."

He replied to me. "It's Nico."

His chin nudged the top of Patricia's pulled-back hair. He wore high-rimmed glasses and a bright red T-shirt at home on his tanned body. "Zaffy told us another climber was here. You Rick?"

"Yup. Zafer should be downstairs right now."

Down in the lobby, our guide swung a chained car key around his middle finger, clutching it to a stop when he saw us.

"Zaffy," Nico said, using a nickname that never stuck. "The best-looking Turk."

Zafer made a "follow me" motion with his hand as it closed over the key. He hopped into the driver's seat of a white van, talking as he went. "No rush, but we should get going. Heading east first thing. Fortress. Almost at Iran border, where I need to get gas."

Nico and Patricia took the seat behind the driver's. I sat in the front beside Zafer. "Got a map?" I asked him.

He tapped his forehead. "In here."

"Got one," Nico said from behind. He unfolded a large sheet, closed part of it and smoothed out the area where the city of Van appeared.

South from Lake Van, Zafer drove toward the Çavuştepe fortress. "You must walk through this, as no one else there this morning," he explained. "We go early, for you. It's very old."

The road rose with the hills as we left Van's suburbs. It remained paved until we swung off on a further incline toward piles of fallen stones. Among the rubble were the bricks of a partially excavated, partially restored building that would have once been considered unassailable. Now it was abandoned, defeated by time.

Below us was a small village, all that remained of a once-thriving farm culture that fed the residents of the fortress. Its flat-roofed homes were finished with stucco, long faded.

"Çavuştepe," Zafer announced. "Once imposing. Now not." He parked by a sign showing the archeologist's floor plans of the fortress's original footprint, and we disembarked.

Nico scaled a slanted wall and peered through a window from which men might have fired arrows at assaulting forces or watched the farmers toil below. He was not impressed.

"We can go now," he called out to Zafer.

"You should visit the Necropolis," Zafer replied. "It is part of the museum where the dead live."

"I think no," Nico said on behalf of us all.

But the village's cemetery intrigued me. "Who is buried there?" I asked.

"Part of it is where murdered people are buried from 1915 encounters. And later," Zafer said. "It was when Armenians had Van. It was under their control. You use word *siege*?"

"Yes," I said.

"It was a massacre," Nico said. "Russians with Armenians occupied Van. Many people were murdered. Always we hear of Turks killing Armenians, but it happened both ways."

It felt impossible to overlook this region's long-held grudges and constant retribution. I had encountered it enough times already to realize that nothing numbs history.

"It is one thousand years of seesaw, I think is word," Zafer said. "But thousand years is too long to remember details. Much long thinking becomes legend. So we remember last one hundred years. That is tragedy for Armenia, yes. Also for Turkey. Kurdish too."

He began to hum. Soon there were words in his song. As we walked toward the minibus, he said, "Song is after village name where fighting started between Turks and Kurds." He sang another verse. "Oramar." He let the song go. "Kurdish won."

Back in our vehicle he announced to the others what he had told me yesterday. "You should go see Noah's Ark site. If not today, go when you are back in Van from Ararat. Near."

"I thought the Ark was on Ararat," Patricia said good-humoredly but sarcastically. Zafer would have none of it.

"If you read history, early texts say boat landed in '*Mountains* of Ararat,'" he said. "Not *on* Ararat. Ararat is range of mountains. Ark landed near Mount Ararat. Not on. I can show you exactly where."

"I'm going," I said.

"Do you know the name of Noah's wife?" Patricia again, goading.

"Noah's wife is not named in Qur'an," said Zafer. "She not named in Hebrew Torah. Not Bible either. No name."

"It was Joan of Ark," Patricia said.

Zafer laughed lightly, and I was relieved, not knowing how he might respond.

Nico chimed in. "How high the Ark must have floated to be above the tallest of mountains!" That elicited the setup line he clearly wanted when Patricia replied, "Higher than Everest." Nico filled in the blanks. "Wouldn't that mean a lack of oxygen for the animals and people on board?" He looked at Zafer, mischief in his eyes.

"And the penguins came from . . . ?"

"Nico," scolded Patricia. "Enough."

Admonished, Nico instead asked Zafer, "Are you Muslim?"

"I was born Muslim. Now Christian. I choose my way."

The banter of my new travel companions, all three of them, struck me as amusing until the topic changed from the Ark to religion; Zafer had firmly secured his belief in Noah's voyage, and we needed to respect our host and let the jocularity rest. Ararat is a land of journeys, I thought, the mountain itself a symbol of man's perpetual search for answers.

Zafer remained silent. Patricia, turning serious, asked him, "Do you really believe in Noah's Ark?"

"This has been happen," Zafer replied. "My opinion. A flood not over the entire world. Qur'an says it was local flood."[11]

Patricia persisted. "You believe Noah lived?"

"Yes. He gave us ground back."

"You really believe he had an Ark?"

"There is no proof it isn't true."

---

11 There were unquestionably many floods over the years, even "super floods." Archaeologist Leonard Woolley, who focused much of his work on Sumerian Ur in today's southern Iraq, was among the earliest scientists to propose the Genesis flood as a local rather than global occurrence. He identified 400-mile-long and 100-mile-wide layers of flood plain—for those who lived there seven thousand years ago, an area that would define their entire known world.

Noah's Ark on Mount Ararat, by Dutch painter Simon de Myle, circa 1570 CE. In his book *Great Ascents: A Narrative History of Mountaineering*, **Eric Newby described Noah as "the shipwrecked sailor with an embarrassing cargo, an involuntary man of the mountains—one of the few to descend from a detached peak without having climbed it."**

*   *   *

Two twentieth-century advocates for the reality of Noah's Ark, realtor Eryl Cummings and theologian John Montgomery, stand out for their foundational research work. Cummings' wife, Violet, was the author of *Noah's Ark: Fact or Fable?* That was a book I'd had resting unopened on my shelf for years and only referenced when this trip was coming together. The Cummings and Montgomery focus was on registering "Ark sightings," and their incomparable assembly of newspaper clippings and historic writings relating to the Mountain of the Ark was a first. They collected names and dates, archiving data from disparate sources in half a dozen languages. The Cummingses' compendium of individually modest pieces, when filed and sorted, became the go-to archive of Mount Ararat's ark-related information.

Their archival approach began by chance. In 1945, a guest at the Cummingses' home read a magazine article about the White Russian aviator Vladimir Roskovitsky. The story had been around since 1916, on the eve of the Russian Revolution. Roskovitsky, posted twenty-five miles northwest of Mount Ararat, was regularly dispatched on reconnaissance flights that took him near or around the mountain. After one sortie he returned convinced that he had seen a boat-shaped object on Ararat partially covered by ice and snow, perhaps a retreating glacier. He'd taken photographs of this geological fold, filed a report, and awaited direction from his superiors. The military hierarchy worked this precious find all the way to Czar Nicholas. In response, two groups of soldiers were dispatched to Ararat to determine whether this boat-shaped object might be Noah's Ark.

As the story progressed, they found Roskovitsky's vessel, took samples and photographs of it, and sketched the layout. Everything was provided to the czar. Unfortunately, the revolution occurred soon afterward and the documentation went missing. It has never been recovered.

Roskovitsky's story wound its way through several embellishers, including the Russian troops and officialdom. Various versions of the event drifted into public mention and became regarded as fact. The Cummingses, not indifferent to religion, took up the challenge to verify

(opposite page) There have been various "ark" descriptions in historical documents, including shapes that are square/cube-like, round, or oblong. All are of modest size in comparison to more modern vessels. Noah's Ark, traditionally regarded as oblong, here reflects the dimensions found in Hebrew texts and therefore in Biblical references. The Ark described in the *Epic of Gilgamesh* is in some renditions cube-shaped, less than half the "length" and a few stories higher than the specifications for Noah's boat, yet providing similar capacity. The Ark Tablet includes instructions for a circular craft. The Qur'an does not specify measurements for Nûh's Ark. Illustration © Simon Carr.

Scarf's Comparison of Oceangoing Vessels and Arks

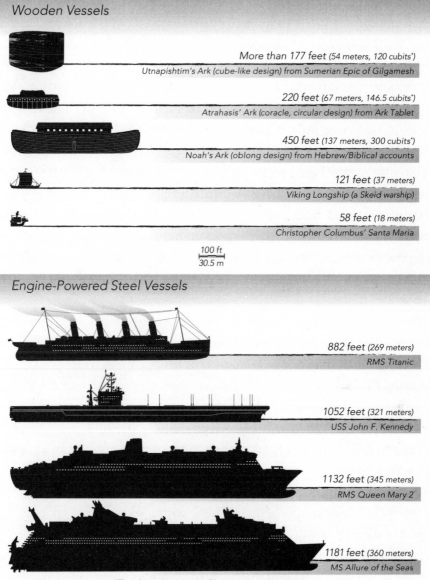

Wooden Vessels

More than 177 feet (54 meters, 120 cubits*)
Utnapishtim's Ark (cube-like design) from Sumerian Epic of Gilgamesh

220 feet (67 meters, 146.5 cubits*)
Atrahasis' Ark (coracle, circular design) from Ark Tablet

450 feet (137 meters, 300 cubits*)
Noah's Ark (oblong design) from Hebrew/Biblical accounts

121 feet (37 meters)
Viking Longship (a Skeid warship)

58 feet (18 meters)
Christopher Columbus' Santa Maria

100 ft
30.5 m

Engine-Powered Steel Vessels

882 feet (269 meters)
RMS Titanic

1052 feet (321 meters)
USS John F. Kennedy

1132 feet (345 meters)
RMS Queen Mary 2

1181 feet (360 meters)
MS Allure of the Seas

*The cubit measurement is subject to various interpretations.

Roskovitsky's tale. As word of their mission became widely known, the informational floodgates opened and amazing stories poured in about all things Ark. They amassed a previously unthought-of repository. Thirty years later, in 1972, they were the published collaborators on the aforementioned book, followed by an updated edition ten years later.

The Cummingses' far-reaching catalogue, which a more academically trained John Montgomery expanded with primary research of his own, was stuffed with documented mentions of Mount Ararat's hidden treasure, much of it bolstering their belief that the ark undoubtedly once existed and indeed landed on Ararat itself. Montgomery's book, *The Quest for Noah's Ark*, included an academic approach to exploration accounts, reviewing each case, indicative of the author's discipline. Cummings and Montgomery traveled to Ararat together, along with other researchers, and their exchange of information appeared harmonious rather than competitive. They both sought proof of an ancient oceangoing vessel, the size, shape, and purpose of which they were confident.

We had headed further east into the mountains for some time when Zafer pulled to a stop. Ahead of us, we saw the rolling climb of a road entering north to south mountains that dropped to barren lands. "That is Iran," he said.

It seemed touchable. Although we could not take that road, traders did; much of their trade was legitimate, some of it not. We drove into a border town where an abandoned lookout tower flying a Turkish flag was surrounded by low-lying buildings. Zafer greeted a muscular youngster in a dark doorway. The boy carried a five-gallon plastic container. He handed Zafer a line of hose with a vacuum pump, one that, when squeezed, created the suction to draw fluid from the can through the hose. The kid placed one cut end of the hose in the container and the other in the fuel intake of Zafer's vehicle. Zafer compressed the pump several times to begin siphoning.

"Young men," he told us, "they bring this gas from Iran on horse. They shouldn't but they do. Very cheap here to buy."

"It's okay?" I asked, not sure why the petrol station was so rudimentary.

"OK, unless they get caught. They carry over mountains. But heavy nighttime work is good for young, strong bodies. If no work for young people, is no good. Young men have too much time. Mornings are sleep, shower. Then sleep, jihad. Work is better."

The boy brought another five-gallon container to where we stood. "It's only pennies," Zafer said.

Nico asked in jest, "And everyone pays taxes?"

"No!" Zafer replied, deriding the concept.

"Then who pays for the road building?"

"The West sends money!" Zafer was enjoying this conversation, as he directed us back into the minibus.

Shifting gears as the vehicle rolled away refueled, he said, "We must go back to Van now to pick up summit team member. Ian got in on ferry."

Entering Van, we drove by a large plaster statue of two cats, one sitting tall, and the other curled at its paws. This was a monument to the city's famous mascot, the Turkish *Vankedisi*. The white-haired "Van cat" has one eye the color of Lake Van's blue waters, the other soft amber, like buttered toast.

Curious to see whether the myth matched the reality, I asked, "Zafer, can we see a Van cat?"

"You mean Cat of Van. Maybe you are lucky, as they are about here. Maybe . . ." He held a thought before rejigging his own day. "Maybe . . . how important is this to you?"

Looking to Nico and Patricia for support, I said, "It would be good to do this. It will impress my cat-loving wife."

"OK, we will do," Zafer said. "First find Ian. Then Akdamar Island is place you go. Ian will come. I will get Charles to meet us at carpet dealer. He has Van cats." He corrected himself. "The carpet dealer has Van cats, not Charles. Charles is flying in this afternoon."

We fought midday traffic in a downtown area riddled with side streets and lacking both traffic signals and directional signs. After long minutes of slow going, Zafer slipped into a side road to stop at a hotel one grade up from a youth hostel, or so it looked from the outside.

Out of the hotel's doorway stepped a middle-aged man wearing a white T-shirt that proclaimed "Mount Rinjani." His sunglasses gave way to a mop of brownish-red hair. He wore an outsized watch with dials that, we were to learn, marked altitude, barometric pressure, and temperatures. His long black pants bulged at the pockets with whatever else he anticipated needing that day. He was self-contained.

"Ian," said Zafer, no doubt in his voice.

With a nod, the man walked around the van with a loner's sense of discipline. No fuss.

In the minibus, Nico's respect showed when he asked Ian, "You've actually been to Rinjani?" This stunning volcano is known outside climbing circles, as its summit is attainable to fit hikers with a penchant for tough treks.

"Last year," Ian replied with some satisfaction.

"Indonesia, right?" Nico asked.

"Yes. Hell of an ascent. Steep volcanic scree. Physically and mentally difficult."

"I envy you that summit," said Nico. "Where else?"

"Fujiyama, in Japan. Beautiful. Year before that, I climbed Kilimanjaro. This year, Ararat—if everything goes well."

"Nico was on Kilimanjaro," Patricia said. "Two years ago too."

"Ararat will be tougher," Ian confided.

His candor was welcome. I liked his sense of self in that it did not show outwardly, as though he knew he could best the coming mountain but did not want to say so, just in case . . .

Nico agreed. "Climbing to the roof of Africa is longer and higher, but climbers say it's the steepness and the weather that make Ararat more dangerous."

"Kilimanjaro is nineteen thousand feet, Ararat seventeen," said Ian. "We need to remember the advice I got trekking on Kili: 'Go slow.'"

Nico asked, "Why Ararat?"

"The highest peaks interest me," Ian said. "I don't want it to sound like a checklist, but Ararat is the highest peak in Turkey. Where next for you?"

"I follow my reading," Nico replied. "Right now I'm reading Richard Dawkins' book *The God Delusion*, so maybe I'll go where atheists travel—a place without the religious connotations of Ararat."

South of Van, back the way I'd come in by the taxi ride, our vehicle drifted over to the roadside near a shanty and a concrete pier leading into Lake Van. The dock was for passengers boarding the boat for Akdamar Island, where the church is another relic of national definition lost by Armenia to Turkey, but not forgotten. It was here, on our ride from Tatvan to Van two days before, that Naim had suggested I visit. Zafer passed coins to the custodian, who pointed us toward a small motorized passenger boat. As we boarded, Zafer said he'd stay behind. "You must walk the island. Be peaceful there. Think lots. It is important. You can hear the stones cry."

After nearly half an hour of breathing the boat's diesel fumes, we hopped onto a wooden dock into fresh air and the island's monuments. Ian lit out on his own and went up past the church; I walked along a path to the island's outer rim, but halfway around we ran into each other and sat down in the heat.

"I hear you took the train to get here," I said. "Did you have to get off at the Elazig track repairs and come by bus?"

He looked perplexed. "There were no repairs. No disruption. I was on the train to Tatvan. We were put straight onto the ferry. It arrived this morning."

"I was told there were construction crews along the tracks, and we had to take a bus."

He asked the date my train was canceled. "Ah, I heard about that," he said when I told him. "It was not for repairs, Rick. It was the anniversary date of the Kurdish movement's uprising. There were threats of violence to the train."

"Violence . . ." I let it drift off, the tenor becoming clearer to me with every day.

"I glided through." He'd even met the ferry on time! "I live in Beijing," he explained. "Flew out of Hong Kong to Istanbul, then Ankara by plane. That's where I got on the train. Not a problem. Well, except I haven't had much sleep."

We walked uphill toward the center of the island and saw Patricia and Nico coming toward us. Nico was enthusiastic: "Go into the church and see the frescoes!"

Surp Haç, the Cathedral of the Holy Cross, was an Armenian church built in 915 CE. This is reason enough for restoration, though the Turkish flag fluttering over the island seemed much more like revisionism. Bas-reliefs on the outside walls portray religious occasions in which some scholars identify Islamic influences. Others say the friezes present a Christian artist's work. The church's inside walls and its ceiling of faded frescoes have been embellished through refurbishment and retell Biblical stories.

Zafer had told us that the island's name came from a lover's dying words, "*Ach Tamar*," distorted to *Aght'amar* and eventually to Akdamar. "A man had love of a beautiful woman, her name Tamar," he said. "She waited for her lover's boat on the island. Storms come. He shouts of his love, '*Ach Tamar*,' from the waters after boat capsizes. He drowns."

Back on the mainland, Zafer was determined to take us to the Muradiye waterfalls. "You will not have time to do this tomorrow when we go to Doğubeyazit, so I think we should go now." With the pride that locals know, he announced, "It is see-must.

"First, though," he said, "carpets, cats, and Charles."

Reentering Van, we veered into an industrial area and drove through the half-open chain-link gate into an empty lot. Well, not quite vacant: a

In Lake Van, Turkey, Akdamar Island is home to Holy Cross Cathedral, now a museum, built in the tenth century CE, when the island and surrounding territory was part of Greater Armenia. Controversy continues over the decision in 2006 not to allow a cross atop the renovated structure.

man in his fifties was waiting for us, relaxing in a chair, his legs out, one foot lodged loosely over the other. He wore a woven straw cowboy hat above a face that looked happy to be exactly where he was. He stood as we stepped out of the minibus.

"Charlie," he said with an Irish lilt. "Just flew in. Zafer's friend dropped me here." There was an easy tension in his stance. "I'm ready."

"Do you climb mountains?" Patricia asked, and I detected skepticism in her voice.

"Hike often. Walking about is what I like. Not mountains. Least not Ararat's size. Never done anything like this. Wondered if I could."

"Don't die wondering," said Nico.

Motivations are complex. Why here? Why now? Nico had said that morning that climbing Ararat was a "once in a lifetime possibility" for him. Patricia was candid; Mount Ararat had "popped up" in her life because of Nico. "I'm not a mountain climber. Never was. I came for Nico. But now I climb for myself." Determination colored her cheeks. "It might be my only mountain. Once my mind's set, I'm set." She embodied the conviction needed to conquer the seventeen-thousand-foot level of an unwelcoming climb.

I wondered what my own motivation was, beyond reading *Forbidden Mountain* as a boy. I began to think it might be: "Climb this to prove to myself that I can climb this . . ."

Zafer distracted us. "Carpets in Van are art form." He led us toward the building. "Crafters are Kurdish nomads—women not educated. They put expressions into design. You will see that. Now."

There are worlds of people who are "not educated" yet are brilliantly creative, intuitive, and majestic, I thought. He glowed with pride and I realized he did not mean his phrasing to sound pejorative.

Half a dozen white-haired cats slumbered beside the wooden posts that propped up the shade roof. Two of them rolled up as we neared, paying us the type of feline attention they reserve for a source of treats.

"Rick, your cats," Zafer announced. Then, "There is inside tea and Turkish baking. It is time." With that he left us.

I hadn't quite believed that I would actually find white furred cats with one blue eye and a contrasting almond one, yet each cat I saw sported exactly that pairing, a duality that captivated me with each eye's separate stare. As a woman served us tea, the cats followed her, knowing there might be spilled milk or a visitor who could be meowed into sharing.

Tea done, we followed Zafer into the building and found ourselves in a showroom strewn with carpets of all sizes. Over the years, I've found that politeness sometimes leads travelers into situations they'd not have chosen themselves. Our deference to Zafer, I realized, had led us into the sales pitch of a carpet entrepreneur.

"Where are the pastries?" Nico asked suspiciously, and I knew I wasn't the only one feeling tricked. To reach the pastries meant entering a zone of layered carpets on the floor. Others hung from strong metal beams so that they could be viewed with ease.

The salesman was talking quickly—one part information and one part pitch. When he paused for a moment to let two women serve the pastries, he observed: "They are very beautiful—both the women and the carpets."

Ian, seasoned with such ploys, was fascinated by a dark red carpet with lovely gold lines streaming in it. "How would I get it home?" he wondered aloud, not at all bothered by the ruse.

The salesman was quick to respond: "We ship wherever."

"I should have a smaller one I can take with me," Ian countered. The salesman brought more, smaller but of the same design.

Ian was delighted and purchased one on the spot. The salesman was equally delighted: "You help hand up the economy!"

With that, Charlie saw the benefits of an unwanted carpet and purchased one. The rest of us declined, but respectfully.

Zafer drove into the parking area as we left the showroom. With him in the minibus was a man in his mid-thirties, I guessed. He had a good-humored face conveying confidence, and on his head was a baseball cap made of unusual blue cloth, displaying the entwined N and Y emblem of the New York Yankees. It had a smooth cream peak. As a kid, I'd grown up rooting for Mickey Mantle and Roger Maris, two Yankees who often dueled each other for the league's batting titles. I set my sights on owning this man's hat before we left Turkey. But how?

"Looks like you're Goran," Charlie greeted him. They clasped hands.

"Actually, it's Goran-without-luggage," the new arrival replied. "I've dreamed of seeing Ararat since I was a kid and packed all the climbing gear I needed. Packed two days before leaving New York, I was so excited." We could see his heart was sinking. "That bag didn't make the plane out of Istanbul. It's lost. If it doesn't arrive, then just for starters I'm jacket-less, sweater-less, and boot-less."

"Don't worry," Ian said. "We won't leave you behind. 'One for all, all for nothing . . .'" he paused.

"And every man for himself," completed Nico with a laugh.

"Whatever the saying is . . ." retorted Ian.

"Goran, I've got an extra sweater you can have," said Nico.

"Not much of mine will fit you," Patricia said. "Though I've got an extra hiking pole if you need it. And a flashlight."

"Remember, Amy said we could rent gear," Charlie reminded us. "What's your size?"

I've never been one to pass up a good opening, and I thought of my packed headwear. "I'll trade you a knitted toque for that Yankees cap," I offered.

"Team's all here," Zafer announced.

EIGHT

DOĞUBEYAZIT

"Mount Ararat, upon which Noah's Ark rested after the deluge,
and which the Armenians call Messina, the Persians Agri,
and the Arabians Subeilah, is without comparison . . ."
—Adam Olearius, *The Voyages and Travels of the Ambassadors*, 1647

Morning brought the arrival of two minibuses outside our hotel. Each van could seat ten passengers. Zafer moved between the two vehicles, arranging for them to be loaded.

The night before, I'd met two American men of Armenian descent at the hotel. One had told me, "We're part of a group visiting Mount Ararat. Some have traveled from Armenia, others—Armenian as well, but living elsewhere—have come from the United States. And Europe. There are twelve of us." I immediately thought it a good "nation" to have on the mountain at the same time but climbing separate from us. Until he added, "We will trek with a guide named Zafer."

I realized our expedition of six was not going to be alone on the mountain. Our group had been kept small, as promised by Zafer. But he'd not been forthcoming that there was a companion climb under his simultaneous command.

Part of the Armenian contingent was sequestered at another hotel in Van. One of the vehicles left to pick them up and would meet Ian and

Charlie at their respective hotels as well. Our minibus would pick up Goran near Van Castle in an hour and rejig the seating arrangements there.

When Zafer mentioned the castle visit, I felt castled/fortressed/churched-out. "Maybe we could just head to Doğubeyazıt?" I suggested, still working on my pronunciation, slowly letting it out. Dohh-ouhh-bay-ahh-zit. "Everyone is keen to get sorted out for tomorrow's start on Ararat." I didn't think that selfish.

"Old Van Castle is important." Zafer was adamant. "You will be only one who doesn't want to see it."

I felt selfish.

After driving a road that sputtered out before the high-walled history that was Van Castle, the two minibuses met up again. Zafer arrived in his own vehicle, alone. Charlie came over to our vehicle in a shot. "Let's get organized and be on the mountain first," he urged. "There are twelve of them. It could be a crowded climb."

Goran was optimistic. "It won't be crowded after an hour of climbing. I don't see them as fit as our six. The gap between us and them could show quickly." I didn't say it out loud, but our own group, with the exception of Ian, didn't consist of climbers either. We were hikers and trekkers experienced on ridges, not rock-scaling mountaineers.

Zafer shouted for everyone's attention.

"I have made arrangements for two groups to be on Mount Ararat these coming days," he explained. "You are all here. We know a Spanish climbing party is ahead of us, as they left yesterday. A Russian team has been on the mountain for two days. They attempt summit tonight if weather holds. It's been windy. Snow at top. Rain too. All bad."

Nico, Patricia, Goran, Charlie, and I were standing near Zafer. We had all placed our confidence in his abilities. Ian, walking over to us with daypack in hand, set it down in the dirt. Our team stood together.

"There are many people in the Armenian group here," Zafer said, unnecessarily. "They should please stand over there. Other group we call 'the internationals'—they are from all over." He let out a nervous cough when saying that. "Patricia, Charlie, all of you, will go in that minibus.

Four of the Armenians will travel with you to the base of the mountain. When you start hike tomorrow, you will have two different guides and set out at two different times. Nico's group goes up first."

"And you will be our guide," Patricia added, looking for confirmation.

"Actually," Zafer said, "I have to return to Van. It is unfortunate, but it is business. I have no choice." Clearly there was not going to be a discussion. "Ahmet will be your guide. He is what you would call a mountain man." Zafer shouted to a man, happily transferring our packs to the group's vehicle, who smiled our way. "Ahmet, come and meet your expedition!"

I winced. Then I winced again. I hardly knew Zafer but had felt I'd had a reading of the man and his competence. This new guide was a mystery—his mannerisms, his ability to harness our enthusiasm into mountain climbing, or his willingness to straddle two camps of hikers. Uncertain characteristics could determine success or disaster on the mountain. He was capable-looking, but that surface was yet to be scratched. The second wince was for the subtle movement of the Armenians' guide to our group, as though Zafer implied an unhelpful ranking.

Zafer's move off the leadership roster was more a problem for the Armenians than for us. It meant that Ahmet, who was to have been second in command and had earlier been introduced as their group's leader, was now the main man on the mountain, gifted right there and then by Zafer to lead "the internationals." Before much could be made of this, Zafer addressed the Armenians. "I have a very good guide, name is Kubi, he is next best to Ahmet—and Ahmet is next best to me. Kubi will be the guide now for your group. You will be pleased."

The man who was piling luggage on top of the second minibus stopped his work and came down to meet the restless Armenians. Kubi's face was browned by time and inheritance. He was a Turkish Kurd who looked to be in his thirties, part mountain herder, part mountain guide, and, like Ahmet, looked competent enough. But the change in guides had been so sudden, and I wondered what the odds were that either Ahmet or Kubi would be as inspiring and competent a guide as we'd believed Zafer to be.

*   *   *

As our vehicles were being prepared, an older Armenian said to me, "We are anxious to finally get here. It is the ambition of many Armenians to make a personal visit to Ararat at some point in their lives, a pilgrimage similar to the hajj, the Muslims' journey to Mecca."

"Me too," I said, not realizing where his comment was taking us.

"Armenia's capital, Yerevan, is only thirty miles from the north side of Ararat," he said. "It is a face that watches over us, though it is blocked from access by a wire fence erected by Turkey.[12] We go to Akhaltsikhe in Georgia. From there we enter Turkey and go south to Kars. This route takes many hours." One must allow for the border protocols, he explained, which can cause delays.

His frustration was evident, having just made the trip. "Often you need to overnight. It's four more hours to Doğubeyazıt. Twenty-hour journey all in." I'd traveled a long way to get here, but did not have to endure the emotional disruption that he had, nor did I have to stare at this mountain every day, cut off from the Armenians' state but not their spirit.

"Our trekking permit costs twice as much as yours, because of our last names," he added.

I could only nod in acceptance of his exasperation when he said, "Mount Ararat is Armenia's mountain!"

Ahmet was alone when I approached him. "May I ask a favor?" I said. "I would like to spend a night here in a village. Alone, without the others."

"You are the man Zafer told me to meet," he said, "I will ask my grandfather. It is possible for you to stay with him."

Zafer again called for everyone's attention. With the Van Castle as his backdrop, he announced his intention for all of us to spend the next hour or two walking about the castle. No one shared his enthusiasm.

---

12 Turkey's border with Armenia was blocked in 1993, after Armenian-supported insurgents targeted the oblast—Nakhchivan Autonomous Republic, enclave of Azerbaijan, friendly to Turkey; some say visible from Ararat.

"Can't we just go to Doğubeyazıt straight away?" asked one of the American Armenians I'd met the day before.

"Good idea!" Goran echoed.

"Yes, we are anxious to get settled," said a clerical-looking Armenian.

"Got my vote for that," Ian added. There was a tentative movement of the group toward the vehicles.

Zafer acquiesced. We were on our way to Doğubeyazit.

Our group repacked into one of the minibuses, as directed. The appointed Armenians came with us. Ahmet now drove our vehicle, and Kubi the other. Zafer disappeared without a last word after the Van Castle tour was cancelled.

The road to Doğubeyazit was in good condition, and we made decent time as we began to work our way down into the city. "There it is!" Ian shouted on our descent. "There's Ararat." He was sitting up in the front seat beside Ahmet. Ahmet found the side of the road.

The second minibus stopped alongside us. We fanned out to take photos of Mount Ararat in the purple haze. The giant spread much wider than its noted peak rose. I recalled Eric Newby, in his book *Great Ascents*, describing the majestic scene we were now witnessing: "The whole Ararat massif rises in splendid isolation from the Armenian Plateau."

Ahmet said, "This might be the best view you get of the mountain. It may be the only time you actually see it whole." No one rushed; it got me wondering what message we were to be absorbing—and I realized we were not to be overwhelmed by our own ambitions.

More than 150 years earlier, British mountaineer Robert Stuart's account of his approach to Ararat conveyed the same awe we all felt: "the snow-clad cone stood out in distant relief." His arrival onto the mountain brought a discipline necessary for all who moved from awe to ascent—a difficult set of decisions we ourselves were to be called upon to make, and to watch unfold with our mountain companions.

In 1856, Stuart's attempt to summit Mount Ararat demonstrated a willingness to let those climbers capable of success attempt the peak separately. It also showed the personal diligence to stay on the mountain until the entire team had completed what it came for.

Stuart's book, *Early Ascents of Ararat*, derided the claims of both Friedrich Parrot and his contemporary Herman Abich, to have ascended Ararat. It was an attempt to relegate them to the margins of mountaineering. This assertion left Great Britain the bragging rights if its climbers led by Stuart could achieve the feat, placing the burden on the shoulders of the good major. Masked vanity is a danger in mountaineering. Armenians, who had provided support resources for both Parrot and Abich, curiously sided with the British, declaring that no one they knew of had reached the peak prior to the Stuart party attempt.

On the day they hoped to summit as a team, Stuart lagged behind his fellow climbers. Not feeling well, he became fatigued. He had the prudence to seek shelter and waited alone while two of his cohorts, experienced alpinists James Theobald and John Evans, "crowned the final difficulty."

The fourth climber that day, Major Alick Fraser, had decided to take a more southeastern line of ascent and moved on his own. Less experienced in snow climbing than the other three, he gauged an "easier" approach that ironically nearly cost him his life. He was within a hundred feet of the summit when, misjudging the sparse layer of snow covering the ice, he lost his footing. Fraser slipped onto his back. He "shot downwards with the speed of lightning upwards of 1,000 feet," until a build-up of snow between his legs brought him to a halt. Later he would say that only because he had kept his "ice-staff" was he able to get off the glacier. He not only regained his lost ground but also eventually achieved the summit.

A fifth member of the expedition, Reverend Walter Thursby, along with a refreshed Stuart, made arrangements to summit within two days, climbing all day to gain a favorable position by nightfall. In a dispute over the appropriateness of staying overnight at such a height, their Kurd-ish helpers left Thursby and Stuart alone on the mountainside, where they rolled themselves up in carpets to keep warm. In the morning, they left their rugs behind and climbed to the peak of Mount Ararat. The Stuart expedition illustrated Ararat's demands: the necessity of deferred authority, the strictness of good judgment, and the honest evaluation of climber abilities and priorities. Both our group and the Armenians' group would learn from that.

Doğubeyazit was more bustling than I'd anticipated; I'd pictured it in my mind as a remote rural community that prepped mountain trekkers. I'd failed to consider its key location in an agricultural area, and with trade routes crossing through here north to south and to the west from the east—though that business was limited now by Iran's embargoed abili-ties for imports and exports—it had once been a prosperous city. How many innocent people, I wondered, do such Western sanctions harm? Fewer, I supposed, than war.

Across from our hotel was a pile of weathered building materials that had been there for some time. Many buildings appeared abandoned mid-way through construction. We learned that owners built piece-meal in Doğubeyazit: only when they had enough money in hand for the next step in the process to add a wall or complete a floor. At the street level, the partially finished building would be in use as residence or a business, while steel rods thrust out of the second or third unfinished floor—a rebar marker signaling eventual completion—and in many cases conveniently qualifying a building as unfinished and therefore not subject to taxes.

The desk clerk at the Hotel Isfahan was caught unaware by our arrival and began assigning accommodation without any room listing, taking down names as if seeing them for the first time.

"Antonson," I said, being the last to sign in. "I'd like to leave a pack here in storage while I'm away on Ararat."

121

"Yes. You can leave everything in your room."

"After tomorrow morning, I will be gone for five or six days. Won't you need the room?"

"You can leave everything in your room."

I asked him if there was a message for me from Zafer. Before he had disappeared at Van Castle, I'd again asked him to help me reach Paraşut, in hopes of seeing for myself the cave where he claimed an ancient wooden formation was locked in ice. But Zafer didn't share my amusement.

After stowing my packs in the room, I looked around the Isfahan's lobby and saw a couch from which I could eavesdrop on the Armenians. I was curious about their approach to the climb. Plunking myself down, the unfinished Gilgamesh book in hand, I listened in on our companion group. Three of the Armenian climbers were particularly serious about the physical demands. All their talk was in English, and it began with reference to the day's exercise earlier in the morning. They debated what to leave behind at the hotel: "I can jettison all my trip material for later, except medication." "The weather report says high winds, maybe snow. I'll put my rain gear in the horse's pack."

"We need to sort out our guide," said one of them. "He is not talkative." But there was more to it than that. "With Turkish handlers I feel constantly forced to recognize that this mountain is no longer Armenian."

Like us, the Armenians had been assured that Zafer would guide them to the summit. They wanted to be led by the person who had made their arrangements, and now felt unmoored. Nerves were fraying. The nearness of departure to the mountain courted moody bouts of anxiety in all of us.

The only woman in the Armenian party, vivacious and in everyone's good favor, seemed, like most in the room, to have worked at being in shape for the climb. I asked her, "How do you feel about Ararat?" She mistook that for a question about its relevance, answering, "It is necessary for Armenians to make this trip, to be on *our* mountain. It is more than symbolic."

"How do you feel about the big mountain itself, about being on the steep side of it, going up, up?" I stressed. "How do you feel about tomorrow?"

"Oh, it will be fine. I want to be here. That is my motivation. We will make it."

Thinking acclimatisation, I asked, "Will you hike around for two days, or—"

She cut me off. "We are going to the top. That is why we came."

It was early evening. Ahmet assembled both climbing teams to brief us about the mountain in the morning. He had the air of an unruffled problem solver, moving around the hotel lobby, telling everyone to gather in the corner of the room for a final talk about safety and organization. I suspected this was not the first time he had been promoted to lead guide at the last minute. The expedition groups clustered near the front door in their own separate groups.

Ahmet spoke about the coming day. "Everyone must put safety first—or mountain has problem with you. Each leave another name with us in case you have difficulty with mountain and we need to notify." I wondered if there were outstanding issues that prompted Ahmet to make this comment.

"All of you will be in tents we provide," he added. I was glad to hear that I could leave the weight of my one-man tent behind at the Isfahan. Ahmet held high a slip-on boot cover for all to see, metal prongs extending from its base. "We will pass out now these crampons to everyone who rent them. Make sure they work. Fit and strap. If you have walking poles, leave them out of your pack, as you will want them for the lowest part of the mountain. If you have an ice axe, strap it away until the final ascent."

He assured us that they would be providing food, but if we wanted energy bars or chocolate or fruit while hiking up, then we should make

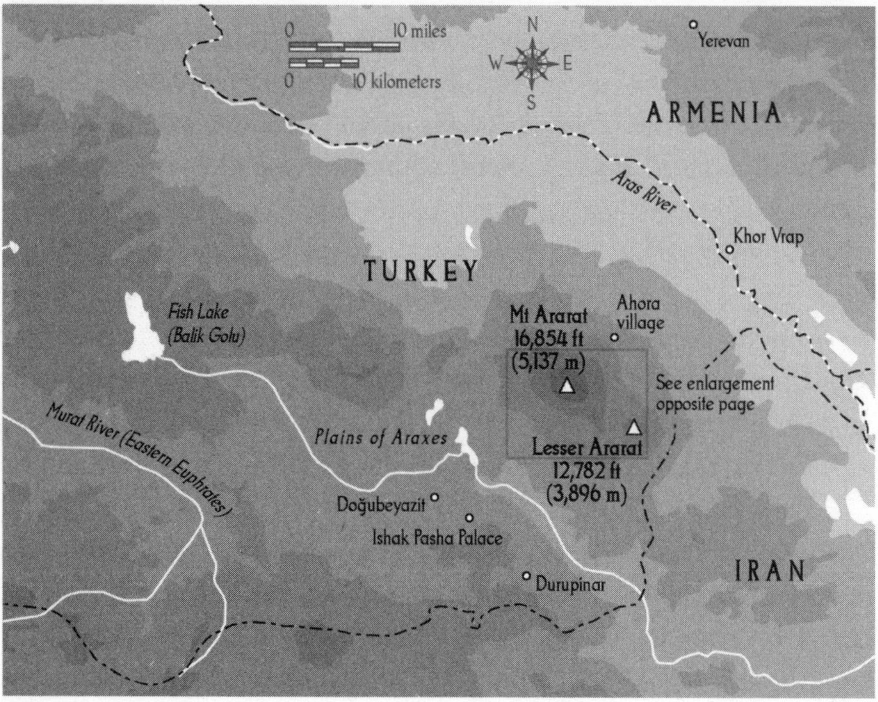
0
10 miles
0
10 kilometers
N
W
E
S
Yerevan
ARMENIA
Aras River
Khor Vrap
TURKEY
Fish Lake
(Balik Golu)
Mt Ararat
16,854 ft
(5,137 m)
Ahora
village
See enlargement
opposite page
Murat River (Eastern Euphrates)
Plains of Araxes
Lesser Ararat
12,782 ft
(3,896 m)
Doğubeyazit
Ishak Pasha Palace
Durupinar
IRAN

The Eastern Anatolia vicinity of Mount Ararat and Lesser Ararat, in Turkey, shows the two volcanic cones and their proximity to the Iranian and Armenian borders.

sure we had these in a day pack. "All your main packs will be put on horses. They will carry them up the mountain. Our cooks will go ahead and set up food camp for when you arrive."

To me it sounded like Ahmet was rattling about in his memory to dredge up lecture notes for a speech he just found out he had to deliver.

"Remember," he said with the opening enthusiasm of someone who knows you may not yet know what he's about to say, "that in the morning we drive first. Once on mountain we hike many hours. Up. Camp we do around 10,000 foot. Be ready for rain. Wind. If not, enjoy. Next day more hours. Also up. We camp at 14,000 feet. You are high then. Air is low then. Maybe take extra day. Get to know the air. Personally, each

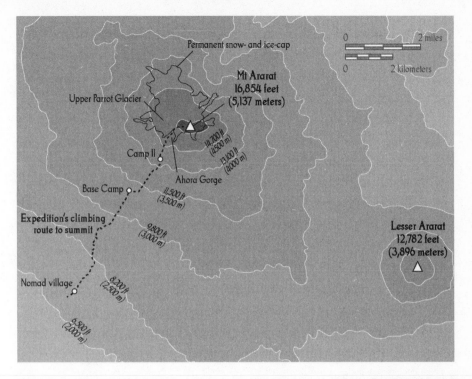

The expedition's climbing route on Mount Ararat, in the Turkish province of Ağrı. Southern routes to the summit were determined by Navarra and others to be less forbidding than Parrot's northern attempts. Over the years, it has been refined to this long, arduous approach used in summer, fit for "climbers who are familiar with the use of axe and crampons."

different. All need air. Nighttime, then or next day, we climb long hours to summit. That's top."

There was a murmur of wincing in the room.

"Ararat is unorganized mountain. You ask for six horses to pack up, three show. This we may find. Stop if your heart hurts. If you have headache, guide must be told. It is difficult to get a sick person down, the higher you go."

Someone asked, "Who brings a sick person off the mountain?"

"The same people trying to take you up," said Ahmet. He considered the mood, wanting to motivate us but also to be practical. "The mountain will say if it wants you." That philosophy fit with the room's psyche about Ararat lore, a tribute to an inanimate object with godlike powers, but it left me feeling disenfranchised and less independent. None of us had previously considered the idea of being unwanted by the mountain.

"For night of climb to summit, you need flashlight," Ahmet said. "Flashlights need batteries. Check tonight. The store down the street sells batteries. You are a danger to us if you don't have light on the mountain. Please."

Ahmet was direct and abrupt. He was also gaining everyone's respect, mine included. Tension decreased as we realized an experienced mountaineer would be leading our ascent. I was starting to feel more comfortable under Ahmet's leadership.

"There is change," Ahmet suddenly added, in a twist of ironic fate. "My father is ill. I cannot go with you as your main mountain man." He looked at Nico. "Not, too, as Nico's group guide. Kubi will be going instead of me. He is here. Get to know him."

He looked around. "Kubi?"

A man put his hand up but stayed standing where he was, away from us. He had been the Armenians' replacement guide when Ahmet moved over to lead our group in Zafer's absence. If we had felt abandoned before, how must the Armenian group feel *now*?

Ahmet continued. "You all have two cooks with you. Cooking for everyone here. They are brothers; one is Fesih, the other is Niecit. You can tell them apart because Niecit sings. They know mountain. Whenever you see them, know you are OK. You will meet them before mountain time. In morning.

"For the Armenians, I will introduce you to your guide when he gets here later tonight. Or tomorrow morning."

There were mutters of discontent. One Armenian said, "We were told Zafer would be on the mountain."

Into the silence, Ahmet said simply, "That is not to be."

The Armenians caucused, and a man stepped forward. "Ahmet, we are not satisfied." Their frustration was palpable. "You know we have come from many places to be here. You need to assure us we will have a proper guide and mountain safety, all meals and proper care."

"Of course," said Ahmet, "of course."

"I tell you of thunderstorm weather. Today it was rain. Misty mountain. Tonight lightning. Tomorrow, we don't know."

With a mistaken air of having deflected criticism and discontent, he moved to our group. "I realize you just getting to know other. You sharing tents, by twos." He smiled at Patricia. "You change mind and want one of these guys instead of Nico?"

Beside her were four anxious, unshaven faces, each atop a badly dressed body, which would soon court days-old smell. She smiled at Ahmet and us. "I'll keep Nico."

Ian and I were standing together. Goran and Charlie had just returned with their refilled cups of coffee. "You okay as you stand?" Ahmet asked.

"Yup," came the collective response.

When Ahmet left us, Nico was the first to rebuild group confidence. "This is how it is on treks in remote places. We'll be fine."

"Seems they don't have consistency," said Patricia. "Makes me uneasy."

"I'd sure feel that way if I was in the Armenian group," said Goran.

"It is most unfair to them," I said. "Something's amiss."

Charlie summed it up succinctly: "Kurds. Armenians. Turks."

One wall in the room had been tacked with a framed photograph of a giant mountain. "That's Damavand," Ian sighed, shifting our attention to a new topic. "It's in Iran. The country's highest. It's over eighteen thousand feet. Maybe that's next for us?"

"First Ararat, OK?" Charlie said what we were all thinking: focus.

Nico looked over Goran's shoulder to the opposite wall, taking the topic shift a step further, ensuring we didn't dwell on something we could not change. "I'm feeling more inclined toward that picture right now." It was a reproduction of Da Vinci's *The Last Supper*, surprising to those of us who thought of eastern Turkey as fully Muslim. "Is anyone else hungry?"

*　　*　　*

People drifted up to Ahmet with questions about their gear or to ensure the equipment they'd rented was available. He addressed all requests patiently. He and Kubi worked the room, distributing crampons. Mostly they spent time with the Armenians, aware that additional support and interest would need to be given to their group. Ahmet paying attention to them under the banner of safety helped ease the mood. Kubi tipped up boots and pressed the crampons so they could be sized and locked in place, ready for on-mountain assembly.

Three people were sent to their rooms to bring back the hiking boots they'd wear. Goran took the opportunity to dance on the stairs, showing off his newly rented boots—the rental was new, not the boots. "I've got myself outfitted," he announced happily. "At least my feet will be warm."

He told us that his luggage would remain missing, for the time being. It was scheduled to arrive in Van after we'd left Doğubeyazit for the mountain. Zafer had helped assemble his replacement gear. "I've got a nice sweater from Nico, and they also rented me a headlamp. I'm good to go up." He would spend his mountain nights in a borrowed sleeping bag.

When the flurry of preparations waned, many of the trekkers went to their rooms for a restless night of anticipation. Ahmet restarted our aborted conversation. "You can stay with my grandfather in his village. I have spoken with him already."

"And who will make that happen?" I asked. "When we come off the mountain, you won't be there."

"I promise to meet you at Base Camp on your return down the mountain."

His face said he meant it. He put a firm hand on my shoulder, just as I'd earlier watched him do with one of the Armenians, calming a worry.

Later in the evening, lounging alone on a stuffed chair in the corner of the hotel's lobby, I reflected on the fact that climbing Ararat is fraught as often with distress and danger as with reward. In my reading, one chilling account stood out as a warning; in nervous anticipation of the climb the next day, I began to fear that we, too, might get *close to* but *not on* the top.

American mountaineer Oliver Sexsmith "Mike" Crosby's cautionary tale should have been required reading for both our crew and the Armenians. Thirty-one years old, Crosby was vice consul at the US consulate in Tabriz, Iran, from where he journeyed to Turkey with consulate clerk Pierce Bahnsen and a friend, Hermann Dietrich. About their 1951 attempt to summit Mount Ararat, he wrote: "the challenge of the peak filled us with quick, suffocating eagerness."

Their arrival at a Kurdish shepherd camp at about eleven thousand feet after a long day's climb drew unwanted attention. They were up the next morning by four o'clock, dressed, breakfasted, and ready to leave camp before daybreak. Three armed guards confronted them: "the nomads did not want us to climb their mountain."

The delay defeated their early start and altered their route, yet they failed to make adjustments to their timelines; they set off to the east as they would have if they'd embarked at their scheduled time, climbing across "countless gullies, lava streams, and fields of jumbled black blocks."

Novice Bahnsen was exhausted by noon, admitted defeat, and returned to the nomads. Crosby and Dietrich gained altitude over the coming hours, trudging through slushy snow. The sun's heat bounced back in their faces from "the great white reflector." After crossing a glacier they stopped to ponder the dangers awaiting them, complicated by the late time of day and growling weather. Resolving to reach the peak, they continued. By five o'clock they were within 150 feet of the summit but faced a dilemma. They lacked sufficient time to reach the peak *and* return safely down the mountainside.

Crosby and Dietrich stared at the summit and had the courage to abandon their ascent. Ice replaced the soft snow on their descent, requiring them to use their ice axes to hack steps before they could proceed. With Crosby not far behind him, Dietrich fell into a crevasse. His arms braced him against the top as he slipped, his extended elbows preventing a terrible plummet and likely death. Extricated from the gaping hole by Crosby, the two moved more cautiously.

Once below the snowline and free of the slippery perils, the climbers also lost the comparable lightness of the snow's glow. For much of the rest of their chilling descent through narrow gullies, their way was found "entirely by feel, we traversed buttress after buttress, couloir after couloir." They arrived at the shepherds' camp at six o'clock in the morning.

Crosby's experience served to remind all pretenders—and currently that meant us—that even prepared climbers can be tossed about (or down) Ararat, at its will. Modest proficiency in climbing is often sufficient when all goes according to plan, but when it doesn't, the slightest misjudgment can put everyone in your climbing party in peril.

After a kebab dinner with our summit team, and sobered by those thoughts, I went for a late-night walk alone along the unlit streets of Doğubeyazit. I'm a stroller, and evening walks are a pensive time for me, particularly if something looms on the horizon. Kubi had stayed with the Armenians as our own group left for dinner, none of us having so much as a handshake with our new leader, a handshake which could have gone a long way to ease anxieties. The night would have to soothe them instead.

The fresh air, along with the uncertainty of the streetscape, was particularly pleasant. Over Doğubeyazit that night was the "waxing gibbous" phase of the moon, an occurrence which happens a few nights before a full moon. My positive anticipation returned; I thought again of the possibility of seeing a full moon over Mount Ararat, and the mental image acted as a salve over my day's travels.

Back in my room, I stripped everything out of my kit and spread it over the bed for a final review. Anything not needed on the mountain went into a stow-bag, along with laundry. I double-checked the headlamp and flashlight batteries as well as an LED tag that hung off my smaller pack.

I lay down and fell asleep. I might have slept in worse beds, but I can't remember when.

NINE

BASE CAMP

"[Ararat] has the appearance of an independent uplift rising abruptly in a single mass, and this isolation lends it an incomparable grandeur which serves to heighten one's impression that it is one of the highest peaks in the world."
—Fernand Navarra, *The Forbidden Mountain*

A drummer outside the Hotel Isfahan at 5 a.m. provided the daily reminder that this was Ramadan. Once awakened, at a time earlier than any of us had planned to get up, excitement about Ararat made it impossible to go back to sleep.

By sunrise, the Isfahan's forecourt was bustling with trekkers. "Give me your pack, Rick." It was Ian, wearing long pants with hiker's pockets and a blue windbreaker. "Mine's up on the bus roof. Patricia's loading Nico's." When he, the ultimate compact packer, saw the size of my pack, he chided, "Hand me Big Bertha!"

As I pushed it up to him, he kept organizing aloud. "We'll be first off, once Goran and Charlie get here. Coffee's over there. One for me too, please." He pointed to a hotplate and a pot of boiling water. I went over to make up two hot drinks, well aware that I was getting the easier chore.

Outside, the loading was inefficient but practical. Everyone wanted to help. Goran and Charlie arrived. A cluster of people and packs gathered alongside the vehicles. Two experienced packers worked as a tag team atop the first vehicle. I took them to be the cook brothers, silent Fesih and a humming Niecit. They moved in sync, taking packs passed up by many hands, laying them out individually by weight so the setup atop the vehicle would not wobble. Once sorted, the dozen bags were strung tight to the roof's aluminum carrier by elasticized ropes snaked through handles and lashed across each pack before being pulled taut and clipped to the frame with eyehooks.

Job done, the brothers stood for the first time, a pair of stocky men, keg-chested and with big hands, standing a little less than six feet tall. Satisfied, they turned to the other vehicle's loading progress. Two trekkers had climbed to the roof of this minibus and packed the bags too high, too fast, resulting in a lopsided, half-full roof rack. Below, hikers kept feeding bags to the rooftop crew faster than they could handle. Anticipating problems on the road, the cooks-turned-porters were off one vehicle and onto the other's ladder in no time, replacing the well-meaning stackers.

Kubi worked to get everyone into an orderly calm but had yet to discuss anything specifically with any member of our group. We boarded the mini-buses.

Mount Ararat's base was ten miles away. I was the last to get in the bus and sat next to an Armenian from the United States. He reached out his hand. "I'm Eric. Got in late last night. I waited in vain in Van for my luggage."

"One of our gang had the same disappointment," I said—consolingly, I hoped—"but we were able to gear him up. He'll be good." Goran had had the foresight to take his daypack of basics with him on the plane. What he lacked were warm clothing, hiking poles, and readily replaceable things like flashlights and toiletries.

"My boots are not here," Eric said. "Nor my hiking clothes. I've borrowed things but don't feel they fit. I'm not sure this makeshift approach will work for me."

We turned onto a road of rubble rocks. The bus's engine revved to keep up. We were rising from the Plain of Araxes, a plateau already 2,627 feet (800 meters) above sea level. True to Zafer's first predictions over email, the vehicle gave up trying to master the road around the 7,000-foot (2,100-meter) mark, on a slope that was quickly to become our challenging mountainside. From here we would trek up to Base Camp.

Five packhorses were waiting, with two teenage boys and a younger kid to handle them. The horses had blankets across their backs. On the ground was a packsaddle frame for each, ready to take on the groceries, cooking equipment, tents, and our individual packs.

For Kubi and the six of us, it was an orderly unpacking. The Armenians were a larger party and in need of more organization before they set out. Two were repacking their goods. Zafer had said we'd pace the two groups apart, and our group was soon ready to leave. It was not much of a head start, but we jumped at the chance to put space between us and anyone else on the mountain. The Spaniards were well ahead of us on the climb; the Russians were days advanced. We wanted our affair with the mountain to feel like ours alone.

The expedition's first day of hiking began without the eventual steepness that confronts climbers on the second day. Our group spread out in respectful portions of individual space on the open mountainside, yet near enough to provide assistance if needed.

*   *   *

Finally, we were on the trail. Charlie was in the lead, followed closely by Nico and Patricia, then Goran and Ian, with me last in line. I prefer being in the front or the back on a hike or when canoeing; it gives me a clear perspective on what the landscape is and where my companions are. Coming up from behind, aiming to move to the front of the line, was Kubi. It was the first time he and our group had shared space, and we were keen to hear from our leader. Once he was ahead of us, he called for an announcement.

"The trail is one you'll see. It is worn. There have been no big rains this low on the mountain, so the trail is obvious if you stay with it." He hesitated. "I must help the other guide get ready. I will be there for while. I'll catch up with you." This was not open to debate. Kubi now became the third person to back away from our team at the last moment.

We felt leaderless on Mount Ararat.

"The brother cooks will be with the pack horses," he said, verbally passing the leadership baton their way. "They are fast. I tell them not take shortcuts. You always have them in sight. If not, they know where you are."

Zafer had earlier passed off our concerns about the Zafer–Ahmet handoffs by saying, "What becomes, becomes." So it was that the brothers Fesih and Niecit became our expedition's fourth "guide" in less than twenty-four hours.

Goran had changed from jeans to hiking shorts at the trailhead and laced up his borrowed boots. He moved up the trail without hesitation, and we followed him confidently along the narrow path. Within the first half-mile it curved into long, deep furrows caused by rains.

The six of us put comfortable room between one another, letting our individual quests settle in. The backdrop ahead was the flank of Ararat, neither lush nor barren, but with occasional stunted shrubs.

We kept our heads down as we each got used to the feel of our day-pack. We came over a high point on a meadow that went on for a few hundred level yards before rolling upwards. Seasonally dry creek beds

A nomad woman in traditional dress goes about her day's chores, aware she might encounter trekkers. Observing such a settlements in 1856, Major Robert Stuart wrote, "The dwellers therein, with their swart faces, piercing eyes and outlandish dresses, gave the finish of life to the whole."

were at the base of the oncoming rise, and beyond was a nomad camp, watched over by two women. Their men were out herding goats and sheep. The boys who were helping our group with their horses and donkeys had likely come from here.

Their homes were fashioned from the land. Cleared twenty-pound boulders provided rocks for the house construction, stones stacked chest high to make three walls. Atop them were blue and green tarps as current iterations of animal skin coverings, draped across and down the respective rock walls to form a roof for the shelter. Ropes secured the tarps to staves and lashed the roof in position.

A nomad camp has a temporary look about it but is settled in for all eventualities. Stacking dung chips dries them out for later use as fuel in open fires or cooking stoves, such as this one at the front of a stone home.

With their men absent, the women looked hesitant to greet us. Trekkers represent awkward engagement for the mountain dwellers. They offered us canisters of coffee and milk. We accepted them gratefully and walked on through, each of us nodding our acknowledgement. As we left, Nico said, "We are to them like snow; it comes, it melts, it goes."

Our goal of the peak was more in our minds than in actual view, hidden by protective clouds. Our eyes kept to the near trail, which was clear to follow but with rocks that could trip a hiker, and water-washed moguls that needed care to navigate. The steepness was less than I'd expected, but consistent—we didn't plateau or come to level walking very often, and where we did it was brief.

"I could hike like this for a few days," said Goran.

"You won't say that tomorrow," came back Ian.

The running and hiking I'd done in preparation for this trek made the going enjoyable—no huffing or drawing down of breath—and the rate of climbing only became a concern when Charlie, Ian, Goran, and I created an unexpected gap between ourselves and Nico and Patricia.

After climbing nearly an hour, we took a rest. Below us, we saw the dust of two departing minibuses. Why were we happy to see the Armenians lagging behind? It did grant us a distorted sense of being on our own with the mountain. Was it really more special to be one of six rather than in a cluster hike? I realized that segregating ourselves from our fellow hikers risked creating a clique mentality that would do nothing for mountain safety, let alone camaraderie.

Ahead of us, on a shortcut trail, the brothers with two packhorses were making a steeper climb. Having been delayed in their start, they now wanted to be ahead of us; they waved but did not slow.

We shouldered our packs and continued along. Eventually, the brothers' route intersected with ours, and they stepped in front. We had leaders.

The terrain turned calf-burningly steep. It meant a hiker's eyes were less level with the surroundings, always wanting to look up. And there, piercing the cumulus, was Ararat's peak. We stopped, proud our motivator had decided to appear and look down upon us. I felt it was the mountain's decision, not the weather's.

"I think I can climb that," said Charlie, not at all overconfident.

"If you do, I will be with you," said Ian, knowing more than the rest of us how uncertain such ambitions could be.

"Me too, I hope," said Goran.

I felt as they did; their measured response to the shiny steel of Ararat's glaring peak was appropriate humbleness.

One of Ararat's more enduring stories of vainglory unfolded near the mountain's Parrot Glacier, and it resulted in the book that initiated my own journey. The rainbow chaser Fernando Navarra had been here six decades ago seeking fame.

Navarra was with an expedition led by Jean de Riquer. The Turkish government supported their mission; the watchful government of the USSR was less enthusiastic, as their empire included the Armenian Soviet Socialist Republic, which disputed neighboring Turkey's claim to Mount Ararat. The Russo-Turkish border was a menacing zone.

Initially they approached Ararat's northern side from the vicinity of Ahora, where the devastating earth tremors in 1840 had altered parts of the mountain—perhaps, Navarra hoped, exposing the ark. After an initial climbing attempt pulled up short, the group made a second foray, this one to a "moraine front" (implying the end of a former glacier) at 7,375 feet, a location "whose sloping sides ended in gullies." Unsuccessful in reaching the summit via the northern face, Navarra nevertheless speculated that he climbed "down the slopes that Noah and the Ark's passengers trod to reach the plain."

Within a week, the party attempted a south side ascent from a new operational base in Bayazid (Doğubeyazit). On their third attempt they encountered lightning, a blizzard, and hail. They camped at 14,000 feet. "We had the feeling that the mountain was defending itself." Roped together, they moved cautiously. "Under our feet, nothing was solid, neither rocks nor ice." Exhausted, their tenacious clawing proved successful, and the climbers were able to "touch the summit of Noah's Mountain."

Another day, hiking high on the mountain near a glacier, Navarra claimed to have encountered exactly what he sought. "On one side, I could see a mountain of ice lined with crevasses, on the other, a sheer wall. At the bottom, I saw a dark mass." The frozen shape, which "resembled that of a ship," Navarra said, could be explained in no other way than as the remnants of the long lost Ark. Lacking on-site assistance, proper equipment, and the wherewithal to excavate, the camera-less Navarra marked the location in his mind, vowing to return. His intention was to keep his discovery secret until it best served his purposes.

The result was a dispatch datelined Istanbul, August 18, 1952, that read: "Not a single trace of Noah's Ark was discovered by a French expedition which battled its way to the top of Mount Ararat. The expedition was led by Jean de Riquer, Polar explorer who raised the French flag atop the Old Testament peak."

Back in France, Navarra penned his bestselling book, *The Forbidden Mountain,* translated to English and published four years later. It earned him respect as a mountaineer, and finally revealed the ice-captured ship shape that he hoped to explore further.

Fernand Navarra returned to Ararat the year after his first expedition (before his book's publication), hoping to retrieve a sample of wood that would demonstrate to the world that he had found Noah's Ark. Punishing headaches, mountain sickness, and numbness assailed him when he was "within a hundred yards of the site of the timbers," forcing him to leave the mountain.

In 1955, Navarra's third expedition would claim proof that the mountain provided the wood sample he sought.

With his first-hand knowledge of the danger-laden journey to Ararat, along with his

Fernand Navarra was untroubled by smuggling an artifact off Mount Ararat and out of Turkey. Navarra first sought to verify the age of a timber through an Egyptian "expert at the Cairo Museum," who pronounced the wood "4,000 to 6,000 years old." Over time, Navarra's "beam" attracted less friendly scientific estimates of between 535 and 725 years old. However, an official of the Spanish Ministry of Agriculture, corroborating the first results, gave a rounded age of 5,000 years, placing it circa 3000 BCE. Portrait © Simon Carr.

experience facing this mountain's threatening circumstances, it was curious that Navarra chose that expedition's team to be composed solely of his family—his wife[13] and their sons Jose, age nine, Raphael, eleven, and Fernand, thirteen. Perhaps it was Navarra's fascination with Noah's family-based adventures that influenced his decision.

The family ventured into a restricted military zone, Navarra posing as a research archeologist whenever asked of his intentions. His gumption got the family onto the lower reaches of Ararat. There, on the first afternoon of their expedition, the family concluded it would be safest for Navarra's wife and two of their boys to return to Karakose, fifty miles away, where they would have proper accommodation.

Navarra and Raphael were left alone at the 7,850-foot level to begin the arduous tasks of exploration. They did not have mules or porters, and their packs were large. The journey would demand brute strength, extraordinary survival skills, and agility. Their survival required total interdependence.

Throughout the rest of that day and into the evening, the partners climbed, stopping to rest, at 10 p.m., around 11,500 feet.

The next day was tougher. Fernand would climb and secure a position, then let down a sixty-foot ladder of light steel. Raphael would work his way up this until "by three in the afternoon we had reached the everlasting snowfields 13,750 feet high."

Later that afternoon, while a fatigued Raphael slept, Navarra took cocaine. "All at once I felt lucid, sure of myself, filled with energy—artificial energy, but as useful as the real thing." Emboldened, he took a reconnoitering hike on the Parrot Glacier. Hundreds of feet above their camp, vast clouds parted to reveal the enfolded ice he'd discovered in 1952. The glacier had, to his happy astonishment, receded an estimated three hundred feet from when he'd seen it just three years earlier.

---

13 Although Navarra's wife accompanied her husband and their three sons to the foothills of Mount Ararat, she—like Noah's wife—remains nameless in her husband's story.

Navarra returned to camp and settled in with his son for warmth. In the middle of the night, a loosened eighty-pound rock, caught in a storm of severe gusts, edged away from its mooring and tumbled onto the tent, injuring Navarra's knee. Half in and half out of sleep after the incident (and perhaps still under the influence), he later wrote, "I dreamed that the snow was pink."

In the morning, Raphael was eager to find the Ark, saying, "I wish it were already tomorrow today." Navarra spotted timbers in the cavern he'd visited the day before. They were exhilarated. Bitterly cold and fatigued, the two trekkers took shelter in an ice cave overnight.

After a meager breakfast, they lowered themselves and their equipment into the cavern using a rope and ladder to get forty feet under the glacier. Navarra hacked into the ice, his pickaxe revealing "a black piece of wood," which he determined had been "hand-hewn." Convinced that this was from the framework of Noah's Ark, Navarra sawed off a water-soaked five-foot length of beam and filmed the ever-remarkable Raphael "hoisting up this ancient piece of wreckage."

Navarra's resulting second book, aggrandizing his reputed ice cave discovery of 1955, as well as trips in 1968 and 1969, was titled *Noah's Ark: I Touched It*. However, he would be haunted by allegations that he'd bought the wood in a nearby town and relocated it to Ararat so that it could be "discovered." Unfortunately, neither Raphael nor the intrepid photographer Navarra had taken any "locator" images of identifiable landmarks to corroborate their claim.

Our own Mount Ararat ascent trudged on. I forgot about meeting up with Paraşut, the possibility of which had long seemed more and more remote, despite being intrigued by his claims of an ice cave and ancient wooden timbers.

We headed up the mountain's southern side, six climbers led by the cooks visible only in the distance as two cantering pole stars.

The grandeur of the mountain empowered us. As we wound through another boulder-strewn section of the trail, Fesih was waiting for us around a bend. "Rest," he said. Niecit was humming to himself a few feet away. Further up the slope, clouds parted to reveal the peak. I felt overwhelmed by the size of it, even when partially draped by cumulous. The rock went gray near snow that could not quite become white in the light, and I recalled Parrot calling it "the austere, silvery head of Old Ararat." It looked indifferent to our being here, the summit tucked back out of sight as though testing our belief that it even existed at all. It seemed insurmountable.

The two teenage boys had moved on ahead with the horses, using steep short cuts. Niecit got up to leave us and said, "See you at camp. Keep as you are. On path. On mountain."

On our own again, we meandered through small boulders, only partially rounded by erosion. Sometimes one of us would hike a straight-up shortcut, as the brothers had done. The tactic brought that sense of singleness, a comfortable feeling of aloneness with the mountain, one that following a worn path did not. Only Nico and Patricia stayed on the path. When we looked back, Nico raised his hand to wave us on. An experienced adventurer, he was confident in trailing us, not wanting his pace to set ours. Realizing that it was best not to splinter the group, we stopped to wait out of Nico's line of sight. We all needed a rest.

When Nico caught up, he said, "It's becoming difficult for me on this climb."

I was surprised. I sensed Nico's humor flagging; a tenseness was evident in his voice. Remembering Charlie's comment about having trained by walking, I tried to find his eyes, thinking they might be foreshadowing the same concern. None there.

"Nico, we will keep you in sight," Ian said.

Nico nodded in agreement. "Stay with your pace. I'm not far behind."

Within thirty minutes the first of our group arrived at Base Camp. The cook tent was set close to the fire, with preparations under way for a meal. The boys were erecting a third trekker's tent, making homes for us.

They'd started far away from the cook tent and fire. Each new tent moved them closer. Ian and I walked toward the first tent, its opening flap faced the mountain slope.

"This'll do," Ian said. He set his daypack down. I tossed mine beside a second tent. "This is a marker for Patricia and Nico."

Charlie came over the lip of land that created this plateau, saw where we were, and claimed a tent for himself and Goran. Belatedly realizing that we risked socially separating ourselves from our fellow climbers, the Armenians, Goran and Charlie chose a newly set tent, infiltrating the other tribe's grounds and ensuring that kinship would develop. Ian moved my pack to mark a more integrated tent for Patricia and Nico.

Base Camp: The pack horses made the difference between an arduous hike and an enjoyable trek for the expedition members. Here they've been unpacked as Ian and Nico survey the site of Base Camp and contemplate the next day's climb.

The walk had changed my thinking, and I accepted that we were fortunate to share a mountain, meals, and a quest with the second group.

Though the Armenians had left the drop-point well after we'd departed, their two lead hikers gained enough ground to keep company with Nico and Patricia. They arrived onto the hem of our campsite together, their camaraderie strengthening Nico's stride.

"Welcome," said Charlie. All four acknowledged his flourish. All the tents were now sprung up for the evening's community.

The sound of bickering reached camp before the remaining hikers did. Kubi was the last to schlep his way into camp, lines of irascibility showing in the squint of his eyes. Disappointment in their guiding arrangements had not dissipated for some during the Armenian troop's climb.

Two six-foot makeshift tables were set end-to-end, pressed-wood sheets lain across sawhorses. There were assorted stools, plastic or wood. Everyone grabbed a prop and sat near the food. The blue and white stools tilted with the contour of the ground. Goran looked oversize in his small chair, but Ian, sitting at a slant, appeared content. On one side of the table, Patricia, the only one of us who was well-groomed, sat awkwardly on her chair, leaning toward Nico, who leaned toward Charlie, still wearing his cowboy hat, now tilted on his head in alignment with the sloping table. We clustered toward one end of the dinner table, Ian, Goran, and I sitting between newfound friends from Armenia.

Appetizers were set in bowls on the table. And here, nine thousand feet up on Mount Ararat, were two baskets of Wagon Wheels for the picking. There were salami and cheese sandwiches. Also on offer were toffee-colored cheddar cheese, salted crackers, and pretzels. Lots of pretzels. The carbohydrate top-up for the end of the day was accompanied by orange juice, prepared from concentrate.

Goran seemed downcast. "I was dreaming of a barbecue on the mountainside."

"And a cold, cleansing ale?" It was Charlie.

Goran continued fantasizing. "A friend of mine hiked a mountain in Africa. At night there was always meat over open fire. One night their guide slaughtered a sheep right in front of the hiking party. Within an hour they had this amazing barbecue. It just makes me think . . . maybe . . ."

"Hold that thought," said Nico, motioning toward the cook's tent.

Fesih came out with a large aluminum bowl of spaghetti and started serving. Niecit brought a second large bowl of spaghetti from the kitchen tent to the table, also cradling a pan of steaming hot tomato sauce. To complete this, just as the food was losing heat to the cool air, he came back out with another pan of sauce and another load of spaghetti.

The sharing was uneven at first, as uncertainty about supply resulted in everyone taking modest portions on the first go-around. When Fesih came with a fourth bowl, we knew we were going to have enough. Then he returned with a platter of fire-crisped chicken. It's hard for me to think of a meal tasting better than that one did after our long day.

Eric arrived near the end and walked over to sit beside Ian and me as Niecit put out sliced watermelon. "Looks like an interesting dinner. You'll need it for tomorrow's climb."

"You'll need it too, Eric. There's lots left," Ian said.

"I won't need it unless I get better sorted on my decomposing foot-wear. It was rough coming up today. It'll be steeper tomorrow."

Ian asked what size of shoe Eric wore.

"Ten."

Ian shook his head. I added, "Mine are ten and a half. You're wel-come to my runners, but there's no ankle support. That'd be dangerous. You need proper boots."

"Right," Eric announced. "About now, they might be at the Van airport."

Dusk descended, and I walked to the side of the plateau, opposite to where we'd climbed onto it. There was a deep canyon, out of range of the glow from the fire pit and flashlights, and I felt peace as I looked out over it.

An angry voice bit the calm. "That is not what it should be!" A woman standing next to Kubi was unhappy. Kubi was now supposed to lead our expedition to the summit instead of the Armenians, but had tried to square their discontent by hiking up the mountain with them today. She raised her voice. "You are the senior guide. You should be with us!"

Kubi's impatience got the better of him. "You should stay at this Base Camp tomorrow. This is how far you should go," he said. "It is safer."

"That is not your business," said another hiker. "We expect you to see us up the mountain."

Frustrated, Kubi walked away to the cook tent. The man and woman trailed him, then thought better of it and left him alone. The fact that a Turkish-Kurdish guide was arguing with Armenian patrons was not lost on me. The cook-tent sanctuary would not protect him for long.

The woman left the camp and came near the fifty-foot drop off into the canyon. It was now so dark that only a flashlight made it safe there. I shone my light on the path, surprising her.

"We are frustrated," she said.

"Why are you on the mountain?" I asked, looking to stay out of their argument.

"For Armenians, this is a sacred place. Ararat was part of Armenia. We lost it. That should not have been. It is a stolen signature of our nationhood. Armenia struggles to become a country defined by what's there, not what's missing."

Trying to tread carefully, I said: "It's been one hundred years—since the atrocities—"

"That is not too long to forget. You seem not to know. You should. After the First World War," she broke in, "Mount Ararat lapsed into Turkish control. That is what new borders did."

Access to Mount Ararat had been restricted to foreigners on and off for many years. It was formally "closed" from 1990 to 1999. Climbers wanting to hike Ararat during the Soviet Union's domination of Armenia were often denied permission or harassed by Russian troops. That much I knew. But clearly I didn't know the whole story.

She turned to face the mountainside. "These guides, they are Turkish and do not want us here. They take our money but do not give respect. The Turks, they killed our people. Many people deny genocide swept here. Turkey certainly does." Her anger put a sting in the tail of her words.

"I should know more of this history," I admitted. The sentiment firmed my resolve to spend time in Armenia, to learn. One might be forgiven for having an imperfect understanding of historical twists and turns of a land that has witnessed vast changes over thousands of years; unless, of course, the topic was genocide.

"The world remembers the Jews and the Holocaust," she replied. "That is important. But it was not the first genocide. Nor was it the last. Think of Rwanda. Bosnia."

With that, she dove into the core of her evening's harsh feeling. "Mount Ararat witnessed genocide. It is a mountain Turks then took from Armenia."

Later, one of the Armenian hikers walked over to where I stood alone near the horses. He'd watched the woman and me talk earlier, heard the exasperation in her voice and my muted responses as the scope of the Armenian accusations settled in on me. I wondered how many others among "the internationals" did not know this horror.

Into the quiet he said, "Do you recognize her?"

"No, we've never met," I replied.

"She is an actress. Her name is Arsinée Khanjian. She has been in many films, but for here, you should know of the movie *Ararat*."[14]

---

14 Core to *Ararat*'s storyline is a film being made within the film, portraying documented events to draw out Turkey's denial of the genocide. As the *New York Times* said, "the film is ultimately committed to the belief that anguished remembrance is far preferable to willful amnesia." The UK's *Independent* reported that Turkey's deputy prime minister chaired a meeting of the Commission Against False Genocide Accusations, during which "a decision was taken to utilize all the resources of Turkey's culture and foreign ministries to prevent the

(Footnote continued on next page)

Bolts of understanding fell into place for me. Travelers should not visit this part of the world without viewing this movie, and I hadn't. Knowing of the film's existence was not enough; I'd seen the preview in my trip research, but what is ninety seconds? If I had viewed the movie, I'd have been aware of the Siege of Van and of why so much anxiety filled our campsite.

Charlie was the first one I met heading back to the camp. He was in a contorted pose. He was a yoga instructor. Beside him was an Armenian from America, wearing a denim shirt over brown cords that were tucked into his wool socks. His boots were off. "I'm taking instruction," he said before folding to the ground and rolling to a sitting position. Out of his shirt pocket he pulled a cigar. "Saving this for the summit."

When his student was gone, Charlie told me, "I had a wonderful conversation with the woman. She's an actress. We talked about MOPE—the Most Oppressed People Ever. Oppressed peoples talk about MOPE. She feels MOPE are the Armenians. I feel the Irish. You?"

"My ancestors are Norwegian," I sighed. "*They* were the oppressors."

Earlier, I'd asked Ian where to stow my pack in the empty tent. He'd said, "On the mountain up-side, in case a rock tumbles down toward us." I lay thinking about such a prospect. Ian nodded off, his feet up on Big Bertha. Near to our shelter, Goran and Charlie sorted out their own difficulties posed by the limited space with all the alacrity of a marriage squabble.

"Great. Zipper stuck in my sleeping bag," Charlie complained.

"Should have brought your own, instead of renting," Goran said. "Sleep warm."

"If you'd move your bag, I'd have more room," Charlie replied, laughing like he was gargling.

---

movie's opening." Khanjian's husband, Atom Egoyan, wrote and directed the 2002 film.

"If you didn't need so much room," Goran said, "my pack would be just fine."

Before he finished, Charlie kept at him: "If you don't like it here, hang your clothes in another tent. You're old enough to move out."

Goran softened. "I need to borrow your sweater vest for tomorrow, and those extra pants you offered. I'm cold."

"Stay cold!" Charlie scolded.

"If you want room, put your pillow and head outside the flap."

Mountain silence descended amid the guffaws.

TEN

MOUNTAIN OF PAIN

"There is not enough water on the earth now and there would
not have been [then] to actually submerge most of the earth."
—Dr. Bülent Atalay, University of Mary Washington

The campsite was quiet when I awoke around 5:30. I went looking for a coffee to warm me up. A quiet chant softened the
morning. Niecit poked his head out of the cook tent and held
a mug, anticipating my request. I was grateful to accept; it was hot and
flavorful, brewed from his private stock.

I walked up the slope to exercise my legs. Ararat's upper reaches
appeared only in brief glimpses, teasing me. The closer we got to the
peak, the more unknowable it seemed.

Ian showed up, rubbing his eyes. "You snore."

"No," I parried, used to it now. "I'm cured."

"You are *not* cured."

Breakfast sorted itself out much as dinner had. Those who were
around early took the seats they wanted. Last night's shared angst about
today's climb had melded the two expeditions. Charlie sat talking with
Arsinée and an Armenian man, both of them with daypacks at the
ready. Ian and I matched up with Armenians at our end of the table. A
squat man talked about the simple joy of being on the mountain. "It is

here I have wanted to be. It is here I now am." An Armenian and Goran helped serve instant coffee, watery tea, and hot chocolate. Flat, beige biscuits were on offer. Ian passed them over, joking with us, "These might make the difference between a successful summit and a missed opportunity. Eat up." I looked around; Nico and Patricia were nowhere to be seen.

Fesih moved with quick steps over to the table with a pan of scrambled eggs. He walked around the table swiftly, mindful that everyone wanted them hot, ladling a steaming spoonful on each plate. He began the circuit again, continuing to share wisely until they were gone. Goran emerged from the cook tent with a plate of fried ground meat that he placed in the middle of the table. The piping pile went quickly.

When our extended family was seated, Eric rose from his end of the table. "Everyone," he began, "I'm not going any further up the mountain. I talked with Kubi just now. He's sending one of the cooks down with me this afternoon. You know I don't have my proper gear. The makeshift stuff isn't working."

There was consternation among his Armenian group. A fellow traveler said, "Let us work to fix it. There's no need to leave."

Eric was firm: "It's my decision to take. It's taken. I will leave."

Goran said, "We can find a way to help."

One joker interjected, "I've got extra stuff I don't need. Can you take it back to the hotel for me?"

Eric was content in his situation. "I'd be happy to. I'll wait till you've all gone up the mountain and rifle your packs before I head down."

Everyone laughed. Eric would leave with our best wishes. Many years earlier, Fernando Navarra had written of a teammate turning back once partway up Ararat, noting that the man simply announced, "I have never climbed so far before. I shall not go farther." Navarra felt that "these were the words of an honest man. They meant that he could climb farther, that he would be able to reach the summit, but that he did not want to."

Ian leaned over to me. "And then there were eleven," he said.

Charlie and Goran sat down in the empty chairs across from us. Goran said, "I think the guide is right. Yesterday showed a strain on some. Some climbers should wait at this camp while the rest of their group climbs further."

"Have you seen Nico?" I asked.

"I saw him and Patricia on a walkabout." Charlie pointed. "They're coming down from the rise."

Nico gestured us to come to them. With coffee mugs refilled, we scrambled up the embankment to their tent.

"This is not my mountain," said Nico. With unflinching honesty he admitted, "Yesterday was tough on me. I know mountains, and sometimes they don't want you. Not sure why. This is as far as I'm going."

"*Ağrı Dağı*," breathed Charlie, drawing out the Turkish name for Ararat with an Irish accent. "It means 'mountain of pain.'"

"We're in no rush. We've an extra day to acclimatize," Ian said. "Take your time."

"For sure, Nico. We can pace ourselves differently today," Goran agreed.

Nico's weather-beaten soul was resolute. "You can't out-source your adult decisions. I'm going out this morning."

Ian said, "We hear you, Nico. You could stay here at Base Camp, and we'll pick you up on the way down."

Nico: a man and a mountain. As James Salter wrote in his mountain-grounded book, *Solo Faces*, "The classic decision is always the same, whether to retreat or go on."

Nico shook his head. "Guys, I'll see you at the hotel in a few days." He added, "Patricia told me she's going to the summit."

Nico's intention was to ensure that the five of us climbed unhindered. Reduced in size, our group was stronger. It felt like his gift to us.

Nico turned to me. "Rick, take care of Patricia."

"I will." I knew he was leaving his partner on a dangerous mountain and wanted nothing more than a sense of trust and insurance. Everyone respected Patricia's self-contained style and sense of competition.

Nico looked around the camp and back at the four of us. "She keeps her own tent." He winked.

Then his left hand wrapped the back of my neck in a nudge directing me away from the others. We walked among the volcanic debris where it was desolate, stopping to look up the face of a beckoning mountain.

"I was hoping to stand with you at the summit, Nico."

"Rick, I'm sixty-nine," he replied. "Most of my good friends are dead. Two brothers are dead. Relationships are to be treasured. I want our friendship to see another day."

"Me too."

"Living takes skill. I'm going to live by walking down this mountain."

The boy who was loading the packhorses had stacked goods beside them. He tossed the buffer blanket over the horses' bare backs. He'd rolled up the sleeping pads used to cushion us against the rocky ground under sleeping bags. He was ready to strike out as soon as a taller person helped him pile up the gear and tie it down.

Enter Goran—tall, without any horse-packing sense. The boy directed him. With Charlie helping out, they apportioned and secured the load. When it was all done, Kubi pushed hard against the stack of plastic stools that had been lashed across the top of bedding and crammed on one of the packs. The load held. The boy knew he'd passed a test. So had Goran and Charlie.

*　　　*　　　*

We were no longer in the run-up of gentle slopes; now we were on the mountain's steeper slant, and the trail was rough. Ian, clenching two climbing poles, said, "I wished earlier that I'd brought two climbing poles. Now I have Nico's. Right thing. Wrong reason."

Kubi had encouraged the Armenians to split their group in two: those capable of further ascent, and those, in his view, less fit for the day's demanding climb. He'd suggested two or three of them might stay at Base Camp. "I would leave one of the teenage boys here with you for security and to help with meals."

But the Armenians were clear. "We go together," said one of the men.

The horses and handlers were soon out of sight. It was the young men's job to prepare Camp II for our arrival—a lot of work. We followed, down to one cook-guide, Niecit. Fesih was descending with Eric and Nico.

Kubi saw off the Armenian group and climbed fast to catch up with us, leaving the tension between the Armenians and their alternative guide at the 10,000-foot level. The rift would catch up to us by dusk.

The six of us made steady progress until Kubi, who was in the middle of our group, said, "It's midday. I don't see any Armenians below."

"The stronger ones are waiting, I think," Patricia said.

Above, we could see the packhorses, the young boy, and Niecit on the trail. Kubi whistled. With hand signals he communicated that our group was now Niecit's responsibility. They should slow their pace and keep us in sight. Kubi bid us goodbye. "I'm going to help guide. We make two teams for them."

Goran, seeing the cook and his helper seated for rest, made no move to lead us on. Instead he asked, "Do you really think Noah docked his ark on this steep mountain and avoided a shipwreck?"

Patricia responded first: "A barge, hundreds of feet long? I don't see that flat of a surface on the mountain."

Ian, being practical: "Say the Ark had a draft of twenty feet. You couldn't know what formation was below you, mountain cliff or field landing."

Charlie added, "A rough landing would send all the animals tumbling to the front of the boat."

I liked these expedition mates for their sense of selves, their nonplussed attitudes and irreverence. Laughing, we picked up our packs and started up, steeply.

We were a tired group arriving in Camp II. At 14,000 feet, our camp was higher than the 12,782-foot (3,896 meter) peak of Lesser Ararat.

The cook and the boy had commandeered a wide space for our campsite, one where they'd camped on other occasions, though mountain protocol didn't automatically grant them this spot. We could see the Russian tents pitched above us, but they showed no sign of life. "If the Russians left a bit late or faced delays, they should be coming down by now. Sure hope everything is OK for them," Ian wondered aloud.

West of us was the camp of Spaniards, the cook told us. "Weather not good last night. They try tonight." That might explain the Russians' absence. Maybe they'd dodged the bad weather by deciding to make a daytime ascent and descent. Whatever they did, they only had a few hours left before darkness.

The altitude slowed our breathing. We'd felt the drag for the last two hours on the trail. Relaxing at the campsite, we were happy the lad had pitched our tents for us, flaps facing away from the anticipated wind. We unpacked. The boy had taken Patricia's pack to her tent. When she was refreshed, she came over to sit with Ian and me, wearing the same look of tiredness that I felt.

"Me too," was all she said.

Ian was buoyant. He once had to troubleshoot in a mineshaft over ten thousand feet below sea level, and now was standing that many feet above it. Being here was a refined sensation for him, even if it left him a little linguistically altered by the altitude—"This moment. Feel it good."

"We have an extra day built into our ascent. Like the Spanish over there," said Goran. His span took in the orange tents and the smoke of the Spaniards' cooking fire across a valley. "We thought they were ahead of us. They should have been up and down by now, heading lower."

"Today was our day to acclimatize," I said. "It was set for us to climb up here. If the altitude bothers anyone, we could descend and stay again at Base Camp."

"Go back down?" Patricia asked. "Are you serious?"

"That's the option," Goran said. "Then we'd ascend to here again tomorrow, adjusted and in better shape for the summit attempt. That extra day may be why the Spanish expedition is still here."

Ian was emphatic. "There's no need to go back down. You all look fine."

"You all look terrible," Charlie said.

In anticipation of our ascent, these mountain five look more relaxed than we actually felt. From left: author, Goran, Charles, Patricia, and Ian.

We laughed. We were tired, yes, but fine. Dinner would bolster our strength. No one wanted to go back down in order to acclimatize. It had seemed an odd option to me when I'd first heard about it from Zafer. Why head back down when we'd worked so hard to get here? We could walk about an extra day if we needed. Looking back now, it was a mistake to think that way, to assume that it would simply be a matter of time before you adjusted to the altitude. Not so. Altitude illness could come quickly and unfairly. The best antidote was to move to a lower elevation and give your body more time. But at the moment we all felt adequate with the reduced oxygen.

"What this means for us," Ian began—thinking to leave an opening for a delay day if anyone needed it—"is that we might attempt the summit tonight."

"Tonight?" Charlie wasn't hesitating or skeptical, only curious.

"Yes," said Goran. "Leave camp later tonight. It's either that, or we hike around tomorrow, let the altitude work with us and go up tomorrow night."

"Tonight," said Ian. "We should go tonight. We can *see* the mountain. The weather, we think we know. Tomorrow may be bad. Let's take tonight."

"So long as Kubi guides us," Patricia said, settling the question.

Ian asked, "All in?"

There was a round of eye-to-eye checking, one to the other, everyone facing everyone else. It was not a moment for false pride.

Nods came from two of them, followed by two separate yeses.

"Make it five," I said.

"Plus Kubi," said Patricia.

"He may already be planning that," said Ian, "but we have to find the right time to ask him. We should approach him together, but not until he's finished dealing with the day's frustrations. Let him get here and settle down, have dinner."

Anticipating our success with Kubi, and to distract our minds with something a little less serious, Goran jested, "Then if we have an extra day after the summit, let's go looking for Noah's Ark."

*   *   *

In the early 1970s, after rocketing into space aboard Apollo 15's *Endeavour*, American astronaut James Irwin drove the Lunar Roving Vehicle around on the Hadley-Apennine region of the moon, logging more hours on its surface than anyone before him.

When the experienced media spokesman made the first of his several mountaineering visits to Ararat, eleven years had elapsed since his moon landing, and he turned his communication skills toward new messaging. Every trip the one-time aerospace research pilot took to Mount Ararat was part of an organized search for evidence of his childhood hero, Noah, and "his water-weary family." Unfortunately for Irwin and his climbing party, during an excursion to Ararat in 1982, tensions were high between Turkey's border territory and Russian forces to the north. Russian surveillance and the incessant jamming of Turkish radio channels by Russian soldiers, a technique that courted disaster on the mountain, stalked Irwin's entourage, deliberately compromising their walkie-talkies.

Two members of their expedition would succeed in making the summit on their first attempt. They'd come from Doğubeyazit, approaching the south face as we were now doing. They rose at 2:30 a.m., left town, and made their way to the 11,500-foot meadow near Lake Kop. Irwin described their hike as "looking for the prow of the ark behind every rock." From there they were bound toward the Ahora Gorge, considering a search of the North Canyon.

The lead American authority on Noah's Ark at that time was amateur historian, hobbyist researcher, and ardent bibliophile Eryl Cummings. Cummings, who'd already climbed Mount Ararat seventeen times, invited Irwin to lead this 1982 expedition. It was almost the former astronaut's last adventure.

Irwin's near-death on Ararat is a reminder of the uncompromising terrain the mountain has to offer. On the morning that he and other climbers were set to summit, the fifty-two-year old Irwin grew fatigued around the 13,000-foot level. He bid the others go on ahead while he rested. Against his own directives for safety, he headed off alone to return

Astronaut James Irwin's Christian beliefs put him in tune with the creationist logic that God had designed the earth with age "built in"—for example, creation of a mountainside containing the fossils of sea creatures (as an alternative to the theory of evolution and the effect of plate tectonics). He held that the common translation of Hebrew texts is "without error" and does not contradict established geological information. During the lunar landing, Irwin's tasks included collecting moon rocks. From one sample, petrologists determined that the moon and the earth were created at the same time. Irwin was credited with discovering "the Genesis Rock." Portrait © Simon Carr.

to base camp. Tiring more, he spotted a route he took to be a timesaver across the snow. He crouched to unpack his crampons and sat down to harness them onto his boots. It was the last alert thought he had until he regained consciousness hours later, at the bottom of the snowfield. By then it was dusk. Irwin described himself to be "in a pile of sharp rocks and I was a bloody mess."

A falling boulder had crashed against Irwin's skull, propelling him into a tumbling slide down the snow. He broke five teeth. Rocks and ice had lacerated his legs and hands. The mountainside had carved at his face, head, and neck. He was weakening from blood loss, as dehydration and cold set in. Irwin managed to pull his sleeping bag from his backpack and crawl in. He huddled in the dark against the steep and slippery mountainside, crouched behind a boulder for shelter, protected from the sporadic tumbling of rocks from above.

Alarms were not raised until the summiteers at the 14,000-foot camp connected with the Lake Kop base below, over radio channels still hampered by the Russians. Eventually everyone realized Irwin was missing. The rescue mission began immediately, but with great uncertainty about where to start looking. Their search area was *somewhere* on Mount Ararat, "one of the largest land masses of any single mountain in the world," according to Irwin himself. The searchers wondered if Russians "disguised as shepherds" had kidnapped him. No one knew he'd drifted off the trail around the 12,500-foot level, let alone that his descent route was distorted by a long fall off the track. Teams descended the mountain from the high camp like lines of longitude, while others fanned out across the Parrot Glacier's lower rim.

"James?!" The call went out repeatedly, echoing false hopes: "James . . . James . . ." Incredibly, one of the echoes reached him. He responded weakly and was heard. Attempts to climb down to him resulted in serious accidents for two other climbers. Finally he was reached. Bandaged on-site, he was transported to camp and loaded on a horse. A four-hour, bone-jarring carryout followed. A Turkish commando team ensured that they arrived at a military first-aid post, where Irwin was transferred to a hospital.

Undeterred, Irwin returned to Ararat later that same year, following up on a reported sighting of Ark evidence. He was back again in 1983, and flew around Mount Ararat several times in a Turkish army airplane, taking hundreds of photographs, particularly of the Ahora Gorge. The crew "didn't sight anything that looked like Noah's Ark," and decided to conduct a ground search. They camped on the northeast side of the gorge, exploring from there. Irwin remained enthusiastic throughout, always reporting with confidence that this expedition or the next would discover evidence of the Ark and put a world of disbelief to rest.

Irwin made a final trip in 1986, then announced that his days on the mountain were over. "It's easier to walk on the moon. I've done all I possibly can, but the Ark continues to elude us," he said. "I think it is time others take up the search."

*   *   *

Brightly colored plastic stools were arranged around our dinner table, similar to the previous night. The table was made using planks left behind by other groups, and I wondered how often a table was burned when the firewood that was carried in ran scarce and the cold became unbearable. Colored cups decorated the table, our tents were all red, and our packs were a crayon box of hues. It was as though a rainbow carpeted our campsite.

We five sat at one end of the table. The other end was not yet occupied, as only a few of the Armenians had made camp, and they were still waiting for the others. It'd been half an hour since Kubi had shown up with four men, faster walkers he'd hived off from the Armenian group. When they arrived, he had turned to us and raised his shoulders, as if to shift stress off them and up to the clouds. Then he returned down the mountain to help the other guide ensure that everyone got to camp.

When the four Armenians finally sat down at the table, realizing it might be a while before the rest of their group joined them, we shared stories of how the day's climb had bushed us all. There was an ease between everyone, much like our muscles relaxing after a climb.

"This is Armenia's mountain," said one climber I'd overheard was a man of the cloth. The day's climb had removed any erect bearing such a religious role might give someone; he was as weary and slouched as the rest of us. "We have been forced to share it," he added, and the tone struck me as somewhat defeatist. It was then I realized there was nothing particularly "Turkish" about Ararat, save for the border. Everything I'd read, aside from the geographic and political victors of present day, affirmed my view that I was hiking in or near ancient Mesopotamia, and historic Urartu, and a one-time Greater Armenia—place names themselves as old as the name "Ararat." The Armenians were our hosts on Mount Ararat, more so than the Kurds and the Turks.

Niecit emerged from the mess tent with two large bowls in his hands. Looking quickly at the mountain peak, as though asking a blessing for the meal, he served spaghetti again, this time with chicken and a sauce that was white but not creamy. Tomato soup arrived in a cauldron carried by a teenage boy and was scooped into tin bowls at each place setting. Our table dug in, not waiting for the others to arrive. Polite restraint was too much to ask of hungry people.

Daylight was leaving. The mountain above gave a ragged bow our way as though it knew this was the last we'd see of it; next, we hoped, was a midnight climb through the dark with restricted visibility. Clouds played as though taking turns to pirouette protectively for the massif, denying us a panorama of our lofty goal.

Goran pointed up to where we'd be climbing later and sang, "The Russians are coming. The Russians are coming." As if conjured by his song, ten Russians descended the trail in loose formation. They had an

Camp II: The angle of the expedition's tents contemplated the prevailing winds as well as the mountain's lack of hospitable terrain. Lesser Ararat is in the distance.

array of equipment styles—some backpacks appeared quite large for the ascent, while a few climbers had only small satchels strapped to their waists. Yet this irregularly outfitted group could only have achieved the summit if they were fully reliant on one another's skills. Clearly they'd shared the loads and the responsibilities among each person, dependent on ability. They slid into their higher campsite, disappeared into their tents, and went quiet.

The remaining Armenians and Kubi arrived. The climbers freshened up, and soon they too had eaten, but Kubi was nowhere to be seen. Darkness enveloped our camp, and the five of us went back to our respective tents, fidgeting with our gear in anticipation of a midnight climb. We knew that if Kubi was game to go, we'd be heading up the mountain. I had to admit, as excited as I was at the prospect of summiting in only a few hours, I couldn't help feeling like something was off, that it wasn't supposed to be like this.

"I wanted to summit under tomorrow's full moon," I admitted to Ian.

"I heard that," he replied. "Amy told me it's why we changed the original schedule and left the day we did."

"And . . ."

"And what? And now you'll miss that?" He repeated his earlier concern. "You can wait. We can all wait. But what if tomorrow the weather is terrible? If tonight we cannot make it, we have tomorrow night as backup. It's better this way."

I had to admit he was right. The romantic in me had lost perspective.

The air and the climb had drained me of energy. I napped. It might have been 7:30. I woke to see Ian snoozing. He snored. I crawled out of the tent and, walking around, saw the Russians' campfire a few hundred feet up the hill. They were sitting on the ground, in a circle, singing. It was pleasant, not boisterous, and it sounded, to my ears, like patriotic or religious songs. I walked up the trail toward them. As I neared the group, a burly man who was wrapped in a blanket and seemed too big to have climbed this mountain shouted to me, "Come here! Come over!" As I got closer, he said, "Come in," and made space in their circle for me to sit near him.

"My name is Mutashat," he said, "and this is my son." He pointed further. "Him, my cousin." And so it went, around the circle.

"Did you summit Ararat?" I asked.

Mutashat spoke in Russian to the men and they laughed. *Yes!* They were cheerful after their triumph and boastful. They all raised their mugs, toasting their success.

One of them saw that I did not have a mug. "For you," he said, handing me one. I sipped. It tasted hot and smoky, black and strong, sweet tea from a Russian caravan. They had me in their thrall.

I asked, "What was it like?"

Again in Russian, the older man translated my question, and they rapidly swapped stories all at once, as if I would be able filter their individual excitement. The patron of it all calmed everyone down. He stared at me with eyes hooded in weariness yet aglow with satisfaction. "First, I ask you. Do you summit tonight?"

"That is the plan."

"Then I cannot tell you what it feels like, because that would spoil it. We wanted to summit night before. We could not, with wind. Rain. Waiting was difficult. Two stayed behind when rest of us summited." He sipped his tea. His eyes lost their tiredness. "You will feel on top of the world."

Through his grin he told the other climbers in Russian what he'd told me in English. Their heads bobbed. I'm sure what I heard next was a Russian chorus of, "You will feel on top of the world!" They leaned away from the fire in laughter, as though it was the greatest line imaginable, and continued celebrating among themselves. Only when I stood to leave, much later, did they realize that their guest was still among them. I returned to our camp feeling buoyed by unmistakable good wishes in a language I could not understand.

ELEVEN

FINAL ASCENT

*"The noble thing about Ararat is not the parts but the whole.
I know nothing so sublime as the general aspect of this huge yet
graceful mass seen from the surrounding plains . . ."*
—James Bryce, Mountaineer, *Transcaucasia and Ararat*

It must have been after nine o'clock in the evening when Kubi appeared from within the cook's tent, rubbing his eyes and stretching his arms, waking from a nap of his own. He finally sat down for dinner. He'd had only a little time to himself when the five of us gathered round his chair, anxious. Ian decided this was a good time to make our pitch: "Kubi, are you tired from the day's hiking, or do you feel like attempting the peak tonight?"

"Tired, yes, of people." Kubi looked at us and smiled. "Nico was brave to know that you five will make it better without him."

Encouraged, Ian continued. "We're acclimatized. We don't need another day to explore around here. We want to climb tonight, to summit. We are ready."

"You look ready," Kubi said, keeping our spirits up. "Tonight we climb. Go prepare your ascent packs before sleep. Get rests. Remember energy—juice and chocolate bars. Make easy to access. It will terribly be cold. Check batteries on headlamps. You all headlamps?"

"We will be ready," Patricia announced.

I reckoned we'd summit under a bright moon and not need headlamps.

"I ask once more, all needs," Kubi added. And he went through the checklist: crampons, walking sticks. He did not need to cover the basics—gloves, extra socks, first aid, and toiletries—but he did remind us, "Anyone taking altitude pills, it is now you should take for final ascent."

"The Armenians," he sighed, "are set in hearts to climb tonight too. They should wait day. But they are of mind to go. I tell guide leave with them before we go."

As we left him to his coffee and contemplation, he said, "I wake you after midnight. Be readying by 12:30. We will away at 1:30 in summit hope. Hope of seeing the sun rise over Iran and Armenia and Turkey, all at once."

I wasn't sure I would be able to sleep at all. There was a sweet, exhilarating smell of risk in the air. I'd read enough about success sidestepping mountaineers on this peak to realize danger loomed and failure was its companion.

"It's midnight," Ian announced from his sleeping bag next to me, his hand shaking my shoulder. He bolted upright with an experienced alertness. "Get up."

I opened my eyes wide.

"I can't sense the moon," he said. He leaned forward, pulling on his jacket and loosening the tent's flap to peek outside. "Covered sky," he announced.

Kubi walked our way, his steps crunching pebbles. "You are eager," he said.

There was no need for him to waken any of us. Just after 1:00 a.m., we assembled. Goran came to our tent, ski goggles braced over his toque and flaps down to his ears, a small pack hung at his left side. Charlie wore a thick ski jacket with a hood that he'd pulled up and over a front-rimmed

167

hat. Topping it all was his headlight, shining brightly into my eyes. I reached over and flipped it downward. "You might have to go first," I joked, "and light the mountainside for us." He took a swig from one of his two water bottles and wondered aloud, "Might this freeze?"

Patricia was dressed in a puffy white parka, a white woolen hat, dark winter pants, and black boots. It was good camouflage. Goran said to her, "Don't fall off the trail, or we might not find you in the snow."

Ian had a trained eye and comprehensive kit, and was the most ready of us all: sunglasses tucked into the outer chest pocket of a red ski suit. His backpack was the largest of anyone's. It looked to include everything he might need, from first aid to extra warmth.

Goran clapped both his hands on my shoulders. "Rick, you all geared up?"

"Ready," I said, not entirely certain this was true.

"Look up there!" Patricia pointed up the mountain to a rising line of lights, the headlamps of the Armenian group.

Kubi said, "They go too fast too early. They have unequal fitness."

We shuffled and stomped our feet, anxious to climb and wanting to leave his rift with them behind.

"About Spaniards," Kubi said, "I talk with Spanish guide. He says group very fit and experienced. They are eight. Six of them climb with guide; two will stay down. All are here for some of team to summit. They decamp same time we do." He pointed to a place above us in the dark. "Expect them to pass us, and give way when they near."

"I think we should beat them up the mountain," Goran said.

"A race?" Charlie asked.

To me this sounded like the type of unnecessary fun that enlivens an escapade and makes a motivating mood.

"Either we follow or we lead. If we go now, they'll be on our heels right away. If our stride is good, we can take the lead and keep it," Ian said.

"Let's go," Patricia said. The challenge was on.

*   *   *

Mount Ararat brooded. The clouds broke up now and then, revealing occasional stars. The moon, swallowed by a heavenly mist, cast a low glow toward the peak, or at least the angled view we took in.

As we started to hike, the incline from camp covered ground we'd walked earlier in the evening, as our nerves settled. Large rocks and narrow footholds soon forced us to use our walking poles for leverage and balance.

Our goal was to reach the summit before sunrise. That meant over a three-thousand-foot elevation gain, climbed on a mile and a half of switchback trails ending with a straight-on ascent. Kubi looked back at us frequently as we jostled into rhythm, no doubt thinking through the dangers and inconveniences. If one of us had to return, we'd all have to return.

He stopped after twenty minutes. "Short rest. If the mountain welcomes us, the mountain will let us climb. We need not rush."

"Do not let the tiring tire you out," said Ian. I wasn't entirely sure what he meant by this.

Charlie leaned his pack against a rock and looked down the mountain. "The Spanish are on the climb," he said. We looked to where he pointed. Their formation kept them tight and moving as a single unit. Their headlamps flickered when the large rocks briefly blocked them from our view, and veered as a trekker looked for footing. Their guide was like a tracer, light steady and pointed ahead. We started up.

In what seemed a little over an hour out of camp, we caught up with the Armenians, who clustered together where the trail widened. They rested as if settled into chairs made of rock. Three of them and their guide were arguing.

Kubi looked back at us and directed, "Keep going. Pass through."

We breathed hellos. A hundred yards past them, Kubi slackened, and fifty feet later he stopped at a bend in the path, out of their sight. "Wait here," he said. "I will talk with guide." He threaded through us and headed back down the trail.

Ten minutes later he was back with us. "They have raging debate," he said. "They left camp too quickly."

"Why the hurry?" Charlie asked.

"Anybody can rush. It takes experience to go slow," Ian said.

Kubi said, "Ian is right. Some struggle soon on the ascent. Others want to continue. They are committed one to all. No one goes ahead unless everyone does."

"That we understand," Goran said. "It is the same for the five of us."

Kubi caught his breath from his ascent, descent and ascent; even someone with so much experience on Ararat was not immune to the increasing altitude. "Yes, but you five . . ." He said he was worried the Armenian group would spread out. "It dangerous to climb with mixed skill levels. Stragglers could get hurt and take a wrong turn. Fall."

"Their guide says tonight is not the night for any summit. He says weather probably terrible. He says should *all* turn back. Now."

There was a moment of silence, everyone mulling over what Kubi had just said, no one wanting to speak first.

"How terrible is it?" I asked. "If you feel we can make it, we want to keep going."

"Me too," Kubi said. He looked down the trail. "Not all of them can. I have to let him know decision." He looked at each of us in turn, and we nodded.

"We five keep going," Patricia said. Echoes stirred among us.

"Wait here." Kubi took to the trail to deliver that message to the Armenians and their guide.

"Hurry!" Goran shouted after him. "The Spanish are closing in on us."

Goran's competitiveness was infectious. I liked the sense of focus it brought to our group. It was not about rushing. Rather, it was sport, a sense of bettering another nation—with no prize for success. Intuitively, he knew this gave us a measure of our own progress, kept us attentive and honed on the climb.

And climb we did. The mountain's demands were sent our way with a path twisting as though the trailblazer had thrown a lash of spaghetti at the mountain map and followed the resulting route.

Night-time climb: Mountain guide Kubi adjusts one of Patricia's climbing poles as the expedition makes its way up Mount Ararat at 2:30 in the morning, planning to reach the peak for sunrise.

*   *   *

Our climb continued along a craggy mountainside. The dark distorted our perception of depth and, being on a mountainside, I felt at times like the path might drop off into nothing. It was impossible to gauge the surroundings, and we had only our own steep steps to define the angle of climb. Thirty minutes after leaving the Armenians, we sensed the Spaniards' presence; it would be prudent to let them pass if they got much closer. Instead, we heard Goran's admonition: "Onward. Upward."

I slipped on an icy rock, my foot catching the dry underside of a boulder as a prop. I gripped another rock to steady myself, but the hand I reached with also held a walking pole, and the grasp was tentative, only barely enough to right me.

Gusts of wind whipped us as we searched fickle footings and avoided slippery props. Slivers of ice blew viciously in the air, finding a crevice in my hood where they could slap exposed skin. Snow had fallen intermittently, and the brown rocks below our feet were dusted white.

Over the hours, frozen rain slowed our movement, pelting and chipping at my goggles. Momentarily it abated, so Kubi brought us to a rest against the cold, wet rocks. Patricia fumbled in her pocket, finding a chocolate bar, and shared it. A swift wind cleared the view. Below us the Spaniards' headlamps were grouped together, shining inward at their own rest stop. Their lights went out in unison. We doused our own headlamps as a cloud-covered dawn arrived. We rested our lungs and legs as a penumbra beat back the darkness. The path behind us was eked out from shadows, and as its significant incline grew visible, it became clear why our legs burned from effort. Looking down, I recalled we'd left a campsite perched on an angle, tents askew. The trail's vertical abruptness below made that inconvenient setting feel level by comparison.

Day broke, and Kubi led us on. The rocks about us felt closer in the sun's definition, but shedding darkness did not make the ascent any easier. We climbed without a flat patch. Snow fell steadily for a while, then that cloud passed. The expanse beyond and below opened to view for the first time. The mountainside flashed long and round, and hinted of a precipice. In the daylight, the mountain felt larger—huge, in fact, and powerful. We paused only a moment for the vista, assuming it was here to stay and that wonderment could be digested when we next stopped. Fresh snow crunched beneath our boots, and then we were through it and onto frozen dirt. Kubi stepped off the sharp path. There was a difficult incline just ahead of us, but dawn's tricky light made it seem like the trail leveled off beyond that.

Kubi motioned that we should go ahead of him. It was the first time he'd done so on the climb. He waited at the side, pressed against a rock, to allow each of us an unexpected moment of discovery.

Ian scrambled up the slope, stopped, and stared. Patricia was next, bracing herself with a walking pole and pushing herself up to where Ian stood. Her gaze was brief, but she looked back at the rest of us with encouragement, flipping up her goggles. Charlie moved hand over hand up the path until he was beside her, as did Goran. I closed the gap and became part of an expedition struck by awe. Big dreams live on big mountains. Against a momentary blue sky, the majestic summit of Mount Ararat beckoned us over a distance and up a striking ascent angle.

On the snow terrace where we stopped to reconnoiter and prepare, we knew we'd been blessed with good leadership, from within and without. We were a strong team of climbers facing harsh elements that had defeated many of our more experienced predecessors.

Kubi, ever about discipline, became a verbal minimalist. "*Wait*," he said, flashing his mitts at Ian. "*Down*," he said to all of us. "*Crampons*." There was no oxygen to waste on sentences. "*Quick*." Kubi had now used four of the five English words he'd bother with at this high altitude. The fifth, minutes away, would be "*Follow*."

I reached into my backpack to pull loose the crampons, untangling their prongs and tugging where a clip had wedged in the spokes. Despite my pocketing them carefully and individually in my pack, they'd become entangled. My glove flapped open to the wrist and shards of sleet pecked the skin as my fingers went clumsy trying to clamp the device onto the snow-smoothed sole of my boot. My earlier practice routines had not involved clumps of heel-packed snow.

Ian slumped beside me in a red mound of toque, jacket, and pants. Unshaken, he scraped snow off his boot. He heeled his boot hard into the base of a crampon, securing it. He forced his full foot into the metal sleeve—the move of experience. His other one slid in the snow until it flipped over and the prongs took grip outside his reach.

Kubi retrieved the errant crampon and sat between us, lifted Ian's foot and fashioned the support onto it effortlessly. With his other hand he stopped my attempt to lengthen my own set of crampons, a sizing chore that we should have secured better back at Base Camp. With a twist of his wrist he got the adjustment perfect and handed it back to me. None of us had brought our own crampons, accepting the outfitter's promise to provide them, which they did—bent, rusting, and overused though they might be.

Kubi dropped his mitts. With bare hands hardened to the bitter air, he fit Goran's boots, only once smarting at the metal's cold against his fingers. Goran stood and pressed the aluminum holder tight with his foot. Kubi looped a lace, buckled another, and then pointed to both of my companions' feet as if to imply, "Done." Instead he said, "Wait."

In misguided imitation, I'd pulled off one of my gloves. Any dexterity I'd hoped for was flash frozen. Numbness swelled my hands. Movement brought a pain that disappeared as quickly as it was sharp. "This must be what arthritis feels like," I thought in the unfamiliarity of the instant. I was about to pull the glove back on, but instead Kubi reached out, took it from my hand, propped it up as a shield for wind protection, and lit a cigarette. He drew deeply on the thin air and thick smoke, exhaled nothing, and returned my glove. His cigarette's glow blew orange and out, and then he resumed his work.

Only fifteen hundred feet remained, straight along a snow trail packed down by yesterday's French and Russian expeditions. It led into more swirls of snow. We moved on the slow climb, glimpsing through the fast-moving clouds what Parrot had called the "icy head of Ararat."

The Spaniards arrived five minutes after us. Six climbers and their guide continued on a bit before resting fifty yards away from us to strap on their crampons. We sensed stern looks, accented by the rarefied air; we were not the only ones competing for the post position, a lead that was of innocuous benefit. We recognized their stance, their gain of ground. We had yielded command. Kubi did not convey loss of advantage. Fatigue had made most of us indifferent to the competition, but not everyone. Two of the Spaniards talked animatedly, their stares alternating between where our party stood and the mountaintop. They plotted their next move while the others clamped on their footwear with élan then rose in unison, stomping and tugging at their straps and holsters.

Our quintet was nearly ready. Kubi fastened the claws onto Patricia's boots and adjusted Charlie's ill-fitting clasps. He jumped from one of us to the other until all our crampons were fastened to his satisfaction. Finally, we traded our snow goggles for sunglasses, a temporary luxury.

Rest for the Spanish was briefer than ours, and it made them appear better trained. Grabbing their ice axes, they formed a line and started toward their final climb, angled ahead of us. Then one climber's crampon came unfastened.

"Let's go!" Goran said, seeing them falter.

"We have a chance to be first," Patricia needled.

"Follow," said Kubi, before the Spanish Armada could regroup. He took long strides, and although he never said anything, I suspect that with Goran's repeated urges to beat the Spanish, Kubi had caught our competitive spirit. Within minutes, he had positioned us in command of the ascending path. The Spaniards fell in line a respectful distance behind. Unless we collapsed, the pseudo-race was over. All our attention now was on safety.

What are we doing here? I wondered, not for the first time. We hoped to find in ourselves whatever was necessary to ascend the peak—not to fail, as had many others, but to triumph. Exhausted, the climb up ankle-buckling trails had sapped our strength. But now we were encouraged by the fresh snow at our feet, sunrise, and the summit, less than thirty minutes away.

The snowfield immediately ahead looked deceptively level—it was in fact steadily rising. Where that section ended began a thousand-step incline to the peak. The east side of the mountain brightened slightly as the early sun shone through light cloud cover, coaxing our approach with a muted glow. There were glimpses of blue sky, and I wondered if the view from the summit might well deliver the country trio of Iran, Armenia, and Turkey we all hoped to see.

We were on the rise.

The air stilled as if it weren't there, and it fought me as I tried to pull depleting oxygen into my lungs. At times our tribe of six slowed to a crawl to catch what we could of the thinning air. I recalled reading Navarra's telling of his expedition "going forward in bursts of twenty-five or thirty paces, and then stopping for lack of breath," one among them moaning, "I'm spitting my lungs up," as another feared aloud, "My heart is bursting!"

We moved to the base of Ararat's final challenge—an elevation gain of three hundred steep feet to its peak. Kubi retreated to the rearguard position. It was his mandate to watch over us as we climbed. Part of his responsibility was to be below our team should anyone fall and begin to slide off the mountain.

Goran, now in the lead, took the first steps up the sharp gradient. His left foot slipped off the icy path. He knelt into the snow to break his fall, regained his balance, and stood up. He looked at the rest of us with feigned assurance. Kubi motioned him on.

We were now on the sharpest incline of the final ascent. We clung to our hopes as much as we clung to the mountainside, repeatedly stopping to ease our pained lungs, to acknowledge the pinch of cold feet and strained backs. *God, where is the air?* I thought. I looked at the peak of Ararat and thought of what Crosby had written before returning to his base camp after a failed attempt: "It loomed before us, tantalizingly close." This was no time to quit.

Ice crystals formed when we exhaled and hung in front of our faces, daring us to breathe in. We caught what we could of the thinning air, nodded to one another, and shuffled on.

Below us was a slope that slipped toward nothingness. The only difference between seeing and not seeing tomorrow was carelessness. Taking his sunglasses off, Kubi winked my way, tapped my ice axe and cocked his head toward the abyss.

An Armenian headwind roared up the mountain's north side and over the summit, where it coupled with an easterly cousin from Iran before slamming us head-on as we climbed, Turkey at our backs.

"The breath of Ararat," Kubi informed us.

Its rage wound through and over us. Then everything went quiet.

More steps. Boot toes into the snow, letting the crampons grip. Someone muttered our jitters: "Will we make it?"

It was a god-awful next ten minutes. I didn't know whether to give up or throw up. White was everywhere and disorienting. Sun made a dawn sky, whisking mist and pallid snow into simple shades of gray. Any denotation of deviation or depth was a blind guess, at best.

Five feet below the pinnacle, Goran stopped and jammed his pole into the snow. He moved off the path and turned to Patricia. "You first."

One by one, we followed Patricia's lead over a sturdy brim of snow and mountain. Patricia, Charlie, Ian, Goran, and I stood as one atop Mount Ararat. Kubi joined us and made it a team.

"Think clearly," he said, reminding us that we needed to preserve our strength for the descent. "The air is thin, the ice is treacherous."

"Five minutes." That came with what sounded like the last of his breath. Each of us moved away from the others to have our singular moment, to feel alone at what felt like the top of the world.

"Rick!" It was a grinning Ian, focusing his camera to catch the exhilaration—I had raised my ice axe and taken one of my gloves off to find my own camera. He handed his to me. "Please." I took the photograph, capturing the mountaineer atop his seventh major summit.

Charlie reached out to shake my hand, but we hugged instead. "Summit," he chuckled.

Goran found the canister that held a book to be signed by successful summiteers and scrawled his name, appending the date, on behalf of us all.

The wind swirled about us, now more efficient than vicious. It lifted snow at our feet and blew the clouds to the side so we could see the vista, but to my disappointment revealed no remnant moon. I pivoted to take in the expanses of Iran, Turkey, and Armenia below us.

Goran greeted the Spanish climbers. "Welcome."

The summit of Mount Ararat, where Charlie and Ian take in the view of Turkey, Iran, and Armenia.

∗   ∗   ∗

Whether one approaches Mount Ararat from the north, the south, the east, or the west—the ascent is only half of the expedition's challenge. One must also get off the mountain safely.

We shared the saddle of the summit with the Spaniards, until Kubi called us together with a warning that corralled our emotions. "We must go down now. Move slowly. Do not trip."

We'd been at the top of Ararat for ten minutes. The Spanish made the first move to depart. We waited until they'd started down the steep incline and, watching their cautious maneuverings, noticed that two of their trekkers were tethered by rope, ice axes in hand. That sight of experienced caution tempered our own speed. The steps we had climbed on the ascent now had a slim ice glaze from the morning's altering warmth and cold; our crampons still gripped, but we felt them catching when lifted. Kubi at one point walked sideways down the trail to avoid catching his crampons.

When we reached the base of that steep incline and the trail leveled out, we saw the Spaniards well ahead of us, unbuckling their snow prongs and stowing them in their packs. They lashed their ice axes on their packs and headed over the embankment and out of view.

For me, it wasn't until our own crampons were off and packed that our accomplishment sank in. Only our poles were left out, to help us balance as we retraced our trail to Camp II. The clouds moved off the mountain-top and the sun took command of the higher skies.

Before moving down from the snowcap onto packed earth, Charlie said to us, "Take it in." We turned once more in a stomping, irregular fashion and all faced the peak of Mount Ararat. Someone bowed, and we each followed in a humble salute to the forbidden mountain. Then we turned to face the rocky terrain below on our descent.

We had made it a fair ways down when suddenly, my eyes blurred. At first I thought it was my sunglasses, so I took them off and opened my jacket to wipe them on my vest. But the blurriness remained. I tried to blink it away, to no avail. Something was very wrong. I'd never had trouble with my vision, not even with age and a family history of glaucoma. The snow's white and the clouds' gray and the rocks' beige blended into each other. I could still sense depth, yet its specifics were difficult to determine. I blinked furiously, trying to dispel the disruption. I could differentiate boulders from the path and Goran from Patricia, because of their heft and heights. Ian and Charlie looked the same to me, their jacket colors opaque.

Not wanting to lose the path ahead, I trailed close to Goran, as he was nearest to me. I was scared to stumble—more scared about what had caused the change and how long my sight damage would last. Permanently? Had I descended too quickly? I shuddered not from cold but from apprehension. When we stopped for a rest, I said nothing while

The descent of Mount Ararat is potentially more dangerous than the ascent. The mountain's steepness and the climbers' tiredness are conducive to mistakes.

removing my sunglasses, but my squinting blinks caught Patricia's attention.

"Something in your eye, Rick?"

I brushed off her question, and stopped the rapid blinking until we were again on the trail where no one could see my efforts. Vanity surely brings more mishaps than it avoids. I worried about the wrong factor. Not acknowledging my handicap kept my teammate image a strong, if inaccurate, one. To compensate, I made sure there was someone behind me; I was no longer interested in being the final one on the trail.

Emotionally, I stumbled down the mountain but somehow managed to keep an even physical pace, and my concerns went unnoticed among the group. When we reached the red blur of our tents, as the team members sauntered into the camp, I chose to follow behind, picking my steps carefully. When we neared our site, I recognized Ian's stance and followed him over. We sat down on the rocks outside our tent and shucked off our packs.

"Ian, I can't see."

"What can't you see?"

"Everything's a blur."

"Ever happen before?"

"Never."

"I'll get Patricia. She knows first aid."

"No." Why was I being stubborn? "Let's leave it a bit. Another hour. Let's settle here. Can you bring me up some food?"

I took orange juice and meat, which I could not identify by sight, only mouth feel. There were eggs on toast. And a Wagon Wheel!

I lay down and slept. My dream was a blurred memory of the descent.

After an hour-long nap, I woke up feeling groggy. I rubbed my face with my hands and elbowed the tent flap out of the way. I could see, and see clearly. Two Armenian men were approaching, Ian close behind them.

High altitude can wreak havoc with a body, fit or not, and play tricks. When a climber's eyes are compromised on a mountain, so is their safety, as well as the well-being of those they hike with. Later I was to learn that a possible side effect of taking medication to avoid acute mountain sickness (I had taken Diamox) could be blurriness of vision. And I would read an article quoting Dr. Fred Edmunds, in *Primary Care Optometry News*, regarding mountain climbing at altitude: "The cornea doesn't get as much oxygen as it would normally like, and it swells up a bit . . . the curvature changes slightly . . . and this brings about a slight myopic shift."

I found all this out later, though. Right then, I had just enough time to realize that my vision had been restored, as the two Armenians, oblivious that anything had been wrong, had news. "We will attempt tonight."

The second one said, "Some of us."

"How many?" Ian asked.

"Not all," said the same man.

"It's what is necessary," I said.

"Yes, the Spanish told us how difficult it was with the ice wind and slippery rocks. Tonight's forecast is snow."

Ian took the conversational pause as a chance to check on me. "Rick, we are planning to go on down to Base Camp this afternoon. Now, actually. You OK to go?" He'd had discussions with Goran, Patricia, and Charlie and did not want to mention my eye condition in front of the Armenians, but clearly he was wondering if I was able to make the trek. If not, the team would wait until I was ready.

"Agreed," I said. "The sleep has cleared everything."

Ian smiled and then turned to the Armenians' planned ascent. "The danger . . . it is dramatic. The sense of achievement is . . . well, it's humbling." And by way of unconditional encouragement, he said, "Of course, you will know all that this time tomorrow."

"Did you see any sign of Noah's Ark?" one of the Armenians asked, only a slight jest in his voice. "I mean, in the daylight, in the distance?"

So Noah came out, together with his sons and his wife and his sons' wives. All the animals and all the creatures that move along the ground

182

and all the birds—everything that moves on land—came out of the ark, one kind after another.

Then Noah built an altar to the Lord and, taking some of all the clean animals and clean birds, he sacrificed burnt offerings on it. The Lord smelled the pleasing aroma and said in his heart: "Never again will I curse the ground because of humans, even though every inclination of the human heart is evil from childhood.

"And never again will I destroy all living creatures, as I have done.

"As long as the earth endures, seedtime and harvest, cold and heat, summer and winter, day and night will never cease."

Ararat is a big mountain, and there are a lot of places on it to hide a boat—even a large one.

TWELVE

WALKING BONES

*"No conscientious traveller turns homewards on the route by which
he came if a reasonable alternative offers itself."*
—H. W. Tillman, *Two Mountains and a River*

The satisfaction of our ascent infused the rest of the day. We
broke camp after a late brunch. The good cook Fesih, who had
returned to camp, would stay with the Armenians, ensuring
they had sustenance for their climb. Kubi and the Armenians had struck
a peace accord, and he stayed at Camp II with them. The Armenians'
guide was seconded and sent down with us.

"Is there a different direction to descend?" I asked Kubi, thinking
we'd see new parts of the mountain on the afternoon's hike.

"It is as you came up," he replied. "It will feel like new goat path
to you."

For the first hour, our guide stayed close. We were rested some but
tired more. The downward moves jarred our knees. It felt unfamiliar and
a bit cumbersome. When we came upon a boulder jammed into another,
the only path was an up and over. Did we come up this way, I wondered?
Usually the guide went first and watched each of us as we made the leap.
When Patricia's turn came, he reached up and assisted her down, holding her by the waist. Within the next half mile he found a number of

occasions to aid her. Finally one of the crew turned to the rest of us and said, "Maybe if I had nice breasts he'd help me down too."

Whatever shape you feel your body is in, once you begin to push yourself physically, the psychological strain can be onerous. Fighting for oxygen wears on people emotionally, even after the altitude normalizes. That and the difficulty of a climb can strain group dynamics and affect a group's behavior. Our group escaped those repercussions, but another did not.

We were descending with a companionable satisfaction, matching up in twos or threes, taking or providing a helping hand over difficult areas, when we came across a stranded group of eight Frenchmen ahead of us who weren't faring as well.

We'd heard they were on the mountain, but our paths had not yet crossed. Before summiting, we had looked over from Camp II, seeing the yellow tents of "The French" (Kubi's term) spread out on a plateau across the ravine from where we camped. Though hikers milled about, we had not encountered even one of them on the mountain, until now. Ian pointed out during our brunch earlier that day that they'd broken camp and left. We thought they'd be well ahead of us on the trail, but when we came off a straight and moved down among big rocks, we saw they had stopped.

They were scattered along the trail, looking on as one man stood atop a boulder beside a hunched-over man. Both looked dazed. One of them had recently vomited, but it was hard to tell which one.

As we passed, I offered our first aid kit.

The fellow who was standing shouted at me, "What is your job? Are you medical?" There was arrogance in his voice, a tone to ward off any challenge to his leadership role within the group. Or altitude was at play, his brain in want of better oxygen.

"I'm not a doctor," I replied, "but if you need something, we may have it."

He looked at me, then at Patricia and Ian as we moved past, and dismissed us with, "He has height sickness. Is all."

"So long as you're sure it's not a stroke," said Ian.

We left the French force behind us.

The two pack horses with our gear trundled to the east of us, higher up, making their own course down Mount Ararat, half-followed and half-led by a young boy who was singing a ballad-sounding song. They worked down an incline that would eventually cross our trail, catch up, and pass us. The boy lived on the mountain, in a nomad's village tucked out of view.

Trailing me were Charlie and Ian. Patricia was just ahead. Down further, barely in sight, cantered Goran. Around the bend and out of vision was our guide, as though safety was a preoccupation going up but much less so now. As the switchback turned, Goran was near enough for me to reach him with a shout.

"Goran. Goran. Sheep!"

He stopped at my call, and the slope between us narrowed as my own steps quickened off the path toward him. He waited a hundred and fifty feet below me, but hundreds of feet of switchback trail separated us. The guide appeared in front of him and continued along.

"Sheep?" Goran asked.

His story from two nights before, regarding the barbecue during his friend's African mountain hike, had popped back into my mind. "I've a bet," I said. "If you can get the guide to find fresh meat—sheep? *Sheep?* for tonight's fire, I'll find a dozen beer."

It was a time-filling banter between weary hikers, as much an effect of lean air on the brain as of hunger.

"Cold beer?" Goran shouted.

"I'd drink it warm," said Charlie, who had caught up to me.

The prospects of consummating the bet with Goran were not good.

"You're on," said the lively minded Goran, who turned immediately and yelped at the now-you-see him, now-you-don't guide, who had reappeared on a switchback. The guide turned and waited. Goran jogged across the ground between them, his pack jumping all over his back, putting his hand flat on his baseball cap to hold it in place. When he caught up with the guide, the young man stared at the ground, listening to an out-of-breath pitch from Goran. Slowly the man shook his head. Even from higher up, I could see the guide smile an answer that said, "Silly."

Goran shifted his stance, now downhill a step from the guide, but still standing taller. He was using more English words than the Turk understood—I could tell that by the sideways shake of the guide's head. Then Goran reached in his pocket, pulled out some crumpled American dollar bills, and shoved them into a waiting hand. The guide nodded and hurried off. Goran swept a pivot with his left foot and scanned the mountainside to find me. He raised his right hand, thumb up. And his left hand rose, thumb down. On Ararat, nothing was certain.

Why had I said a dozen beers? Why had I said cold?

Still a good distance from Base Camp, our path again came close to the youngster and the horses. He was a hundred yards away and on a friendly slope, his own shortcut. Soon he would forge ahead, getting to the night campsite well ahead of us in order to set chairs, ready tents and light a fire. I left the trail and angled across the mountain slope to cut him off.

"English?" I asked on approach, feeling dumb not to have spoken earlier with the boy who had been doing all this camp work for us. The youngster grabbed the pack rope on the lead horse and halted it. The horse snorted and flicked his head, and his spittle landed on my cheek. Point made.

"Beer," I said, raising my hand in a drinking gesture.

The kid's head shook. The horse's head shook.

I spoke louder, as though that would improve the translation. "Beer. Twelve."

His smile showed that he knew what beer meant, but his head's tilt said, "Not possible." My mentioning twelve was irrelevant.

"Beer," I nodded as though this could make it so, then held up all my fingers to indicate ten and flipped two again. I pushed off my pack and dropped one hand to a side zipper. I had a U. S. $20 bill and he took it eagerly. Now I was the one who was confused. Was this the price? A down payment? A tip? Or did he just accept my money without obligation?

Then he was gone, moving faster to catch up with his coworker.

Goran looked my way, palms out, asking about my success without saying a word. I shrugged, *Wait and see.*

Forty minutes later we took a trailside break. Those in front doffed their packs to rest and waited for us stragglers. The trail was distinct, which explained the guide's confidence in moving ahead and leaving us on our own.

"My prediction?" Charles chuckled. "Cookies, pasta, and orange juice for dinner." He bit into a chocolate bar, looking at Goran and me. "You two just gave away money. You're on Mount Ararat, for heaven's sake, not at a food fair."

"I am walking bones," Ian laughed. "Very much in need of a meaty meal."

Patricia took off a boot and stuck a finger in it, searching for a pebble. She caught it with a fingernail, hooked it free of the padding, and flicked it away.

Intuitive camaraderie came with our exhilaration and exhaustion. So when Goran said a simple, "OK?" our answer was to strap on our packs.

We reached Base Camp, where Niecit was expecting us.

"*Merhaba,*" he said in welcome.

"*Merhaba,*" rolled off our tongues in response.

He had a tumbler of cold water for each of us, backed by the smell of fresh perked coffee—the cooks' tent version.

Our packs were soon off the horses and shunted to where Niecit and the boy had decided they should be placed. Three tents lay flat on the ground in their designated places, waiting to be set up.

There was lots of campsite room—no Russians, no Spaniards, no Armenians. No one else was descending except the French, and there was room across the gulley for them. The Spanish climbers were hell-bent for home. Their guide had told Kubi they'd hike one long day's trek, up from Camp II to the summit, down to Camp II, onward to Base Camp, and out. It was an unnecessary and unhealthy jaunt, favored only by daylight. No one was on the ascent, or they'd be here by now, setting up camp for the night.

We pitched our tents—still shared —as nasty clouds gathered. The wind was up and ruffled the nylon walls, so we opened the flaps and windows so that it could blow through.

Then we relaxed. I was burrowing in the large pack for my windbreaker—it was not cold yet, my sweater underneath was enough, but the breeze had a bite. As I pulled it out of its inside-pack entanglements, I heard "clip clop—clip clop" and looked over my shoulder to see a horse with a rider—a young man, unshaven—and across the neck of his horse lay a dead sheep. Or at least I thought it was dead, until it raised its head in an uncomfortable shift; eyes open, looking straight at Goran.

"Well, well, well . . ." Charlie said.

"I don't believe it," Patricia said.

Ian clapped his hands in applause.

Goran didn't make a noise, but his chest showed he was stifling a smug, though shocked, laugh. He cracked, and we all snickered—until Ian pointed to Niecit, who was unsheathing a knife. Now confronting us was the cold reality of our antics.

"'Die sheep or eat the knife,'" Goran said. I'd never heard that saying. Where'd Goran get it? Croatia? New York? It hardly seemed an architectural term.

The sheep was slid from the horse into the arms of the cook, who grabbed the rope that held it by the neck. The rope was taut.

I walked away to gather scraps of dead scrub brush from the field for the fire, feeling suddenly irresponsible. Even though the sheep's fate was "life on the mountain," we'd instigated this particular slaughter. Ararat was a setting; the scene was our own.

Sheep make a throttling whine when their necks are pulled back, arched for the knife. My back was turned. Ian fussed with tent pegs, Patricia repacked, Charlie made more coffee; Goran alone watched—an obligation to witness?

Silence.

Niecit had moved out back of the cook's tent. There was ample room to place a plank of wood on solid ground, a butcher's block for his carving. The man who'd brought the sheep was there to help the cook. We went back to our chores, the fire brightened and cooking coals glistened. The guide brought out a round metal bowl, scorched by a thousand campfires. He placed the pan inverted near the fire, to be used later as a grill.

Two village boys climbed, from below, up the rise and into camp, sweaty and happy to have found us. They went straight to the guide, who darted behind the big tent to consult with the cook. When he came back he pointed the boys in my direction and called "Rick." They each carried a plastic bag that bulged with hastily packed cans. The bags wept from condensation. The cold beer had arrived.

The older of the boys went to help tend the packhorses, bringing them water and wiping them down with his bare hands. Later he held one hand open and fed both of them carrots from the vegetable tray sitting on the dinner table. The horses nuzzled his hand and licked it, seeking more carrots and the salt of his sweat. The boy rubbed the saliva on his pants and returned to his duties.

Ian loosened the twelve Turkish Efes beer, their distinctive blue label making them immediately recognizable, and cracked one open, handing it to Patricia, who had raised her jacket hood against the cooling breeze. Ian took a swig from another can, stifled a burp, and set it down to open one for Goran and pass two more to Charlie and me. But when he made a move to hand one to the cook and guide, they both declined.

Raising his tin of beer, Goran toasted: "To absent friends."

"And to mothers," added Patricia.

"And Nico," said Charlie.

I immediately wished I'd made Goran's Yankee ball cap a part of our bet.

Niecit came from behind the cook tent, his bloodied hands carrying a wooden platter laden with freshly butchered sheep parts. He kneeled by the fire and set the inverted metal bowl on the heated rocks, its arch heating quickly into a grill. Onto this he placed slices of sheep that sizzled and turned quickly from blood red to gravy gray. The fat crackled. The older boy, fresh from patting down the horses and having them lick his hands, helped the butcher by grabbing meat with those very same hands and placing it on the metal. Without any self-consciousness, he

Last camp: Our guide, along with a horseman and a young packer, attends to the sheep meat cooking atop the fire the evening we returned to Base Camp.

wiped his hands under his nose in a swipe of an itch, then picked up a piece of partly cooked meat and turned it. Over my shoulder I heard, "It's enough to create irritable bowel syndrome."

"I'll cook mine right over here," I said, choosing three pieces off the butcher's platter and laying them across a heated rock that had been left outside the grill. "I'll watch these ones," I added, making sure everyone heard. I reached into the nearby pail to wash off the blood, a last attempt at sanitation—I'd have to rely on the beer to cleanse my gullet.

Niecit chanted as he orchestrated the meal.

The swigging of beer, the mountain setting, the cool evening air, and the warmth of the fire brought everyone close. After a while it no longer mattered which hands picked and moved the meat, lifted it for inspection, or palmed it against a stick for display. In the end we were all happy to eat *very* well-done mutton.

There were no latrines, no trees, and few large boulders for everyone's after-dinner, pre-bedtime rituals. Modesty was elusive on Ararat. Darkness and distance alone enabled one's comfort, and that meant walking far from camp.

When I came back, our errant second-in-command, the disappeared and nearly forgotten Ahmet, nonchalantly hiked into camp from below. He was happy to have arrived, but disappointed to have missed the big meal.

When we had a moment alone, I asked, thinking that he'd forgotten, "Will it still work tomorrow night with Grandfather?"

"That could be. I think better you go night after."

I was disappointed at the delay. "I head back to Van and from there elsewhere and . . ." I stopped myself. I really had nowhere to be. No one expected my appearance. Nobody cared. If the plan to spend a night in his grandfather's village shifted, what did that matter?

Ahmet, amused, watched my mouth twitch in debate with myself, and proposed, "If we all go to Doğubeyazit tomorrow, that is best. Works for everyone. All are off the mountain safely together. Next day, I take you to Grandfather's. It is right."

Clouds, darkening by the hour, hid the full moon that surely hung over Mount Ararat. They threatened us with rain and assured snow further up where our Armenian friends camped. Charlie and Patricia donned wool sweaters and huddled by the fire, chairs and stools brought near for the rest of us. Goran groaned, "I have a lovely camp sweater I'd like to wear right now but it's in the Lost Luggage Department of the Van airport." Ian alone dressed the same as always, but when the idleness of sitting attracted a chill, he accepted the offer of a second sweater I hauled out of my orange pack. Seeing me fishing around in my large rucksack, he asked, "Rick, does Big Bertha fold open into a life raft?"

Later I had a walk away from the group, taking in a calm sense of shared accomplishment. To a person, they'd become friends, one to another—Charlie reliably irreverent, Patricia solidly upbeat, Ian forthright in all things, Goran spontaneity personified. What, I wondered, did I bring to their climb? Wistfulness? My thoughts shifted forward, contemplating where the following weeks might find me. Would I be able to navigate entrance south into Iraq, getting a visa upon entry? I very much wanted to go there. If not, would I instead get to Armenia by the circuitous ground route north through Kars? Was it possible to get a visa upon entry? My only restriction was the purchased ticket for the Trans-Asia Express, set to leave Van in two weeks.

Anticipation of a full moon—this was the actual night—brought with it the realization that I'd been counting on such a sighting for many months now. At last it was here, if only favorable sky conditions would sweep away the cloud cover for a while. In other parts of the world, Janice and my sons Brent and Sean would each find their own time with the full moon that night, thinking it would signal the night of my ascent. We went to bed on Ararat with close cloud coverage still overhead. There was a sense of defeat as much as of disappointment.

I woke in the raw hours of the night and lay still, enjoying a quiet interlude. Not a snore, not the flutter of a fire or ruffle of a breeze. It was bright outside the tent. I sat up and smiled to myself, easing forward to open the tent's flaps, as if afraid my noise might scare away the moon. I crawled out on hands and knees, craned my neck around and up. There it was: a full moon—clasped at its edges by a shroud of dark clouds. It was singularly, if not wholly, visible to me.

My camera was in my bag inside the tent. To retrieve it would surely wake Ian, whose interest in this almost fully visible full moon was considerably less than in having a good sleep. The image had to be held in my mind. I will never forget it.

Raindrops started to sprinkle. The shroud drew closed, as would a camera's shutter, over the moon. The wonderment vanished. The rain hardened. I took shelter in our tent.

Falling asleep, my ambition almost fulfilled, I smiled to myself. If the fabled boat so many believed in was anywhere near, this was as close as I'd ever get to seeing a full moon over Noah's Ark.

THIRTEEN

TURKISH BATH

*"I am sure there are things that can't be cured by
a good bath but I can't think of one."*
—Sylvia Plath, *The Bell Jar*

We had anticipated two-day-old bread and warmed-over instant coffee for breakfast, only to be surprised. The night's drizzle continued, and those of us up first wore plastic slickers to shed it. I walked away from camp to meditate in the rain near a large rock, sipping delicious coffee from the cook's percolator, handed to me by Niecit. Despite our summit success, I felt out of sorts and did not understand why. I was trying to digest the accomplishment but along with it came, for me, a corresponding emotional letdown. It was a curious post-trek funk, and I didn't know what to make of it.

The sky seemed ready to break favorably, hinting at the promise of blue sky. Behind me came a cheery voice. "Nice if we could see a rainbow this morning."

Goran, a cup of brewed coffee in hand, had snuck up on me. "Rainbows mean no more rain," he informed the rock and me. "And that'd help our Armenian compatriots. Wonder if they made the peak. Looks like it's snowing up there."

"Then a rainbow would be news," I said.

"We should ask Zafer if he sees Noah's rainbow here," said Goran.

Never again will the waters become a flood to destroy all life. Whenever the rainbow appears in the clouds, I will see it and remember the everlasting covenant between God and all living creatures of every kind on the earth.

We didn't get a rainbow, but we had other good news. It turned out that Niecit had hiked down the mountain before sunrise and met someone coming up from the parked 4x4 who had breakfast supplies for us and other provisions for the Armenians. The driver brought loaves of fresh baked *simit*, bread that looks like a large doughnut. This we lifted from the campfire, where Niecit had reheated it. The warmth was welcome.

A nomad girl and boy outside their camp offer the descending hikers crocheted and knitted souvenirs—as much household goods as traditional crafts—a rock boundary separating their retail operations.

Patricia spoke. "Today we're off Mount Ararat, back to town. Make your final memories."

I snatched the last Wagon Wheel.

As we hiked down the mountain we encountered the nomad camp, this time prepared with their wares. It was clear they anticipated several climbing parties to be descending that day, some of whom would have an interest in taking home a knitted cap or goat leather purse. There were male nomads about this time, which may have explained the willingness of the women to engage us. They smiled at our arrival but were in no rush to sell their crafts, which were strewn on the ground. They'd spread an ornate patterned carpet for us to sit on, and offered us coffee and warm milk. Charlie and Goran picked among the folk art pieces, each choosing one. "This will have a place in my home," claimed Goran, holding a colorful mitt. I've found that such things seldom see display later unless framed for art or left on a bookshelf as casual memorabilia. We hiked on. "It's over," said Ian, acknowledging Patricia's comment. "It's time to leave the mountain behind." I had the impression they wished to be off of Ararat in order to gain perspective on having summited it.

The first person we saw once we arrived back in Doğubeyazit was Nico. His first hugs were for Patricia, of course, but right away he showered us all with questions. "Did you make the summit? How, without me?" He was jovial. "Was Patricia well behaved? Did you all miss me?" His smiles were an antidote to our tiredness, and he took great satisfaction in personally knowing five friends who had climbed a mountain that was not his.

Amid the reverie I realized I continued to feel a post-summit anxiety, and could not track down its motivating source. Was I anxious being off the mountain already? Frazzled nerves left over from my temporarily diminished eyesight? While wondering if I could make it into Iraq, I was crafting an alternative plan to get into Armenia overland. Was the lack of information on what that would entail maybe creating stress? I usually welcome uncertainty, but this sensation was drawing away my energy.

Despite the bustle of our arrival, the desk clerk was again at a loss for where our keys might be, and seemed confused that we were even due to check back in that day.

Nico was as rested as possible for a sixty-nine-year-old triple-A personality. As we checked in, he chatted about exploring the town in our absence. Top of his telling list was the Turkish bath, which, two days in a row and again this morning, he'd availed himself of. He had the tenor of a changed man.

"You must," he said to me. "This is what you need, Riko. I'll see you in the lobby in fifteen minutes. Drop your pack in your room and skip the shower stall."

Digging through my luggage after the room situation had been sorted, I found my bathing suit. Fifteen minutes later, having washed my face and stared down the temptations of a hot shower, I dropped a flight of stairs and met Nico. I held my bathing suit. He offered a simple, "Come along, Riko. You'll like this."

It might be our only time alone. I had to ask. "Nico. Was it the right decision to leave us on the mountain? Are you OK with it?"

"Life that you look for, you'll never find," came his assessment.

That quote is from Gilgamesh, I immediately recollected, though I couldn't remember who said it to whom. I'd told him where to find that book in my pack left at the hotel. Voracious reader that he was, he had tracked it down.

Nico took me back to a street we'd walked on the first night's outing, and soon, down an alleyway, we were standing out in front of the entrance to the Turkish bath. "I'll get you set up." And in we went. No one was around, so Nico shouted, "Anyone home?"

A near-naked man Nico's age rose from a side room, signed recognition of his returning client, and left. When he came back, he held two towels. Nico passed, saying, "Just my friend." I took my towel and

198

followed them to a change room with open cubicles, single hooks, and pairs of rubber slip-on shoes.

"See you later," said Nico. "Wrap yourself in the towel, fall asleep, and be prepared to come to in a while. A reinvigorated Riko."

The older attendant stood nearby. I palmed him assorted lira and he took what he needed from my hand. He showed me a door. "Next."

Stripped down, towel wrapped, I entered a room where steam rose from a water-filled pool the size of three billiard tables and not much deeper than they would stand. There were stools and knee-high water faucets along the wall. Thin hoses ran on the tiled floor. It's a courtesy to squat and pour tubs of water over your head to cleanse life's grime from your body before bathing in shared waters. The tap water was warm and satisfying rather than cool and invigorating. Tubs of self-served water spilled off me, washing away the grit.

A man came into the room and looked my way with a custodian's authority. He twisted the mid-section of a running hose to stave the flow and pulled it with him while motioning me to follow.

In the other room, he gracelessly tore away my towel and bade me lie down on a workbench. He dropped the hose, and its water ran freely. With precision, he snagged a tub of soap from a nearby counter and slap-splashed it about on my body as I lay face down. It was a massaging, soaping, pummeling process that felt wonderful. He knew the mountain-strained muscles by sight, and he focused his kneading knuckles where pack strap grooves lapped across my shoulders and into the nape of my neck, forcing the muscles to give up tautness. With the push of his thumbs around my lower neck, he forced away my morning's mountain angst.

He picked up the hose and drenched me with cold water. I was skittish and arched in surprise, but did not flee the soothing shock.

I felt a nudge to turn over. Nakedness + innocence = embarrassment. The masseuse spent five fierce minutes lathering my facing-up body thoroughly, top to bottom, with a courtesy fly-by to miss the groin. I was white with the soap and red with the pounding. He patiently worked on my toes one at a time and wedged an angry finger between every pair of them, with the same treatment for my hands. He gave a pushing massage over each climb-toughened leg. My eyes were closed under soap bubbles, but I sensed him bending to pick up the hose and I braced for the cold-water rinse. It washed away worries.

Finally, he was done with me. I retreated behind my curtain of inhibitions.

The water pool was still empty of bathers. He said, "Five minutes in. Rest, out. Then five minutes in. Always rest. Take half hour of that."

Toweling down afterwards, I felt both rejuvenated and exhausted—and blessedly free of my post-mountain anxiety. I was not sure if I next wanted a bed to crash on or time alone in a cafe. As I approached the hotel, Charlie and Goran were leaving. "Nico told us where to get a beer in this non-beer town. Come along."

The drinking destination was off the town's main street. A pastry shop occupied the building's bottom floor, a decoy business. We thought we had it right, but when we got to the second floor the man who met us gave a dismissive glare. Even the tilting of our hands and smacking of our lips did not work. Foiled, we invoked the name of our friend: "Nico." Apparently that was the correct password, as we earned the patron's smile and were shown to a hidden balcony providing a little table with chairs.

Soon, three beers were frothing at the ready and cold sweat was beading on the outside of the glasses. We downed them in quiet gulps, though we did emit giggles of pleasure as we slurped and signaled for more. The tent mates across from me, who'd squabbled cantankerously at night on the mountains, threw arms over each other's shoulders.

Patricia and Nico joined us on the street, with Ian in tow. Patricia was one of few women in a six-block promenade. We chose a wooden table in the middle of the plaza as waiters from competing restaurants lobbied for our dinner orders. A joint won for its sliced kebabs, served with flatbread and rice pilaf. Ordering up, we waited for soda pop and our meals, and talked about our plans for the coming days.

When the sodas arrived, we raised the glasses, clinked them against one another's, and Nico toasted: "Nice to be together again."

This would be the last time the six of us shared a meal. In the morning, before the rest of us were up, Charlie would be off to Kars, bound for Istanbul and then home to Ireland.

"Almost last to arrive," he claimed. "First to leave." He propped his straw cowboy hat between his hands, creating a pensive mood. "My inaugural summit." He looked at each of us around the table and raised his glass our way. "Thanks."

"Ian," I asked, "Do you want to see if we can get into Iraq?"

"Iraq has an image problem slightly worse than Hell," he replied. "At least Hell has a consistent brand. Iraq . . . I don't feel it is for me."

"My flight's out of Van late tomorrow afternoon," Goran said. "Zafer will be here in the morning. He's offered to take me to Ishak Pasha Palace first."

"Ishak Pasha?" I was keen. "Can I come along?"

"We are out early. I have to be back in Doğ by eleven, to get from here to Van's airport and check lost luggage."

"Early works for me," I said. "Zafer offered to show me where he said Noah's Ark is for sure. Maybe he plans to swing that drive together with Ishak?" Suspecting the answers, I still asked, "Anyone want to come to Zafer's ark site?"

"Ishak Pasha, yes. Noah, no," Ian replied.

"Noah, no. Pasha, no," said Patricia. "We want a day alone together. Nico and me. Zafer's taking us to Van tomorrow evening, and we fly home the next day. But we'll be up to see you leave. Will save our goodbyes till morning."

With Charlie going, and Nico and Patricia begging off, our group was disassembling.

"Goran, looks like you've only got Rick and me with you to Ishak Pasha," Ian said. "What time?"

"Seven. Grab breakfast before then." There was a hesitation in Goran's voice. "I'm thinking I might like to see where Zafer says Noah's boat landed."

Nico had the last word, looking in my direction. "All this. It's odyssey stuff, isn't it?"

FOURTEEN

THE LOST SHIP OF NOAH

"Myths do not die suddenly. They pass through a long period of respectable retirement, decorating the background of the imagination."
—Kenneth Clark, *Civilization*

"Ishak—you would call him Isaac on the Anglo tongue—didn't start building this, nor did he finish. His dad, Colak Pasha, needed administration complex for his area of the Ottoman Empire. That in 1685." Zafer bantered on about the palace to those he'd corralled in the Isfahan Hotel's lobby and persuaded to come along: Goran, of course, and me, but also Ian, and at the last moment Patricia and Nico, who had both become inquisitive.

We were driving a few miles south and east of Doğubeyazit. "This palace was center of town, but you won't see that town now," Zafer continued. "Ishak got his name on the door, but he was only like midwife for project. His son Mehmet got job done."

"We are on spur of the Silk Road," he said. "Through here, by Ararat. Marco Polo."

As the high sloping sides of cut stone came into view, Patricia said, "Lovely place to stay if you were traveling three hundred years ago."

The hillside around the palace was desolate, and as a result of having nothing to compare it to, the mausoleum, already quite big enough on its own, really affected you by its colossus size. Eight smooth barriers angled around an uneven rectangle, forming a continuous octagonal base. I'd seen beautiful photographs of the palace in advance of my trip and looked back to see they'd been taken from a vantage point a long hike from where we were, one I was confident we wouldn't be taking.

Walking toward the arched gate of Ishak Pasha Palace, I saw a table of trinkets, one of which was a woman's powder makeup case that would fit in the palm of my hand. It bore an image of a full moon over Mount Ararat. It was the first such image I'd seen. As I purchased it, I could see the real Ararat in the distance, majestic and almost touchable in the clear air.

Not until I ventured inside did the openness of courtyards and narrowness of passageways leading to domed rooms make the place feel charmed in its semi-restored state. The mansion was light and airy, much of it open to the sky. The interior plaza was sided by ornate stonework that

The Ishak Pasha Palace, outside Doğubeyazıt, commands a view of the surrounding lands, as befits a former administration center that began construction in 1685 but only saw full function and completion in 1784. Today it is in semi-ruin.

rose above arches. There were a hundred windows without coverings. The barricades looked to never have taken cannon or rifle fire. Ian said it felt "over-restored."

"Let's go see Noah's Ark," Nico said to Zafer, jesting only a little.

Ignoring Nico and seeking a sympathetic listener, Zafer looked at Goran, disappointed by the lightheartedness. "It is serious, Goran. I believe Noah's Ark landed where I will take you. It can be nothing else."

In the vehicle, Zafer prepared us for what he felt to be a contentious destination. "We are going to the Durupinar site, which you will have heard about."

"Not me," said Ian.

"Me neither," said Goran, looking at Patricia, who shook her head.

I had. It was common lore in even peripheral research about the Ark—a landmark that begged for explanation, and had often been given an intentionally erroneous one. It was that interpretation that Zafer believed in.

The others who came along were skeptical, even cynical—reluctant pilgrims. Like so much in these travels, old images were becoming real for me. Photos from books became land I walked on, and this visit would bring old magazine articles to life for me.

A patient but perturbed Zafer continued. "What I show you, I am exploring. I have on order special drill from United States. I believe it will show below this ground is Noah's Ark."

Our road was rolling, the hillside craggy as though a cover of dirt had been pulled back from the rocks, leaving them mostly bare, but for the occasional shrub or patch of mountain grass. With Mount Ararat eighteen miles off on our horizon, Zafer turned from the pavement, where a sign in Turkish promised us "Noah's Ship," the white lettering stating *Nuhun Gemisi*. He pulled up at a deserted orientation center and looked over a long valley toward rocky outcrops in the distance. It was the valley that would reach up and grab our throats with its unorthodox appearance.

Around the building and away from the road, we were stunned by the archeological oddity that swept to massive proportions in the acreage below. We were gazing on what looked very much like a giant houseboat embedded in the earth: an ark.

As we were silent, Zafer attempted to explain, himself agog at the sight. "Noah's Ark story has its own reasoning. Not all is for us to know. It is beyond understanding."

Even though I'd seen online photographs of this while researching Ark matters, it was hard to ignore the visual impact of the grassed-over evidence of a ship-shaped formation that looked high enough off the surrounding ground to have "landed" there, now settled in bloated relief.

"You see?" Zafer asked.

"I . . . Yes . . . I . . . do," Goran said, paying homage to the concept.

"I'm glad I came," Ian said. "I don't know what to think. An astonishing coincidence, I'd guess. It looks like the hulk of a really big boat."

"Nico?" asked Zafer, prodding.

"The mound looks like something you'd see on National Geographic. Or Fox News."

Patricia stared at the bulging ground the longest. "It's . . . um . . . hard to dispute it's shaped like a . . . ocean vessel . . . a boat. It looks like paintings that portray Noah's Ark."

"It is a rock formation, through and through. It looks like a landed barge that has sunk slowly onto the earth over the ages. But it's not," I said.

Zafer took umbrage at my comment; in his mind it would be Noah's folly not to land here. "That is not true, Rick. You are wrong. Sorry. This actually is Noah's Ark. Been proven. I will prove further."

To help us think through the logic, Zafer found the site custodian, asleep in the rear of the building. Bringing the man around to us, he said, "Inside." We obeyed.

Inside the visitor center, displays and poster boards were pinned with claims of facts and excavation work. The storyboards foreshadowed further digging into the artifact, planned to prove that this was not a freak of nature but instead a man-built object that explained the outcropping's shape. But I'd done my research: even from a distance it had the tell-marks of rock folds, the synclines where the formations dip inward as though aiming to display an S, and rising in places, the anticlines that morph to a capital A design. These formations take many millennia to come about and don't happen to former wooden structures. Overlooking geological truths has been a hallmark of this site's popularity.

The site before us was one of the best known sites that claimed to be the landing place of Noah's Ark. First reports go back to 1948, when a Kurdish shepherd, Reşit Sarihan, came across a formation of rock that "looked

The Durupinar site is captivating. Although this boat-shaped geological formation has been debunked as the site of the ark's landing, it is a visually compelling structure resembling the hull of a ship, perhaps one bloated by centuries and the earth's upheaving, conveniently approximating the Noah's Ark measurements, including a length of 450 to 500 feet (137 to 150 m). It is 18 miles (29 km) south of Mount Ararat. Photo © John Dawson.

like Noah's Ark." Sarihan thought a series of earthquakes had rattled the boat loose from the mud in which it was concealed. The earth's rumblings dropped the starboard, he reasoned, leaving the sides of the "boat" exposed. Adding further excitement, a split in the middle of the formation spurred rumors that the boat's timbered ribs were visible. Building on the appearance of a shipwreck, the relic's proximity to Mount Ararat gave it special meaning. As awareness of the site grew, those who visited proposed that the form had been hidden within the earth until erosion and centuries of rain allowed it to slide down from a higher site until it came to rest here.

But it wasn't until ten years after the shepherd's discovery that the world took popular notice. A routine mapping exercise of a Turkish Air Force flight over Mount Ararat in 1959 ended up profiling this geographical oddity. Turkish army captain and air photo specialist İlhan Durupinar, analyzing aerial photographs taken at ten thousand feet over the Akyayla range near the Tendürek mountains, discovered an unusual oval, boat-shaped mound of earth. His interpretation of a particular uplift of land attracted the interest of his military superiors; Durupinar speculated that it was the hull of a ship. In support of his assumption, the ridges in the pictures were identified as gunwales. Turkish officials brooded over the image, but Durupinar went so far as to propose that the photographs revealed the petrified wood remains of Noah's Ark (despite petrification being a process of fossilization ostensibly at odds with Biblical timelines).

The military dispatched engineers for a two-day reconnaissance under the aegis of the Archeological Research Foundation. Among their preliminary findings were measurements indicating a length of 500 feet, a height of 45 feet, and a midsection width of 150 feet. If one allowed for thousands of years of ground swelling and seismic upheaval, these enlarged figures were thought to compare favorably with the accepted conversion of Noah's cubits as recorded in the Book of Genesis within both the Torah and the Bible.

To those engineers on the ground, though, the preliminary findings were insufficient and inconclusive. In a departure from archeological protocols, the assembled brain trust decided to dynamite part of the formation to determine if there were fossilized timbers or if the demolition's debris held pasted tar or indications of metal braces used in boat construction—anything that would be grounds for further exploration. When they sifted through the demolition's rubble there was nothing of the sort, just lava, stone, and soil.

Not even a polite hunch remained that the formation had ever been a boat, but Captain Durupinar's legacy was that the site became his namesake. And despite the lack of any concrete evidence, the site gained notoriety as the "Phantom Ark."

Word spread widely in the United States with the September 5, 1960, issue of *Life* magazine, which ran aerial photographs under the banner: "NOAH'S ARK? Boat-like form is seen near Ararat." *Life*'s reputation for integrity lent an aura of fact-finding sincerity to the speculation.

For two decades, enthusiasm for the Durupinar site as the home of the Ark bubbled below the surface, with the occasional news report. Although fraud-mongers and tricksters had been involved with Noah's Ark sightings for over a century, American Ronald Wyatt's "I found Noah's Ark" caper courted plausibility of this site by distorting facts better than anyone before him. The impetuous Wyatt resuscitated international awareness in the Durupinar site.

A novice in every respect, the self-described "researcher" Wyatt first visited the formation in 1977, a site to which he'd return nearly two dozen times in twenty years. He recounted his preliminary investigations in a widely distributed, creatively phrased pamphlet, *Noah's Ark Found*, which attracted funding for further exploration. Wyatt returned two years later amid claims that earthquakes (as first suggested by Reşit Sarihan in 1948) had indeed exposed timbers of petrified wood, aligned to resemble those of a massive boat.

Wyatt's storyline had the aura of truth. In the summer of 1984, he brought American space hero James Irwin to the site, one of many celebrities and scientists, including archeologists, geophysicists, and brigades of religious embellishers. The "dig" site was mapped with elaborate tools, such as "penetrating radar," and with equipment said to be capable of generating data about fossils or isotopes for dating whatever was found, as well as determining what remains of construction might be retrieved from beneath the surface.

Asserting that he had unearthed proof of the Ark's existence, Wyatt showered the outside world with so-called evidence from his findings, reporting data from elementary metal-detection devices that he claimed revealed a grid of fastenings required at specific structure points in the Ark's erection. He assured that man-made braces and peg-secured joints would be found. To the surprise of accompanying professionals, he even removed samples purported to be artifacts and smuggled them out of the country, without the permission of the Turkish authorities.

Wyatt's bewildering publicity tactics became more intricate as he scrambled to sustain funding, expand support, and court public interest. As a Biblical literalist, Wyatt's popularity relied on the idea that Noah's story was not a metaphorical tale, let alone improbable folklore.

As Wyatt's contrived story failed scrutiny, participants with serious academic credentials fell by the wayside and declined further engagement in his project. The duplicitous Wyatt was an evangelist with no hesitation about promoting himself as a modern-day Indiana Jones (using a parody of the movie poster for his book and video covers, floppy explorer's hat atop a face with a graying beard, neatly trimmed on a tanned face). He maintained his pledges of pending discovery. Accusations of farce and fraud abounded, including those stating Wyatt placed relics on-site to be found later. Undeterred, the sensationalist circulated photographs showing a grid of professional survey strips over the "ship's" earthly casting. He maintained that their placement was based upon scientific soundings taken with sophisticated equipment. The strips outlined, unmistakably, an ark-like ship.

None of this was true.

The location has much visually—and only visually—to commend it to a succession of believers and proponents. But soundings and core samples have proven without a scientific doubt that this amazing piece of geography was just that—an amazing piece of geography. At the core of every claim made by the cherubic Wyatt was fabrication.

Dr. David Merling of Andrews University says of one claim that "the lack of growth rings in what Wyatt thinks is wood is evidence that the Durupinar site was created by molten rock, not made of wood." A 1997 Australian court case drew in a disenchanted Wyatt supporter and one-time collaborator, fellow American David Fasold, author of *The Ark of Noah*. The case pitted Dr. Ian Plimer, respected geologist and formal skeptic about Ark claims, as court foe with a group of "creationists." Fasold, having repudiated his earlier endorsement of the Durupinar site's prospects of being Noah's Ark, testified that claims the Ark had been found were "absolute BS."

Still, despite all the real evidence to the contrary, Wyatt's charade was so successful that many today still believe the Durupinar site to be Noah's Ark, and regardless if visitors believe it to be the ark or not, the unique and natural rock formation is fascinating. Local officials, whether as preservationists or opportunists, set the Durupinar site aside for protection, and by June 1987 it was being called "Noah's Ark National Park"—though the Turkish government did not officially adopt the name. Located two miles from the Iranian border, less than twenty miles from Mount Ararat and within ten miles of Doğubeyazit, the attraction extends the length of stay of visitors to the region and increases economic impact to the area.

Zafer weathered the dismissive comments from our group. "It was from here that the animals again went to earth. And the sons of Noah who left this site four thousand years ago were fathers of Iran, and Iraq, and also Armenia. Of course, Turkey too."

Or, as the Bible puts it:

The sons of Noah who came out of the ark were Shem, Ham and Japheth. These were the three sons of Noah, and from them came the people who were scattered over the whole earth.

According to the Hebrew records, Japheth had seven sons, whose descendants peopled Europe and Asia, while Ham's four sons populated Asia's southwest and Africa, leaving the Middle East (western or southwestern Asia) to Shem's descendants.

Nico did not accept that. "So all five races, every ethnic group on earth, share a common descent from one family on the ark?"

"It is so." Zafer did not blush or hesitate.

"Rick?" It was Nico seeking an intervention. My mind raced, as I preferred observing them and not participating. Should I ask, "So Noah's small, two generation family repopulated the earth by having sex with one another?" Or, "So, after the flood, the kangaroos hopped without breeding-stops all the way from here to Australia in order to be a one-continent animal?" I didn't. It was not a discussion with a resolution, and the two of them let it drop, for the moment.

I inferred that Zafer's adherence to literal interpretations reflected the religious landscape hereabouts where Noah stories (or those of Nûh, for those of Islamic faith) were perceived less as folklore and more as hand-me-down truths. He knew things, like that the old village Ahora's name translated to "vine plantation," reinforcing that Noah planted the first off-ark vines there. With such traditional information, many people had no need for indecision.

Eventually Zafer double-edged us: "I said I will drill next year," he said. "Many of us believe. We know. We will prove."

Zafer's bravado did not, in my mind, stand up against the information I knew, like the competing story information found in the Flood Tablet, a small storyboard I hoped to see with my own eyes at the British Museum in a couple of weeks. Nor did it pass muster with science. Still, it didn't matter one iota what I believed. *He* believed.

In front of the Isfahan Hotel, Ahmet's vehicle idled in preparation for the drive to Fish Lake and his grandfather's village.

"We have guests," I said to him. "Nico and Patricia are coming to Fish Lake." Just the three of us.

The timing meant a further parting of the ways. Goran, Ian, Patricia, Nico, and I hugged awkwardly, wanting to say meaningful words. Instead, we mumbled goodbyes: "It's been great." "Keep in touch." "Share those photographs."

I heard from Ian, "I hope your snoring heals."

Just before he left, Goran took off his Yankees baseball cap and stuck it on my head.

FIFTEEN

FISH LAKE

"You think you understand. You don't. If you get bad driver at border
and get caught with something, my phone number no good for help.
You'll be . . . the American term? . . . Screwed."
—Ahmet, mountain guide

"Maybe once a year, two times most, other people from the West come on this road," Ahmet informed us as he drove out of Doğubeyazit, Fish Lake-bound. I was sitting beside him. Patricia and Nico were behind us, on one of the minibus's bench seats. We were on a paved road making reasonable time when such a concept mattered not at all. Ahmet waved to bystanders as we passed through a village of twenty homes. Ahmet honked. Kids waved.

"Rick," he said once we were through, "that is where you'll be tonight. My grandfather lives there. It is the way we return." He suddenly turned off the paved road, admitting, "If you wish, we go straight to Fish Lake. More you should see where I take you first. Then to Balık Gölü!" He laughed to himself, then explained, "That is proper name for you call Fish Lake."

It was his whim. He'd talked of Fish Lake being "up the road" from his grandfather's home. On the dirt road he asked, "Is OK, this detour? It is good road, just not today, as rains. We will slip, but you will see remote Turkey. Do?"

"Yes," Patricia answered for all of us. "Bad roads are more interesting." The countryside eased into greens and ambers. The low-lying fields were spot-flooded, and shallow pools were everywhere as streams spread away from their main flow and formed giant puddles along their course. Rivulets corrugated the narrow road. Stones once laid as part of a gravel base had long since washed away, and traction was tough for the vehicle.

Hay was stacked in yards and behind stone holding walls in the small village we approached. All this remained from the last harvest and, it being August, new seeding was taking hold in hopes of an autumn season as well. An orange tractor stowed in a yard was the bright spot in the scene.

"If we can make it higher, the road takes us up," Ahmet said. "You will see far. But clouds hang over the picture today."

Our vehicle's tires slipped in the soft dirt, not because we were speeding and not because we were slow; it was simply a poor road for this light a vehicle. In response, Ahmet accelerated and the vehicle's back end slid sideways. We were propelled forward and into another curve, wider than expected. As Ahmed fought to straighten out, the minibus's rear wheels dipped into a ditch. We shuddered to a stop.

"I don't think I'll forget this little corner of Turkey," Nico said as he got out to assess the situation. To the assembled faithful he said, "Yup, we're stuck."

We were not only stuck, we looked set to slip further. As Ahmet gunned the motor, his three passengers pushed. We tried a rocking motion, in hopes of a grip for the tires—to no avail.

"It is that we sit here or not," Ahmet said.

"Not," responded Nico.

I suggested, "Why don't I walk back to the farm where we saw the tractor? Ask for a tow?"

"I'll go with you," Patricia offered, and we walked back down the road. After much slipping and almost falling on the muddy road, we reached the farm.

"Hello!" I shouted into the farmyard. Behind a fence and off the roadway was a brick house, all one level and square, with space inside for two rooms. "Anyone there?"

Patricia strolled over to the orange tractor and noticed an official-looking yellow light on the top. "Maybe part of a road crew?" she said.

Across the street, a man in a sweater vest and long-sleeved shirt shouted at us. It was a language I did not understand, but he was pointing at a gritty farmer nearer to us.

"Can you help us?" I asked the young man. His overalls implied he could do things with machinery that I could not. It was likely the orange tractor was his. "Stuck," I said. "We're stuck." I sang the last bit so poorly that Patricia laughed. The man laughed too. He saw that Ahmet, far behind us, had his arms in the air.

"Tractor?" said the man. His English was impeccable.

"Tractor," Patricia agreed.

He let her (but not me) into the tractor's cab with him, and they drove slowly out of the yard and toward the trapped vehicle. Trying not to read too much into this gallantry, I trotted alongside the tractor.

Ahmet and the man shook hands and laughed through their language in a way that implied, "Hey, it could be you stuck in the mud instead of me." Or maybe it was, "Yes, she's pretty, but she's with that tall guy over there."

The man chained his tractor to the minibus and hauled it out of the ditch in no time. His body language said it all, and his Turkish sounded emphatic when Ahmet translated: "Don't even think of going further. It is worse, and you will get stuck again. And it's a long walk back to my tractor."

We got in the minibus, Nico moving to the rear seat behind Patricia so he could stretch his legs. Ahmet turned our vehicle around and headed down the slope into a valley, onto the pavement, toward Fish Lake.

"It is not that it is all pavement, I should have said." Ahmet was describing the end of the paved road to Fish Lake, just as we again hit dirt road.

Nico sang, "*Que sera, sera*. Whatever will be, will be."

Overhanging trees shaded the road from sun-brightened clouds. We slowed as we approached a bench at the side of the road where a man of long years sat with a cane supporting his right hand, in turn supporting his chin. He wore a rumpled suit jacket over a tartan shirt of red and gray. Between these layers was a cardigan vest with its entire button row done up. A beret put a slight shadow over his flinty eyes. If Humphrey Bogart had been of Kurdish stock, he would have looked like this man.

A teenager stood beside him at the bench and flagged us down.

Ahmet stopped and lowered his window, interpreting for us. "I ask what they need. And boy says, 'Old man needs to go,' and I say, 'Go where?' and he says, 'Go with you.' I want to say OK. Is that OK with you?" That last was a question to the three of us.

Nico looked forward at Patricia and nodded back at me and said, "There is room."

I got out to help the boy help the Kurdish Bogart into the seat beside Patricia.

"Phew," she exhaled under her breath, an unintended whisper in response to the man's odor that would be unmistakable in any language. Fortunately the old man did not hear her. He smiled, showing a few teeth, all on the upper part of his mouth.

Ahmet turned to him and asked, "Where are you going?"

Bogart nodded. Off we drove.

And drove.

The old man did not remove his beret. It sat square on his head, inches between it and the minibus's ceiling. His ears were the size and shape of Portobello mushrooms, hugging the sides of his face.

As we came to a lake, Ahmet said, without irony, "Fish Lake. Do you want to fish?"

Whatever his intention, we did not stop, only kept cruising this back road, much to the amusement of the old man. He was happily humming a tune.

"Do you know what song he hums?" I asked Ahmet.

"It is an old man's song. Many songs melted to one."

"It's pretty," said Patricia.

As if he'd heard this, Bogart got louder in his humming. Every once in a while, as though his mind was taking him back to a dance party of long ago, he stabbed his cane at the floor in time with his humming.

Going over a slight hill, we came upon a bay and were gliding toward a few homes along the road. We slowed at the lakeside, entering a village. Ahead was a road full of sheep, led by small boys and prodded from behind by a broad woman. She wrapped a headscarf around her cheeks and draped it down the back of her neck. Behind her was a mosque. Ahmet parked the minibus beside the lake, giving wide berth to the commanding flock.

Six or so young men, all wearing jeans, sweatshirts, and running shoes, shuffled at a roadside work project, but stopped working when they saw us approach. Walking past the young men, I received "Hellos" as I made my way toward the flock of sheep and the other end of town. When I neared the shepherd, she forced me to the side; it was her road and her sheep, and neither moved for a stranger. The animals brushed against me, friendly but directing.

I wanted to see the mosque up close. It was a fair walk to the aqua-green painted building with a white conical mantle and minaret, or as the Turkish call it, a *minare*. In any language, it is a lighthouse of sorts, in recognition of its role in the call to prayer.

After circumnavigating the mosque, I saw that Bogart was out of the minibus as well, and was standing with the young men, though not speaking to them. Everyone was watching the mid-afternoon shuttle of animals.

With no rush, my walk back to the minibus took me to the stone fence around the shepherd lady's yard, where she'd marshaled her charges. Her husband came out of their house through a fly-screen door. The lady, now seated on a stool, was about to begin milking their sheep when she looked at her old man, quipped, and he sniggered. She pulled a sheep's teat to begin the chore. Her husband acknowledged me and then moved, corralling the sheep to within his wife's yanking range. He signaled me over with both his hands. She said something to him I didn't understand, but her expression was all invitation to me. I hopped the fence (I'm sure there was a gate, but this leap was to indicate enthusiasm) and walked toward them as though I knew how to milk sheep.

The man gestured me to bend, to squat in the same stance as his wife. I took it up. The woman demonstrated the simplicity of a downward pinch she'd been doing for half a century or more.

My bare knees sank into the soft ground under my weight. While her husband laughed, the woman smiled a mother's worry at me, implying I might not be comfortable. The side-glance to her husband was a reprimand for his giggles. He said something to her in Turkish, probably "Oh come on, Fatima. Looks like he's from America. Who cares if he's kneeling in sheep shit and doesn't know it?"

From the other side of the fence I heard, "Ah, Riko, when you're finished milking the herd, you wanna wash yourself off before getting back on the bus?"

"Nico, come here," I said. "Ya gotta try this."

In a shot he was through the gate (without the fence-leaping exhibitionism).

"You're not exactly lowering the average age of local sheep milkers by joining us," I said. "If you can harken back to your high school years of fondling, Nico, I think you'll have fun with this."

The woman offered us a taste of our work, direct from the bucket of milk. I pretended to take a sip, knowing better, keeping my lips tight to the rim as I lifted the pail to fake my tasting. Then I passed the pail over to my friend with this advice: "Nico, the old man told me it's best taken as a mouthful; tastes better."

"OK," said Nico, taking a gulp.

"Nico, I'm so proud of you," I said as he tried to swallow, visibly torn between courtesy and the urge to spit it out.

"*R-i-k-o*," he spewed.

At Fish Lake, Nico befriends the shepherdess and her husband in their home corral, then receives a milking lesson.

*   *   *

Ahmet got us into the minibus with the promise of lunch. He said, "I've brought chicken to cook. And bread. We have soup to warm up. We will light fire. By the lake."

He drove far into a field and parked. He said, "We should eat closer to the lake. It is good to walk there." I'm a Boy Scout from way back, and any chance to have a campfire is welcome. Ahmet had brought firewood with him in the vehicle, but while we were walking to the lakeshore he told us to search for kindling. We picked up damp branches. He carried a plastic bag of dung chips. It would be a cooking fire, not one that would rouse us to campfire songs, but there would be warmth and heat and camaraderie.

"Where is the old man?" Nico asked. "Did you leave him in the village?"

Ahmet said, "I told him, 'I thought you were going to go out,' meaning at village. He says to me, 'I just go with you.' I think he came for ride. Is all."

I turned and saw the man ambling behind us, without his cane. To our surprise, Bogart must have gotten back into the minibus first at the village and fallen asleep on the last bench seat. We had all popped into the vehicle, Nico beside Patricia, and left for the lakeside without realizing he was with us.

"Hey, wait for him," I said, turning toward the minibus. "You okay?" He started a smile but caught himself before his lips revealed his poor teeth again, and nodded. We walked, step for slow step, through the grassy field and to the shoreline, where Ahmet fanned smoke, hoping it would become a fire.

Ahmet unpacked his containers and prepared to cook. The old man was content to watch, and settled into grass near the pebbled beach. Over the next twenty minutes I made my way to an upper reach of land, a finger of a hill alongside this near-bay crescent on the lake. A boat with two men in it was moving well out on the lake. One of them cast a net while the other one rowed.

When I returned to the fire, Ahmet, respecting Ramadan for himself, and Patricia were dishing out a lunch of cabbage, bell peppers, and spinach, along with skewers of chicken that had the flavor of smoked dung.

There was no hurry to our meal. Bogart's appetite matched our own. He spoke sparingly with Ahmet and only gestured to the three of us if he wanted food passed to him. Suddenly he pointed to the boat on the lake and tapped Ahmet on the shoulder. He pointed again. "*Tekne.*" He could not raise his arms himself, not high enough anyway. Ahmet stood up, waved, and shouted, bringing the *tekne* to our shore.

Just before it beached, a lad jumped out, rubber coveralls up to his chest. He took a bowline to steady the craft so his mate could get out. They were like the other young men in town, a bearing of confidence to them. Their first greetings were for the old man, who, it was clear, if he was not family, was held in high esteem in the area. He was why they came ashore. As the real Bogart once said, "I've been around a long time. Maybe people like me." Next, the fishers greeted Ahmet as a long-time friend.

"You'll fish now," Ahmet said.

Nico, never one to miss a turn of interest, said, "I'm in," and made for the boat, with me close behind.

"I'll stay by the fire," Patricia said. "Off you go, boys. Promise to bring back fish and I'll keep the fire burning. We'll cook it here."

Ahmet decided to stay with her. Nico and I each swung a foot up and into the boat, hoisting ourselves aboard. The old man was right behind us, and the fishers helped him up and in. Nico went to a flat landing aft, and the old man signaled him to make room. With Bogart ensconced behind him, Nico looked set to find us fish.

Once we were out from shore, one of the young men started the inboard motor and set us on a course to a distant point of land. When the water was deep enough, he cut the engine and set me to the oars. I pulled them steadily, my eyes on Nico, who periodically ordered an adjusting tack. When our quiet craft was near the fishing grounds, the lad tossed the net and set it with buoys.

One young man cocked his head toward another buoy and the other took back the oars. They got me to help the lad pull in the fish net they'd lined out earlier. We pulled together against the weight of water. I watched the master curl the arriving net at his feet, away from mine and into an untangled mesh that would easily spool out later.

He handed me the net stream, where a large chub-looking fish flopped, hoping for freedom. The fisherman killed and filleted it, and another one as well. He cleaned both fish on board, tossing the guts into the water for the birds and hand-washing the fillets in the lake.

Nico arm-wrestled the other boatman on a landing at the aft of our boat. Soon the young fellow was wearing Nico's leather hat, the wide brims flopping fashionably over his dark skin and clothing. I wondered if he'd won it in the arm-wrestle game, or if their temporary friendship made it a loan.

In all of our days together I'd not seen Nico as carefree and happy. It was a found day for him, with unexpected adventures and a boat full of friends he'd never see again.

When the boat arrived near shore, Ahmet and Patricia came within rope-tossing distance and pulled us toward them. The young fisherman bounced out and held the two fish high, pointing my way as if to give me undue credit for catching lunch. Ahmet speared them with sharpened branches.

The fresh fish sizzled as the fire took hold. The searing was quick but Ahmet let them cook through, blackening the skin and producing a delicious smell. Paper plates were passed around when the grilling was done.

"Thanks, everyone!" Patricia said, helping herself to a final mouthful.

"Thank me," Nico chuckled. "I charted the boat's course to where I knew the fish were waiting."

Nobody wanted the fire to die. No one wanted the sun to hide. I looked over at Bogart, who was enjoying himself enormously. More than any of us perhaps, he knew that all lovely moments end and that he'd soon be alone again on his roadside bench.

As we headed back in the direction of Doğubeyazit, Ahmet's grandfather's house was on the right side of the road. "Here my grandfather was born," he said. "Not in this house, of course. It is newer."

"Where is this?" asked Patricia.

"You are in Turkish name Seslitaş. Grandfather is Kurdish, he calls it Çaliğa village."

We slowed as the road we traveled became the village's main street.

"If you need it," Ahmet began, "*when* you need it, bathroom outside behind house. You meet my family. There are many. Come for tea. They expect you. Well, expecting Rick. Patricia is bonus. Nico too, maybe."

Nico replied, "Maybe they'll want me to stay instead of Rick." My thought was they might want Patricia instead of Rick.

The house had been in a state of construction for years; no one had borrowed to finance this home's completion.

Children milled about the minibus, chattering and pushing each other in order to be closest to the strangers. Grandfather stood on the plywood-covered porch. My host's face was serene, his cheeks covered with a bristly gray beard. He didn't greet us and would hardly speak during my visit. He wore an argyle sweater and long pants tucked into his socks, in turn tucked into his slippers. Ahmet introduced us. "His name is Mohammed. He is eighty-five." He muffled a cough and sniffled.

"That is grandmother, mine," said Ahmet. She carried a year-old baby. "Asile is her name. You call her Grandmother." Grandmother wore a floor-length brown skirt around a notable girth. Her bosom overflowed everywhere; wide and down. She owned her age.

It was İlhan, Ahmet's uncle, who delivered the greetings on everyone's behalf—"*Hoşgeldiniz*," first to Patricia, then to Nico and me.

In Çaliğa village, en route from Fish Lake, at the home of Ahmet's grandfather Mohammed (his hands on Mem's shoulders) and grandmother Asile (holding the baby), beside Nico and Patricia, at the back. Ahmet (center) and his nephew kneel beside İlhan.

Grandmother disappeared. Ahmet took us inside, where tea was set for the infidels, the others respecting Ramadan. There was room for two on the couch, and I sat on the floor by the serving utensils. Nico tripped on a fold in the carpet and pointed to how it was rolled in a low and loose wave across the floor in little humps, not tacked down.

Ahmet caught up with family gossip. Once in a while he motioned to one of us, as his stories brought us into his grandfather and grandmother's world.

Nico and I talked of friendship, with pledges to meet again. He said, "I'm not much good with emails, but if you're in my city I'm good with a skillet and serve nice wines. There's a spare couch."

İlhan took us outside to walk around the yard, pointing out future walls, and plans for the expansion of the house, and the toilet. Ahmet was with us. "Rick, you and İlhan should walk when we leave. He will show you everywhere that is village. Grandmother has prepared family dinner for you. Then you sleep in room with others."

Looking across the road, I saw that Ararat imposed itself on this village. It dominated the eastern horizon. Mown hay and piles of building lumber were set alongside the road. A mile away was a collection of homes, but not many. Our side of the road had more residences, irregularly placed, and strung out over half a mile. The villagers were walking along the road to see us, the visitors. They paused and stood respectfully near Grandfather and Grandmother's place.

Ahmet, Patricia, and Nico readied themselves to leave. "In the morning my cousin drives a bus to Doğubeyazit. He starts by Fish Lake. Comes through here at 5:00 a.m. on way to the city. You need be on that bus. Is only way to leave. Grandfather will wake you."

"Thanks, Ahmet. I've wanted this to happen, and you made it so."

"You will be comfortable. Safe."

"Just don't stub your toe on the carpet," Patricia said, and Ahmet laughed.

"Patricia," I said, looking at Nico, "Make sure this guy keeps breathing." I put my hand up onto Nico's shoulder as I said it; he pulled me into a hug.

"Nico . . ."

"*Riko . . .*"

I hugged Patricia. "Safe passage."

Nico and Patricia got into the minibus, and Ahmet drove them out of my life.

İlhan was fortyish and lean, with black hair that lapped his head in a long comb. His left wrist sported a gold watch. He did not speak English but was a willing listener, and it was not long before he'd taken me on the street for Ahmet's promised walkabout. There, a small group of men and children wanted to say hi and practice their English on me.

"Where are you from?"

"Did you climb Ağrı with Ahmet?"

"Will you stay tomorrow?"

"Do you play soccer?"

I answered each question slowly, knowing my audience wanted to hear a native speaker of English. The middle-aged men were more interested in my handshake or canvassing my face, reddened by sun and wind. Kids strayed behind us as we walked, but one came abreast of me and remained there. Mem was Ahmet's five-year-old nephew. He became my companion on the walk with İlhan, at the dinner, and throughout the evening. He was inventive at getting attention; tugging at the cuff of my pullover or bouncing a red rubber ball on the road so that it veered into my hands—a game of catch that lasted, in various settings, until midnight.

Dinner was at dusk. The comfortable place to sit was on the living room floor, which was covered wall to wall with the unsecured carpet that bubbled everywhere. Grandfather, İlhan, Mem, and I sat cross-legged, each male facing a setting of cutlery, plates, and mugs.

Food kept coming to us over the course of an hour. Flatbread was served first and often replenished, always kept warm until eaten. Dishes of roasted vegetables were first passed my way and then put down for others to reach—eggplant, potatoes, cooked tomatoes, and grilled red peppers, accompanied by bowls of yogurt and several cheeses set out on a plate, all similarly white but cut differently to define their type. We helped ourselves by using our hands for the hard pieces and a spoon on the soft cheese.

All this without conversation. The women, including İlhan's wife Rahime, were in the other room preparing the next serving, also silent. I wondered if they'd have spoken were I not there. Or would their dining ritual be one of silence? Maybe they held back words as a courtesy toward their visitor, who would not be able to join in.

Sliced roast of lamb arrived, prepared earlier in the day, and was placed before me. Lettuce was provided, torn by mother's hand and in a glass bowl, ready for each diner to wrap the lamb and garnishes individually.

After our evening meal, I signaled to İlhan that I was happy to walk on my own. I went up the road, flashlight in hand. When I turned down the way, I saw that he was behind me, perhaps unsure where his hospitality ended and wardenship began.

"*Hoşgeldiniz*," he said again when he caught up to me. *Welcome.*

When we returned, Mem's red ball bounced my way on the lumpy carpet. I tossed it back to him. For an hour this would be a welcome distraction. I was awkward company—we had no conversation to share and so exchanged spattering comments, falling back on smiles and nods to convey serenity in place of observations. Comfort grew from this, and our idleness fell into a rhythm of polite grunts or the occasional "uh huh" from me, which I could only hope was not a vulgarity in their language. There was a television in the corner of the room, but when turned on the picture was just black and white hail. Music came through the low static though, and was pleasant enough. Time passed and nothing was asked of anyone. Tea was served. The red ball bounced between Mem and me.

I was shown my sleeping quarters, which I helped set up by laying out a mattress taken from a closet and putting a blanket on it. I had a corner to myself in a room with two unmade beds in separate corners. Grandmother gave me a comforter and slippers to wear, and soon I was first to bed.

My room's window was closed against the cold and the door left ajar. I'd barely fallen asleep when a red ball bounced in and landed on my bed, waking me. Mem opened the door and went to another corner. A cigarette was lit in the dark corner; İlhan smoked, lying down, and continued to do so throughout the night, even while asleep, it seemed to me. Mem moved close to his father and every few minutes, for over an hour, the red ball landed in my corner. As soon as I felt he thought I would not return it, I bounced it back to Mem, keeping him awake.

An old man's hand shook my shoulder. It was 4:50 a.m. and time to catch the bus. I coughed in the smoke-filled room, clearing my throat as I stepped outside. On the porch, I took in a vista few anywhere in the world could match. Across the fields was Grandfather's neighbor, Mount Ararat. A fresh fall of snow graced the massif's upper reaches. The air sparkled, its crystals reflecting the snow in what I wanted to believe was a white rainbow arching out of the cloud cover.

Who might have tried to summit last night? I wondered. *Would they have made it?* I held the coffee Grandmother had given me before she shooed me out of her kitchen. I sat in a porch chair made of tree branches and squeezed the red rubber ball in my hand, thinking good wishes for the little friend's future and that of his family. Grandfather appeared, dressed as the night before, only with shoes on. Sitting in a side chair on the porch, he was talkative as he drank his coffee, as though to make sure I kept awake. His focus was getting me on the morning bus, as he'd assured Ahmet.

At 5:00 a.m. he and I stood at the roadside as a pair of headlights came down from Fish Lake. We shook hands. "See you," I said, quickly realizing the inaccuracy of that common farewell, and so added "Thank you" in the language he'd understand: "*Sapas Dicam.*"

The bus slowed and stopped beside us. The cousin-driver shook my hand, rejected my offered fare, and closed the front door, all while smiling to indicate that the family's cooperative hosting was nearly complete.

Five passengers snoozed in their seats, and I made my way past them as a woman shifted over to make room for me. "We heard you were staying in Çaliğa. You're from America. Which part? USA? Canada? Mexico?"

Such encounters satisfy an urge to reach across a cultural divide, reminding us that we can. All night, Grandfather and Grandmother had seen to my comfort, intuiting something about their grandson's life from the stranger in their home. That was more than sufficient for me. Mem earned an undemanding—if temporary—friendship by initiating a game of ball catch. I'd fallen asleep without returning the last pitch. Along with İlhan, Mem had overslept my quiet departure. Just before leaving the porch with Grandfather that morning, I'd gone back in the house, poked my arm into the quiet bedroom, and ricocheted the red ball into Mem's corner.

Now, as the bus pulled away, I saw Mem, red ball in hand, waving goodbye from the porch.

Ahmet's cousin dropped me off a few blocks from the Isfahan Hotel. I walked the quiet town with all its closed shops. Bakeries were busy, however, as evidenced by the delightful aroma. I was lured into an alleyway with a table featuring a variety of breads, many braided knots and rounded loaves to choose from. At the bakery I pointed to a *naan* I'd become fond of, and on a bench beside the baker's helper I spotted a coffee pot, intended for the workers. One of them poured me a cup. Smiles all around.

I sat on the sidewalk, tore into the warm bread, and sipped my coffee.

A while later, arriving at the Isfahan hotel, I was surprised to see two men from the Armenian climbing group, and wondered how they'd fared.

"When did you get back?" I asked.

"We thought all of you would be gone," was the response.

"Yes, except for me. I leave this morning for Van."

"Us too. Or maybe we go this afternoon instead. Depends—as this whole trip has—on our fellow travelers."

"Did you attempt the summit again?"

One said, "Some of us."

"How many?" I asked.

"Not all," said the same man.

"Those who waited at camp helped the rest of us be successful. It snowed. We went up with two guides. One brought a hiker back from halfway, as he was tuckered out."

The mountain wins, I thought. Really, though, the team won—they did what was right in mountaineering: worked together to enable those most capable of attaining the highest success, and shared in that achievement.

Ahmet greeted me later that morning in the hotel lobby. He treated me as a newly adopted relative. "We drive soon."

"Thank you," I said, and began a deeper explanation of what it all meant to me, but it was not necessary.

"We know. Us too." With that he closed the pleasantries like a verbal handshake.

"The Armenians?" I asked, thinking they'd accompany us.

"Zafer, at noon."

Along the drive, I asked Ahmet about my prospects for traveling overland to Iraq.

"You could," he told me. "No one else goes, you know. Everyone feels dangerous. I don't see Western media, but travelers tell me says eastern Turkey dangerous. Is not. Not too much. Iraq, in north, is sensible part of insensible country. More dangerous is Van to Iraq, short route. You cannot take. You go long way. Two days. Is by bus. Unless rich for taxi."

"I might try to fly. If not, then the long road," I said. I remembered my so-far-unfulfilled commitment to Janice, that I'd get the letter translated or read before I entered Iraq. "Do you read Farsi?"

Shaking his head, he said, "I give you my phone number." He wrote it down as he drove, and handed the paper to me. "I know Iraqis, in north. They are Kurds. My friends. You have troubles, call me. I will help."

Knowing that the Van hotel clerk Aysenur was trying to figure out the air ticket for me, I said, "If I could get to Erbil by air, maybe I could come over land, back into Turkey."

Ahmet was educated at what he called "the University of the Street."

"Rick, I tell you I heard people crossing the border. Brave Europeans. You have caution with border drivers. Please. Some, like with taxis, they also smugglers. One person I trekked, his taxi driver brought cigarettes from Iraq into Turkey. In taxi-car's trunk. The traveler—he was afraid, of being caught. Punishment."

"I understand . . ."

"You think you understand. You don't. If you get bad driver at border and get caught with something, my phone number no good for help. You'll be . . . the American term? . . . *Screwed*."

"I need to get out safely and return to Van. I plan to board the Trans-Asia Express in Van next week."

"You have good adventures. Ararat and Iraq and Iran, *and grandfathers*," he teased.

Aysenur was behind the Şahmaran hotel's check-in desk. He greeted me as a friend, bursting with the news.

"My cousin, he has help for you, Richard. He's airport. Remember? There is flight from Van to Istanbul. Tomorrow. You be on it."

"Istanbul? Aysenur, I was trying to get to Iraq."

"Istanbul. Then Iraq. Two times each week. Flight Istanbul to Erbil. You know Erbil?"

Andam and Taha's family live there, I thought. "Yes. Good news."

"If you want ticket, he has hold for you. You must buy. Decide now," he said, politely but firmly. "Now."

"I will check in and go to my room. I will decide soon."

"No flight left. You will miss. Decide now. Or don't go. I say right? You understand 'now'?"

"I will take the flight," I decided. "Here is my credit card."

"No. Need your cash. I must send cash to cousin."

The moment of hesitation was more a question of trusting my own whim than of trusting Aysenur and his cousin. I gave him the cash I had. "Richard, you are complexed. This, yes, to Istanbul. You want Iraq?"

Of course I did. He pointed me to the ATM tucked around the corner (I wished I'd seen it there my first day here).

He was jubilant for me. "Ticket tonight. Leave tomorrow. Am happy."

Using the computer in the lobby, I emailed Andam and Taha back home: "Will be in Erbil day after tomorrow." I wrote the date I expected to be in Iraq, along with the Turkish Airline flight number and arrival time in Erbil. "From airport I will get taxi and ask the driver to phone your family. I'll use the envelope Taha gave me, with numbers. Is this still ok?"

I sent emails to Janice, Brent, and Sean: "I am going south."

After dinner, there was a reply from Andam. "Taha just spoke with his brother. I spoke with him too. He is my uncle. He will meet you at the airport in Erbil. You will love Iraq. And Kurdistan."

There were three more replies. One of my sons reminded me, "Be safe." The other said, "I wish I was with you." Janice emailed, "I can't believe you are really doing this. What does the letter say?"

SIXTEEN

THE BURIED BOOK

"My mistress still the open road
And the bright eyes of danger."
—Robert Louis Stevenson, *Song of Travel and Other Verses*

Was this a flight into danger?

It was the last Sunday of August when my flight took off from Istanbul, heading to Iraq. I was unprepared for this when I left home. Any cautionary tales I found were on the computer in the lobby of the Şahmaran hotel in Van. One nation's travel advisory concerning its citizens' travel to another nation is often different from that posted by other countries. The United States was adamant that travel into Iraq should be avoided. They felt no need to elaborate. Turkey's advice was clear that they did not like people crossing the Iraq/Turkey borders for personal purposes, only for business. Canada and Britain advised against individuals traveling unless it was for family reasons. I could not find a single advisory online with the words "tourism" and "Iraq" in the same positive sentence; I did find many to the contrary. Such travel alerts are often national hesitations, alarmist, or serve as political insurance policies should something go amiss. Many nations extend broad warnings, while others caution with a less ominous air, a "travel at your own risk" advisory. If there is a bombing in northern India, for example, some countries will advise their citizens to avoid travel to that entire country, which seems to me irresponsible and unhelpful, as well as unnecessary. I carried that mindset with me on the plane to Erbil. Iraq was to be avoided, full stop. However, I'd learned from Taha that parts of the north, Kurdistan, were at that time civil. A safe haven, if I was so inclined. I thought along the lines Ahmet had stated, and felt it to be a reasonable part of an unreasonable country. Mostly.

After two and a half hours of flying southeast from Istanbul, the Turkish Airline flight entered Iraqi airspace, Syria to our right. I was freshly aware that gaining an Iraq entry visa upon arrival was far from assured, and tried not to think about the complications if I were refused entry. I would likely be forced back aboard the same plane, but I had no idea which country this aircraft would be flying to next. I could be stranded, and from outside the aircraft window it looked to be a desert of dubious hospitality.

We soon touched down on the airport's tarmac in Erbil (Arbil, Irbil, and in Kurdish, Hewlêr), Kurdistan. The city of Mosul has long been a troubled part of Kurdistan; its value in oil and location close to Syria has made it an uneasy land. This was true long before I visited, while I was there, and would continue to be in subsequent years, even more so when the evil that is ISIS emerged. Mosul lies fifty miles west from Erbil, toward the Syrian border, which itself is a three-hour drive west of Erbil. The Iranian border is as long a drive in the other direction, to the east. Sixty miles south of Erbil is the oil capital, Kirkuk. Another hundred and fifty miles beyond that is Baghdad. North, sixty or so miles, is the Turkish border. I had landed at the crossroads of history, ambition, conflict, and enterprise—everything except ambivalence.

Kurdistan has been an independently administered region of Iraq since after the first Gulf War in 1991. The region of Kurdistan in Iraq is frequently called Southern Kurdistan, as the southern portion of an envisioned sovereign nation, hoping one day to be a member of the United Nations.

The only other western traveler on the plane had been a young man with a short-whiskered face. He stood in front of me as we latched onto the end of a queue headed for border control. He looked around, saw my face and the nationality of my passport, and spoke in English. "I am from the Netherlands. Here to see friends. Backpacking. You?"

"Do you have a travel visa? Or will you apply here?" I asked.

"Yes. Apply here. I was told maybe." He added his name, Jan.

"Rick," I said, and we shook hands.

To our left was a large sign that said Entry Visa. Jan pointed to it. "Maybe there . . ." We left the regular customs lineup and went through a hallway into a large room with the statement repeated on the sign above an office counter: "Entry Visa." Relieved, we waited for the person ahead of us to finish his paperwork. When he was done, the female clerk motioned us away as soon as we approached. She pointed back to the customs lineup.

"Entry visa?" I asked, holding up my passport. Jan did likewise. The clerk spoke firmly, waving frantically while shaking her head. I pointed at the sign, and she sighed. "Commercial," she said, tapping her counter. "Commercial."

Jan and I retraced our steps and joined the remnants of arriving passengers, my new acquaintance ahead of me in the shortened lineup.

At the customs booth I tendered my passport and said, "Visa? Entry visa?" The official nodded once—up/down, and that was it. He flipped open my passport, stamped it, and said, "Seven days. Renew."

Just like that, I was officially in Iraq.

I carried only my small backpack for these few days, having left my larger pack and other equipment back at the Van hotel, where I'd retrieve it upon my return. I was one of the last from my flight into Erbil International Airport's baggage area, as most people had already cleared away from the carousel. Two friends had been waiting for Jan, and they accompanied him to claim his baggage. I sauntered out the airport's exit doors in hopes of being greeted myself.

No one was there for me. The reception area was empty except for a man with a parcel he'd set on the ground, above which he stood motionless. Jan and his friends came out, and the security doors closed behind them.

"Rick?"

"No one," I said.

"Maybe they are elsewhere," deduced the taller of Jan's friends.

"I have a number but no phone." I reached in my pocket for Taha's envelope.

"Phone? I have phone," the other friend said. "What is number? What do I say?"

When his call was answered, he said what I took to be Arabic for "I am with Rick. Do you know him?"

He listened and smiled and handed me the phone.

"Hello?"

I heard a welcome voice. A man said in English, "We are waiting. You take longer than others. We thought maybe you didn't come after all. We would understand. We are waiting for you at end of the bus ride."

There was a shuttle from the arrival terminal through a second security gate to a parking lot. Jan, his friends, and I boarded the otherwise empty bus. Within minutes we passed through a perimeter check. Jan and his friends stepped off in front of me and headed for the car park while I stood on the lower step of the bus, looking into a crowd of Iraqi men dressed in various shades of black: open-collared shirts and buttonless jackets, long pants. One man stood out from the rest, wearing a flowing and calf-length top over his pants, distinct in his Buddha-like rotundness. This Muslim Buddha smiled. "Mr. Rick."

Buddha's name was Karim, and he had brought quite a number of friends along with him. Everyone reached out a hand in greeting, and I was introduced. Despite my best efforts, many of their names became jumbled in my mind, but their circle of smiles was unforgettable.

We split up and got into three waiting cars. Karim was in the back seat and motioned me to the front. Hemin (the "i" silent) got behind the steering wheel of his car. "Freshly washed for your arrival," he told me, adding, "I am Taha's younger brother."

Huner, sharing the Jabbar family name with Taha and Hemin, sat in the back beside Karim and was quiet, nodding when Karim said, "Huner is Taha's nephew."

"Taha has been very helpful to me," I said. "And Andam. I met Andam before the rest of his family. And Gulie." I turned toward Karim and gave him the envelope. "Taha wrote this letter." Karim opened it and unfolded a letter in beautiful Arabic script. He chuckled as he read.

"Of course you read Farsi," I said to Karim, relieved.

"No, none of us read Farsi. But this letter is in Kurdish. Taha writes to us in Kurdish."

"But I thought . . ." I trailed off, alone in the realization of my ignorance over the letter.

"Taha writes that we should help you in Iraq. He says you are good to know."

Gratified, I said, "He told me you would help me find a hotel to stay in. Can you?"

"Hotel, no. Mr. Rick, you will stay with Taha's oldest brother. Auntie insists. Auntie is Gulie's sister. Her name is Khasyeh Khader, though I would refer to her only as Auntie, as should you, Mr. Rick. She is married to Ali Jabbar, Taha's 'big brother,' as you say in America. You will meet him now. At his home. It is arranged. We are taking you there." The names, all thankfully pronounceable with my Anglo tongue, transfixed me with their originality to my ears.

The airport in Erbil is northwest of the city, and as we drove we passed a suburb. Karim said, "That is Ainkawa, the Christian part of Erbil. Here, different religions are understood. Muslim—Sunni, Sh'ia. Also many Christians fled here from other parts of Iraq under Saddam's persecution. All are welcome in Erbil."

As we passed the Citadel of Erbil, Hemin called it "Castle of Erbil," telling me it goes under either name. One can do that with ancient places. He called Erbil "The oldest city. In world." Karim picked up on this and explained that technically this is true: Erbil is the oldest *continuously lived-in* community known to archeologists.

Hemin offered, "Later in afternoon. We'll bring you back here."

As we turned off the main thoroughfare, the other two cars, including those who had come to greet me, continued on their way home. Our car alone arched around the city, passing by the promenade of shops and a bazaar laden with rugs, tapestries, and ornate household goods—to my relief there were no trinkets visible outside any of them, no T-shirt shacks. No two storefronts were anything alike—not in height of displays or width. It could not be further from the uniformity of American shopping centers, with their predictable brands, controlled signage, ubiquitous similarity—and across the continent, city-to-city commonality; state-to-state sameness. The generic city shopping experience common in Paris or London or Frankfurt has no place in Erbil; here, each store you stare at is unique (with all that word's wonderful implication: "one of a kind").

The traffic was an untenable snarl. "Is always," said Hemin. But it was important to show me their shopping district, so they bore the inconvenience. As we drove by signs designating the Hotel Seever and Tawar Hotel, I gaped at them, increasingly happy to be staying in someone's home.

Cities laid out by engineers and visionaries thousands of years before anyone contemplated the need to accommodate automobiles—as had been Erbil—frequently have grand parkland in the center. If developers have not overridden an old park, such spaces are a heartbeat of civility for residents and visitors. Erbil's blocks-long greenery is mown short, filled with people and activity. Cars surround it, all heading in one way. Aside from the modern intrusions around it, the citadel on the hillside looked how I imagined it had looked centuries earlier. None of the buildings were taller than was the citadel; today did not overshadow the past. Taha had told me, "Erbil is old, but alive." Here, in the oldest settlement on the planet, I sensed that antiquity was the soul of the city.

Eventually we turned east onto Daratu Road and an open expanse. Within ten minutes we'd passed hundreds of partially built homes, many with people living in them. They might have one floor completed but only a strong indication of a second story or appendage to the side. The unfinished walls of ubiquitous gray plaster gave everything a ghostly appearance.

A dirt road led into a sparsely populated community. Long dirt streets spread out before us, some with only four or five homes on them. We stopped in front of a handsome home with a gate open in its cement front wall. A woman wearing a long black dress and purple scarf stood on the second-story balcony.

"That is Auntie," said Karim. I noticed a man standing in the doorway. "That is Ali." The eldest Jabbar son. Three children came out and swarmed us. A few young men stood at the ready in front, waiting. I got out of the car, and they gave me a respectful once-over. Their smiles made me feel at ease.

Protocol demanded that I first meet Ali. He wore tidy, solid green fatigues with an open collar and billowed leggings. In his breast pocket was a silver pen the color of his hair and moustache. His feet were bare. He stepped aside and into their home as I approached the doorway, thereby inviting me to enter. Shaking my hand, he talked to me in Kurdish. He was welcoming, despite the fact that he didn't smile. He motioned me upstairs to a living room. More children and young mothers sat on a long red couch. There were more young men, watching the midday news on the television. I made my way around the room, saying hello and shaking hands, stopping to squat and make eye contact with the children. They all laughed, strangers without shyness.

Ali sat, working beads with his fingers, a nimbleness to which he put his mind while also observing the room.

Auntie arrived from the balcony and I was told, through Karim, about the arrangements. "You will sleep in their big bedroom. It is off this room, right there."

"Karim . . ."

"Mr. Rick, call me Kaka. It is what they call me."

"Kaka, I'm fine with a bed in a corner, or a couch. No need for a big room."

"It is their best room. They say you are to have it. Do not disagree, Mr. Rick. It will not work." He grinned.

Auntie wanted to show me the room. Air conditioning, which I imagined a luxury in Erbil, was on high for my perceived comfort. As Auntie talked, Kaka interpreted. "You are in here, as you have private bathroom and shower."

I looked around the room with its double bed, a baby's bed and pictures of a young husband and wife. Their kindness had me displacing a family of three. As I began to voice my hesitation, Kaka hushed me again. "Do not bother, Mr. Rick. Things are set."

Sons of the family brought tea and biscuits into the living area. One of the servers spoke to Kaka and addressed him as Dubba.

"Dubba?" I asked. "Why did he call you Dubba?"

Karim, who had just become Kaka to me, laughed like only someone with a large belly could. "It is my name, my nickname. Dubba means barrel." He began to explain the notion of his barrel shaped body and saw the look of understanding on my face. We both found it pretty funny.

Before I could ask, he said, "You too. You can call me Dubba. I would be flattered."

And with that, he changed the subject. "Later you will have dinner. First, now, afternoon tea. OK?"

"Very OK," I sat down where he indicated, belatedly realizing I'd be the only one eating. "Kaka, your . . ." I caught myself. "Dubba, your English is very good."

"It should be. I lived for seven years in Halifax, Canada, then Vancouver. But this is home. I want to be here. Kurdistan is an important *country* . . ." he corrected his intentional accented misstatement, ". . . *state*. We have our own parliament. Also have our own flag. Kurdish people see a good future. Saddam is gone. It is very positive here. You will learn that."

I accepted a cup of tea and watched the family interactions in the room. Dubba pointed out who was who, and their inter-relationships. It was a mix of uncles and nieces and brothers and nephews and grandchildren and sisters and sons. As the fifteen of us relaxed, Dubba told me, "Hemin will drive you to Erbil so you can see the Citadel. When you return it will be time for dinner. I will not be here but that is OK. They have English words."

"This is so nice of everyone," was all I could say. I was overwhelmed by their hospitality.

"Tonight others will come to visit and look at you." Dubba laughed from deep in his belly—or was it from deep in his heart? "I'll be back for that. News is out that a visitor is here. They know that you know Taha. Everybody loves Taha. You could trust him with your life."

"I have," I had to admit.

With that, Dubba's phone rang. He spoke in Kurdish and then handed it to me. "It is Taha. He asks if you are here safely."

"Taha!" I said. "You have a wonderful family. They asked me to stay in their home. I am here now." I swallowed. "Thank you, Taha."

"I hear they are taking you for a drive tomorrow," he said. "They are showing you the mountains. You will see where we fought Saddam Hussein. You will learn of Kurdistan. Do not rush to leave them. You are welcome to stay."

He asked to speak with his oldest brother and I passed the phone over to Ali. I listened to this side of the conversation in Kurdish and saw a smile light up the brother's face.

"Citadel of Erbil," said Hemin. We were back in the chaotic traffic beside the bazaar, below where the walls of the citadel rose. As the traffic broke, Hemin took to a side street and drove up to a closed gate at the perimeter. He knocked on the large door. Let into an open area, we walked around the World Heritage Site, once the center of town. A road rings the citadel mound. Within this settlement, artifacts have been found that date from roughly 5000 BCE, though written mention of the site did not occur until much later. Occupied in some fashion or another since then, despite switching hands and loyalties due to wars, commercial rivalries, and strategic needs over the centuries, there must have been a thousand reasons to abandon Erbil—yet it has never happened, over the course of seven thousand years.

In a shop at the site, I saw a Kurdistan flag displayed on the wall. After explaining to Hemin that my son Sean collects flags and I'd like to buy this one for him, Hemin approached the custodian. The man smiled but shook his head, explaining through Hemin that the flag was not for sale, but was on display as a show of pride. I spoke directly to the man, asking if I could look at it more closely—my English was irrelevant, my tone genuine. He stood on a stool and brought it down for me to see. When I folded the flag respectfully and held it to my heart, he nodded in understanding, spoke to Hemin, and they both grinned. I walked around his place, found a book in English about Kurdish history and offered what I hoped was enough to pay for the book.

The man shook his head. He would not take my money. Thinking I had overstepped my push for the flag, I was surprised when he handed it to me, with the book, and pointed to Hemin, who said, "My gift."

Dusk brought dinner. The day of fasting had been long for my hosts and their families. The moment it was technically proper—sundown—we made for the food. The dining area was on the home's main floor, by the kitchen and front door. As we moved there from the second-floor living room, I saw where the women were cooking. Little girls giggled and pointed at me. For our meal, the men sprawled on a carpet with cushions for their backs. Ali handed me a soft pillow to sit on more comfortably, but with none of them using one, I politely declined.

I wondered about their eating customs. Might I stub my social toe through ignorance? The youngest sons came in as attendants, one with tea and the other with flatbread hot from the oven. A delicious dinner, visually fascinating for its array of colors in everything from assorted serving dishes to the vegetables to the spicy sauces thick with onions, began. The tableau was punctuated with large bottles of soda popping up in tints of orange, green, and brown. The setting disassembled at once in a circular passing of platters. With the gregarious dining experience, my concern about offending them with my eating habits was unnecessary.

A neighboring family joined us in the living room after we had eaten. It was a mother and father and their three children, although only the parents moved to sit down. But before they could seat themselves, even more visitors arrived at the front door. Without Dubba there, my linguistic bridge was my camera, so I asked if it was permitted to take pictures of everyone to show to Taha. I did so hesitantly, as in some cultures or settings a camera builds a blunt pier instead of a bridge; here there were immediate nods of permission and curiosity. One of them brought out a camera to reciprocate. Panning the room, I noticed one shy four-year-old tucked in his father's arms. He looked away, even while other kids gently ribbed me and kidded with my camera, posing, and pleased to watch as I played back each video clip for them and their families.

I narrowed in on the youngster, as his father did not mind. I took a photo, and turned the camera towards the boy, who closed his eyes rather than look at his portrait. His father poked his ribs, talking to him. When I played that shot his way though, I could see him look out of the corner of his eyes. I backed away, and then the boy invited my participation by having him film his father and me together. I recognized that this boy, not me, was a bridge builder.

Each face I looked at looked back. No one averted eyes, and some made to speak directly to me. Glances and body language gave away that I was a topic of curious conversation, a novelty to be observed. The lack of one-to-one talking with me did not slow the evening nor did it make me feel anything but fully accepted. They were happy among themselves—pleased that I'd dropped in. The room never went silent. A heartfelt spirit filled the room with people making sure I had food or water or tea or that I knew I was being talked about, as though that conveyed their welcoming; it did.

After the visitors had left, we watched a TV game show and a Kurdish comedy sketch called *Habo Kurdish Komidi*. The sitcom skits were about two men and a woman who were lost on a road to nowhere. Their mishaps in social and political situations brought laughter around the room. I could discern slapstick insincerity, but not the pointed parody. Canned laughter may be a Hollywood invention, but it has gone global.

The next morning, I entered the front room to find Ali sitting alone, the string of beads in hand, his fingers mulling through them. It was still dark outside. He acknowledged my entrance with a happy face and slim smile. I sat across from him and voiced morning pleasantries, as did he. The exchange was about the tones of our voices, not our exact words.

Even before I was settled in my chair, one of the sons entered the room with a tray for each of us. Apparently Ali had waited for my arrival before he would accept his pre-dawn tea. I wondered how long I'd delayed his morning ritual by sleeping in. There were several pieces of warm flatbread for me, along with honey for the bread and tea. And cheese, white and squared, to be eaten by hand. Ali received only tea.

Time spent with Ali was like meditating with a guru. It was a privilege I almost overlooked, at first mistaking his quiet as discomfort, instead of recognizing it as his gift of shared solitude and uncommitted contemplation.

Soon it was time for action. Dubba, Huner, Hemin, and I jumped into Hemin's Toyota. Dubba had swapped his black shirt for a red one with bands of black and white. "Mr. Rick, today we drive far into the country, to the border with Iran, of course not crossing the border—or you would not see home again for quite a while!"

On our route out of town was the Erbil Civilization Museum. We pulled in. To me it was an unexpected sight to see a large stone wheel there in the foreground, with all the clumsy, cartoonish character of the world's first invention (well, if not "first," it might trail right behind "fire" and be just ahead of "string"). It symbolized the dawn of civilization, in my mind. And yet, as I thought about it more, it made perfect sense to be displayed in a place like Erbil. This was Mesopotamia, which we know was a place of tradespeople, farming, grazing animals, developing governance. Fighting. The past was all assembled within Erbil's museum; the displays were static, the statues clean and tall and chipped. There is a dearth of visitor "attractions" in Erbil, this being one near the top of a very short list.

We left the city, heading east up a long incline, frequently slowing at police checkpoints. Only once did a guard approach us. Dubba rolled down his window, and we were flagged on.

In an hour's time we were far beyond the city's outskirts and into winding, hilly roads twisting back upon one another. We came across villages, some of only a few people, the largest having no more than a thousand residents. Often we stopped, and one of my hosts would get out and go in a doorway and bring back a bag of peanuts or biscuits to keep me going, while they stayed true to Ramadan. When I said, "I too will fast," Dubba said, "That is not necessary for you. We must. Here is a bottle of water for you. That, too, we do not have during daylight of fasting."

I had to prod about something, even if to be told no, because I needed to be certain there was not an angle I was overlooking, and so I asked, "Tomorrow, can we head west from Erbil?"

"Not too far. It would not be good."

"To Mosul?"

Huner shook his head. "No, Mr. Rick. Not to Mosul." He spoke to Hemin and Dubba, who responded to him in Kurdish. Dubba turned to me. "Huner once military. He has much experience and many contacts and he says he would not go there, as it is a very dangerous place now."

"It is as I expected. But I hoped . . ."

"Why?"

"The Library of Nineveh. The ruins are there on the other side of the Tigris River, near Mosul. That is what I wish to visit."

"One day you will. Not this week, though; not this year, maybe not this decade."

245

*   *   *

On the east bank of the Tigris River, in 700 BCE Assyria, stood the city of Nineveh, a great trading center three miles across, enough to straddle north-south trading routes while commanding east-west corridors at a propitious intersection. Its perimeter wall was over seven miles long. A river, the Khosr, flowed through Nineveh on its way to meet the Tigris.

Nineveh began as a hamlet before Erbil existed, though its longevity of continuous use fades by comparison. The ruler Sennacherib is the one

NORTH-EASTERN FACADE AND GRAND ENTRANCE OF SENNACHERIB'S PALACE (KOUYUNJIK)
Restored from a Sketch by J. Fergusson, Esq.re

Sennacherib's Palace, Kuyunjik, north-eastern façade and Grand Entrance. King Sennacherib made the minor town of Nineveh the magnificent capital of his Assyrian Empire and, for many years, the largest city in the world. His grandson King Ashurbanipal (reigning 668–627 BCE) constructed a new palace and library at Nineveh to house all of Mesopotamia's written works. In 612, an alliance that included the Medes, Persians, and Babylonians destroyed much of Nineveh. British adventurer Austen Layard excavated the ruins in 1847, rediscovering Sennacherib's seventy-one-room palace in 1849 and unearthing that library, including over 20,000 fragmented clay tablets in cuneiform.

who gave Nineveh its architectural greatness, his palace said to have had seventy rooms or more, including a library of clay tablets he left when he died in 681 BCE.

In archeological legend however, it is the name of a successor king who is remembered for a remarkable library. King Ashurbanipal of Assyria (668–627 BCE) also gave the "royal" designation to the library when he oversaw the gathering of thousands of works written in clay. Scribes were mandated to collect all the texts they could, and to copy every important chronicle they could borrow. These volumes recounted history and the sciences, including botany and chemistry, mathematics and geography, and more. There were correspondence and documents of legal and administrative nature, as well as accounting tallies and registers of people and goods. The Royal Library of Nineveh's[15] collection included stories of legends, myths, and magic.

The ravages of war, the shifting of commercial routes, and the birth of newer cities such as Mosul eventually lessened Nineveh's importance. Its demise came at the end of the Assyrian Empire; in 612 it was "razed to the ground."

Eroded and dissolved by centuries of winds and rainfall, the remaining walls of Nineveh's buildings tumbled into muddy heaps, burying a trove of sculptures as well as the library. Covered by the sands of time, the collapsed city formed mounds, or "tells," the most famous of which is Kuyunjik, which stands sixty-five feet above the desert floor. What survived of Nineveh would lie barely visible, largely hidden beneath twenty feet of sand until its first accurate survey by the Briton Claudius Rich, the father of Mesopotamian archeology, in 1820. Just as Sennacherib and his early Nineveh library is less well remembered today than the

---

15 For anyone who has ever loaned a book and not had it returned, or lost it through the neglect of others, consider Ashurbanipal's posted notice to anyone thinking to borrow from his library: "May all these gods curse anyone who breaks, defaces, or removes this tablet with a curse which cannot be relieved, terrible and merciless as long as he lives, may they let his name, his seed be carried off from the land, and may they put his flesh in a dog's mouth."

later Ashurbanipal collection, so too are Rich's impressive efforts outshone today by the work conducted twenty-five years later by Austen Henry Layard and his colleague Hormuzd Rassam.

Called "one of the great archaeological pioneers of the Victorian Age," at the age of twenty-two Austen Henry Layard set out to travel overland from Europe to Ceylon to work in a completely different profession: law. Meandering to Mosul, he became intrigued with tells said to cover ancient ruins.

Austen Henry Layard partnered with Hormuzd Rassam in exploring the ruins of Ashurbanipal's library and making the discoveries that led to the "Flood Tablet." Portrait © Simon Carr.

Among the "tells," one would become known as Nineveh (Kuyunjik) and the other as Nimrud, twenty miles south of Mosul.[16] "As the sun went down, I saw for the first time the great conical mound of Nimrud rising against the clear evening sky. It was on the opposite side of the river and not very distant, and the impression that it made upon me was one never to be forgotten . . . my thought ran constantly upon the possibility of thoroughly exploring with the spade those great ruins."

---

16 An assault on artifacts begun as profitable looting and black market selling turned to purging and destruction in 2015. Having destroyed collections in the Mosul Museum, ISIS militants bulldozed into Nimrud to rid it of deities worshipped rather than Allah. By April they were tumbling over antiquities, sledgehammering ancient Assyrian ruins, and exploding ninth-century relief sculptures, forever hindering our understanding of those times and peoples.

Inspired, Layard abandoned the lure of Ceylon and instead ventured to Constantinople. It was 1842. There he met the British ambassador, who provided employment and eventual support for his further explorations. In 1845, he left for the rubble and remnants near Mosul that had so enchanted him. He wrote about these "mighty ruins in the midst of deserts, defying, by their very desolation and lack of definite form, the description of the traveller."

In 1847, Layard unearthed discoveries during excavations he could not have undertaken without the local knowledge and deft management of Rassam. Taking advantage of Rassam's good relationship with local tribesmen, Layard's exploration of the ruins would identify the ancient Assyrian capital of Nineveh. During excavation, Layard discovered "walls paneled with stone slabs"—part of the colossal palace. Further burrowing the revealed remains of a magnificent library thought to belong to Ashurbanipal, alternatively designated as the Library of Nineveh, though both are tags of convenience. Found were approximately 32,000 fragments, which after joining and aligning have become some 26,500 different inscribed clay tablets, although the process of fitting the pieces back together continues to this day and may reveal that some of the pieces fit together on single tablets.

Layard knew the resulting cargo they shipped to London from Ottoman Iraq contained stories that were difficult, perhaps impossible, to decipher. The task of interpreting the tablets in the mid-1800s was hampered primarily by the lack of scholars conversant with cuneiform writing. Even expecting surprises, Layard would not have imagined how unbelievable one story concealed among the tablets would prove to be. For that alarming revelation, the archaeologist had to wait twenty-five years for the deciphering talents of the George Smith.

George Smith was a slightly built thirty-two-year-old in 1872 when he earned his supercharged reputation. For the self-taught Assyriologist, his foray into the world of cuneiform interpretation was the start of a brief but exhilarating career.

Smith's early role at the British Museum, as a repairer, was working on the tablets shipped by Layard and Rassam. He was in a junior capacity, running errands and doing miscellaneous chores, his main tasks being cleaning, identifying, and joining fragments.

Henry Rawlinson, Assyriologist extraordinaire and a public presence associated with the museum (though not on its staff), was told of this young man's abilities with cuneiform, a notoriously difficult field of study and a writing form decoded, in part, under Rawlinson's oversight. Smith was brought into Rawlinson's sphere and later promoted to assistant, with increased responsibility for organizing and cataloging the broken clay cylinders and tablets.

Smith became the Assyriology Department's senior assistant by the early 1870s, and his responsibilities grew to include deciphering complicated texts. While studying a set of linked chapters in a book of tales told sequentially on small tablets of baked clay, he realized one tablet told of a flood, a boat, animals, and a landing—along with a hero figure. Smith realized he had discovered a Babylonian flood story that not only predated but possibly presaged the story of Noah's Ark. His astonishment was in his observation. "I am the first man to read this text after two thousand years of oblivion."

Smith's decipherment of *The Epic of Gilgamesh* is recognized in large part because of his work on the surprising eleventh chapter of that book, later designated the Flood Tablet. The tablet's story startled and confused the public when it was announced as a predecessor to the Noah story, foreshadowing everything first written down a thousand years later in Hebrew texts. Here, in cuneiform writing, was everything from a god of wrath and a flood of unimaginable consequences to the building of a survival boat, the rescue vessel's rendezvous with a mountain, and a prophetic rainbow. And a hero named Utnapishtim.

In his monograph *Discovering Gilgamesh*, Vybarr Cregan-Reid portrays Smith's years following the public announcement of his deciphering this story as exciting, lonely, productive, and ultimately tragic. The

Telegraph's hailing of the discovery's importance ensured a standout crowd for Smith's first public reading of the transliterated story at the Society of Biblical Archaeology on December 3, 1872. In the audience was British Prime Minister William Gladstone.

Smith determined that a tablet fragment containing perhaps as much as seventeen lines of the flood epic was missing. He was set on visiting Mosul to explore the tells at Nineveh, believing the remainder of Gilgamesh's eleventh chapter lay hidden there. Unearthing that remnant would bring the rest of the story to light.

Funded for travel and exploration expenses by the *Telegraph* and other supporters, Smith took a leave of absence from the museum. In January 1873, he headed to Iraq to find the lost fragment of the Flood Tablet.

Taha's brother's home was quiet when I woke on my third morning in Iraq, before sunrise. Others were up so a meal could be eaten and Ramadan respected. By mid-morning we were all off to visit Taha's father and stepmother's home, a few miles away. The entire family went along, though I rode over as part of the now-common gang of four. We were in Huner's dark-blue Kia. Dubba, the only one of us to change his clothing each day, now wore a white over-shirt, trim black scarf, and billowing black pants (traditional Kurdish clothing called *schawar*). I liked his sense of fashion—nothing grand but always different. I'd describe it as "natty," if outsized clothes can be.

Taha's father awaited our arrival in the forecourt garden of his home. He rose to acknowledge our entrance and welcomed me with a bend, not a bow. I was impressed with his Kurdish turban. He wore a suit befitting a clothier, the pants smartly pressed but without a pleat. Taha had told me of this man's work life as a "self-taught tailor and stitcher."

"I am a friend of Taha's," I said to introduce myself.

At mention of Taha's name, he gave me a tight-lipped grin, clearly pleased with whatever I was trying to convey about his son who lived in a distant land.

(left) Taha and Ali's step-mother, Iyshyeh Hamd, wore the weight of a country's history and family's ambitions on her beautiful face. When Saddam's henchmen demanded she call her three Kurdish sons home from battling against Saddam, she said, "There are not three. I have four sons fighting for freedom. They'll come home when they have won."

(right) Taha and Ali's father, the Kurdish tailor and patriarch shown here wearing his handsome turban (known as a jamadani), passed away, age 88, in 2015.

Taha's step-mother emerged to greet me, her slenderness accented by the baggy headscarf she wore and a draping one-piece black dress. Her face was lovely, storied and sincere, though not without despair. Its lines reflected eight long decades of life, but she smiled when one of her granddaughters danced behind me, letting loose as a youngster in a way her grandmother might not have experienced herself for seventy years.

Both the elders had endured hard lives in a hard land; but there was food to share because of my visit. It was a generous display, more than morning tea—and set for my enjoyment alone. There was a discussion to the side of me; Ali spoke to Dubba, who turned to explain. "Dinner tonight is here, for you."

"Well . . ."

"It is decided. Father says it is to be. Mother too."

I looked to Mother, whose eyes smiled a little, then brightened.

"It is to be," I said. "Thank you very much."

With Huner driving, the four of us left the parents' home and headed to the mountains. The highway signs showed Baghdad, which puzzled me.

"Are we going to Baghdad?" I asked.

"No. We head partway toward Kirkuk, where we will also not go," Huner explained. "We will go to Sulimaniyah."

We eventually drove through Sulimaniyah and far into the hills, finding mountains. We stopped on a lonely patch of back road.

"It is here that Taha and Gulie fought Saddam Hussein," Dubba said.

We got out of the car and viewed the mountains in reverence. We were far from any village.

"Taha and Gulie were both in the Peshmerga," said Dubba. "You have heard of Peshmerga?" Before I could answer, Dubba said, "They are fierce fighters. Kurdish. Peshmerga means 'one who confronts death.'"

We stood in silence for what seemed a long time. "It was resistance," Dubba eventually said. "When you are home and see them, please tell Taha and Gulie we brought you here."

Dubba turned eastward. "Our fighters camped on the other side of those mountains. For many months we fought troops sent by Saddam. They had more weapons and more food. We had more resilience. The fighting, it seesawed over the hilltops. It took three nights of foot travel for a soldier to find food supplies and return for our army to eat. Battles were fierce. Villagers, at danger, helped us. Many Kurdish died." He paused to recollect. "Hilabja is over other side of those mountains, not many miles away. Bloody Friday, it began as a sky-blue day."

Friday, March 16, 1988, saw over a dozen of Saddam's bombing sorties target Hilabja's public places and civilian homes for five hours. There had never been a bigger use of chemical weapons in an attack on civilians, let alone a leader's fellow countrymen. One account claims the gas that wafted over the city was made to smell like oranges so people would breathe it in for the scent.

Hilabja was a key town for Saddam's army to overrun as it forced the Peshmerga back into the mountains. Saddam's Al-Anfal campaign, of which Hilabja was a part, is thought to have slaughtered 100,000 Kurdish residents of Iraq and destroyed thousands of villages. Said another way, this crime against humanity was genocide. Saddam's preferred approach was to use nerve gas.

Dubba became pensive. He talked to Hemin, and it sounded like they were making new plans.

"Mr. Rick, he said. "I want to see an old friend. He is not well. We fought together in these wars. He lives in a village we can visit."

An hour further into the remote countryside, we navigated a potholed road to a tiny village.

Dubba got out of the car and walked about, asking after his friend. Those he met pointed up a road, and Dubba continued walking as we followed him in the car. I got out, thinking to accompany him on the walk, and then realized I might spoil the reunion. But it was too late to get back in the vehicle, so I made sure to stay a respectful distance behind Dubba.

A man appeared on the road. Behind him a neighbor steered him our way. He looked older than Dubba, and I could see in his hesitant steps and orientation that he was not well. Dubba had offered me no details beyond their comradeship. I confess I had an unwillingness to ask, knowing they'd battled evil together.

Iraq has always been a conundrum for me. A constructed, artificial country held together by tyranny until gifted with democracy, a system peculiar to the surroundings and fraught with instability and abuse. While many observers lack the confidence to call Iraq's central government "democratic," it is also apparent that many Iraqis (other than the Kurds) do not view the new setup as a gift. I knew little about Iraq's Kurdistan before arriving, save for it being an ambitious state, one continually "emerging from" but never "arriving at." I had read of Kurdish victories against Saddam Hussein, and now I stood next to two men who had fought to make them happen. Standing alongside living embodiments of the struggle, Kurdistan and Iraq were changing from merely visual placeholders on the printed map to a very real sense of emotion and respect I could feel inside me.

"*Be kher bi!*" the man exclaimed.

"*Rozh-bash!*" Dubba responded. They embraced.

I stood back until Dubba turned my way and explained to his friend why I had come along. His compatriot shook my hand. They fell into conversation and I backed away from them, and from any sense of Iraq I had previously held. In this corner of the country were stories of brutality and humility, of desperation and destruction, depicting a powerful legacy of Kurdish bravery.

We were in a remote part of a remote land. The surroundings gave me a feeling of both continued poverty and consistent optimism. There were not many people as I walked the length of the village, but those I saw went about their daily chores with a firm resolve. With the exception of our vehicle's presence, this site had likely not changed since the war years; buildings were tired and dry looking, and gardens appeared difficult to tend. Nothing was new. I was struck with the sense that these people put one foot in front of the other on life's long walk, never hoping for too much, so they could not be disappointed. They'd known unfathomable difficulties, painful separations from family and community. They knew about starvation and fear. Now, with relative peace, they could see this day as a good one, without making any assumptions that tomorrow would be as well.

"Mr. Rick." It was Hemin calling me back to the car. I looked over at Dubba and his friend. Two men, whose lives had pitted them against unbeatable odds which they'd beaten, were bidding farewell.

We were in the Zagros Mountains, a rugged range nine hundred miles north to south, forming a border between Iran and Iraq. These mountains carry one particular story from far beyond today, beyond the 1980s, beyond most of recorded history.

It is said that Mount Nisir, in the Zagros range, is another possible resting place for Noah's Ark.

Well away from the Tigris River, near Sulimaniyah and about three hundred miles from Mount Ararat, are foothills that lead to what was once named Mount Nisir (or Mount Nimush), where the *Epic of Gilgamesh* tells us that Utnapishtim moored his ship after the flood began to recede. The names mean "Mount of Salvation." Today the mountain, which has an elevation of nine thousand feet, is often known as Pir Omar Gudrun.

The Zagros Mountains are steep and often treeless, exposing the rock strata. We drove into them on a winding road and pulled over for a lookout. I could see the Mesopotamia of old reaching for the horizon.

Driving alongside a narrow river on our way back to Sulimaniyah, Huner took a sharp pull and stopped beside the road. The river below us trickled at a creek's pace. The water argued its way around rocks, creating white foam before breaking into a deeper calm. We walked a path along the waterway, and peacefulness set in. For twenty minutes we did not talk. I imagined my companions pondering all that had occurred in these mountains, of battles won and lost, and the elusive truce.

The main road in Sulimaniyah branched in two as we returned to the city. We took the street dominated by auto parts shops, used goods stores, and shops offering fresh produce.

"You should have lunch, Mr. Rick." Dubba must have noticed my fatigue.

"I don't see any place to eat," I said. "Besides, you're not eating and I'd prefer to observe your Ramadan."

Dubba pointed to a closed shop. "There, across the street."

Parts of Kurdish Iraq convey a sense of modern ambitions, though many places on the author's drives, such as this thatched barn and out-buildings in a small farm yard—still evoke centuries-old agricultural and living practices.

I protested. "Ramadan. I don't see a place for food."

"Behind the curtain," he insisted. "There is a hidden entrance. That respects Ramadan, because it is not on open display. Go. One of us will come for you later."

I walked across the street, indeed hungry. Intrigued, I lifted the corner of a dusty and dirty white sheet that hung over the entrance to a building. Behind it was a door, ajar. From within came the smell of grilled meat.

"Hello," I said, tentatively, to the first person I saw in the room, and noticed it was crowded. Twenty men seated at their meals went quiet and looked my way. The setting was reminiscent of a speakeasy during prohibition. I was too obviously Western to be an investigator looking for non-compliance with Ramadan. If they were worried about being discovered, that concern was not evident, as they soon turned back to their meals.

"Come here. I will set you up." The manager swerved between the seat backs that made for a narrow passage. I walked sideways to move through the artificial aisle. The patrons pulled their chairs in to let me by, and when we were on the other side of the room I was given a table for four to myself.

"There is beef. There is pasta. Rice, of course. Vegetables cooked on the stove, not boiled. It is as I learned to cook in New York." All this came from the man who had seated me. It was not a list of menu options; it was what would be served.

My only choice was what to drink.

"Orange soda? Coca-Cola?"

"Coke, please."

The meal was filling and tasty, and had a spice I'd not encountered before. Around me, men ate in a humble defiance—Muslims breaking Ramadan without feeling guilty, acknowledging their need for sustenance without wanting to publically flaunt religious prerogatives.

Huner came along later and sat with me, but he did not even have a coffee.

"You should walk off that lunch," Dubba said as we drove away from the restaurant. I knew they had eaten nothing, and wondered from where they drew their energy. We parked high up on a road in the forest. I could hear carnival noises echoing from above. Walking up, we entered a festival set-up of booths filled with toys and hats and barren food kiosks. Hardly anyone was there. "It is empty now, but full at night. So busy you can't move."

The footboards we walked on turned into a bridge over raging water. The Bekhal Falls torrent plunged from a source high above and tumbled down on top of massive boulders, pockmarked with cup-size hollows that had been smoothed out over the centuries.

The author's three Iraq travel friends: Huner and Hemin of the Jabbar family, and Dubba.

Hundreds of feet above us, the river roared over and around a horde of rocks, some having been broken apart and wedged mid-stream, green moss covering many of them. The waterfall was a hundred feet across. A tree shot out of the cascade, dividing its tumultuous streams. "That wouldn't be seen back home," I shouted above the thundering waters, pointing. Two small children were crossing the waterfall. How had they gotten out there? The only way I could see would have been jumping over two-foot-wide rushes of water or using stepping-stones hidden under the powerful current.

One boy stood below the tree, poised to leap over a cascade to where his friend already stood on the only available perch, a slippery rock.

"Wonder where their parents are . . ." I said, looking around.

"There." Dubba pointed to a middle-aged father straddling the rocks farther down the falls, his butt resting against one to steady the hands that held a camera.

Traveling back down into Erbil that evening, we were subject to several military checkpoints. Security seemed to be on heightened alert, and the soldiers never hurried when it was our turn for inspection. At the third interruption there was a protracted discussion between the officer and Dubba. Words passed quickly between Dubba and Hemin, then Dubba and Huner, and back to Dubba through his opened window to the guard.

Dubba looked at me. "Mr. Rick, he wants your passport. Now."

I gave it up and listened to the Kurdish debate escalate between Dubba and the guard. The guard walked away with my passport, showed it to a fellow sentry, and returned to my window, holding up the passport photo for comparison. He flipped my passport closed. Then open. Then closed. He stared at the cover and blurted a question. Dubba responded with a flood of words, during which I heard him say "USA."

Finally, the guard passed back my passport and waved us through. Dubba said something in Kurdish to Hemin and Huner, and they laughed.

"What was that all about?" I asked.

"When I gave him your passport, he told me he doesn't know where Canada is. He said that your passport is no good. I tried to explain Canada. He didn't understand. Finally I told him you are from USA. That is why he let us through."

Chastised, I told them, "We travel with a certain smugness about our Canada passport. It obviously didn't have any cachet here." Though Canada took a strong role in both world wars and the Korean War, it is a country that mostly aims to avoid conflict; indeed the concept of the United Nations "peacekeeping" force was the brainchild of a Canadian prime minister, Lester Pearson, recipient of the Nobel Peace Prize. Canada's is a favorable passport to offer up during an introduction. The country's flag is a backpack emblem that helps travelers get hitched rides that those wearing other flags perhaps wouldn't. Here though, Dubba explained, the opposite was true.

"Here, in northern Iraq," he said, "Kurdistan exists because of the United States. Saddam Hussein killed us, for many years. That Saddam has disappeared is because of Bush the son. He and USA are liked in Kurdistan."

Dinner at Taha's father's home was a spectacle, all under his step-mother's orchestration. The feast was a buffet of grandmother's age-old recipes. With her in the kitchen preparing the food were the women of the extended family. Taha's father was distinguished-looking and solemn as he led the men from the sitting room to where we would dine. The men all sat cross-legged on the floor around a rectangular carpet as the meal arrived via a constant march of young women from the kitchen. A few boys helped with the larger platters and when they were done serving, they sat with the men to have dinner. The girls and women would spend time cooking, serving the men, beginning the cleanup, or—as service intervals allowed—eating, in the kitchen; none joined us.

"*Nositanbe!*" said one of the men, the Kurdish version of *Bon appetit!*

Dinner at the home of Taha's parents was comfortable in every way. The rooms were spacious and nicely furnished. The men, seated on the floor with Father at the head of a carpet of food, were served a menu steeped in tradition, complemented by colored soda waters, teas, and coffee.

Dubba was my culinary tour guide, ensuring that I moved beyond the rice dish and wispy bread. In a land where neither beer nor wine is commonly served, and water is plentiful, the treat drinks were dark cola or the bottles of orange soda, sometimes a sparkling lemon drink. Bottles of each popped their heads above the serving dishes on the carpeted floor.

"Mr. Rick, do you know these foods?"

"Some from last night and before. Most I've never tasted, never seen."

"All is traditional. You know, Taha's mother and other women have cooked this feast because you visit."

"I wish they'd join us for the meal," I said.

"They would, if you stayed longer, but you are new guest to them, Mr. Rick."

He pointed and explained. "That, with peppers, potatoes, is with a sauce from tomatoes and other vegetable. It is *tapsi*. The broth is good for dipping the *pide* in, that thick crust bread."

I could see onions peeking through chilies and green peppers with naan rolled to hold it all together. "*Dolma*," Dubba called it. "The bread is from their old oven. It is clay." Then he snickered. "The oven is clay, not the bread."

SEVENTEEN

KURDISH LANDS

"Be sure this land of nowhere will expel
All those who seek a chance outlandish spell."
—Gavin Maxwell, *A Reed Shaken by the Wind*

The night before, Hemin had said it would be best if we rose early, at 4:00 a.m. He wanted us on the road shortly thereafter. The route back to Turkey would lead close to, but not into, Mosul, then north through Dohuk, to the Iraqi border town of Zakho. It would be a two and a half hour trip, and they had to return to Erbil once they dropped me off. I had argued—well, "put forth"—that they could send me there by other means, as I was already the beneficiary of a great amount of fuel and companionship. But the three of them were set on taking me. Our inseparable foursome would become three the moment they delivered me to the Iraq–Turkey border, but not before.

I was sitting up in my bed, trying to fully wake up, when there was a tap on the door. "Soon," said a man's voice. When I entered the sitting room, Ali was in his chair, working his beads as he'd done every time I'd been with him. It was a ritual I'd come to admire. I understood it was not fidgeting but an observance to ease his mind and deliver a mantra. He cherished those beads and relied on them for serenity and confidence.

When resting in his thoughts, Ali left his mouth ever so slightly open, his tongue pressing to the inside of his upper lips. He was doing that when one of the sons brought us tea and honey, along with the bread and cheese. Ali, because it was still before dawn, ate with me this morning.

We spoke in our own languages. Our words were few. He remained his stoic self; tomorrow morning he would be here. Where would I be? I wondered how I appeared to him. Had time with me in his home, in his land, met his expectations of a brother's friend? I realized that when I'd arrived in Iraq, I'd simply wanted safe passage in a country of complex circumstances. I'd hoped that my concerns about traveling here could be dismissed once I arrived. Ali, his family, and his country had indeed accomplished that.

Ali, Taha's older brother, is the linchpin in an extended family of relatives and friends, most living in Erbil. A calm face often conveyed the seriousness of his role, but here, his smile of confidence and experience broke through.

I heard Dubba's car pull up. It was time to leave. I'd been quiet so as not to wake the rest of the household.

Ali stood first and stepped toward me. I rose and reached to shake his hand. Instead, he placed his beads in the palms of my hands and closed my fingers around them, holding my hands cupped in his, his grip soft yet firm. He smiled.

I moved quietly to the first floor, intending to leave without disturbing anyone. But they were all there to say goodbye. The mothers and their youngsters were in morning clothes, and the boys and young men looked ready for whatever chores awaited them. Their farewell words, even though I didn't know exactly what they said, were clearly prayers of goodwill and safety. I wished them the same, though prayer seems more powerful than wishing. We would miss one another.

Our destination was in the northern part of Iraq: the Ibraheem Khaleel Border Complex, which oversees heavy traffic—both goods and people moving between Iraq and Turkey. A bridge there, over the Khabur River, is the border between the two countries.

"We have one hundred and twenty miles, Mr. Rick. Your last drive with us as bodyguards," joshed Dubba. "We will leave you at the border in very uncertain hands." He said the last part with seriousness. Hemin had already fallen asleep in the back seat, and Dubba added, "You can sleep if you wish."

I was tired, but too excited to sleep. As we drove out of the development, the variety of home construction sites was evidence of a people rising from decades of thwarted plans to live in harmony.

"Mosul," I read aloud as we headed east under a directional sign. I asked one last time, "The Library of Nineveh?"

"It is 'no,' Mr. Rick. We will go to outskirts of Mosul. Highway then turns north toward Dohuk."

Nearing Dohuk, the homes we passed were elaborate; many had several balconies, and their facing stones were in pastel colors ranging from muted purples to pale creams. Some entrance pillars looked like highly ornamented notes of accomplishment for the owner, others like artistic statements by their designers. No two were alike. If I ventured on every city street, I thought, I'd not find a duplicate.

We soon saw signs for Zakho—where I'd weeks before imagined spending a night, on a lark, just to put my foot into Iraq. The border town has the hubbub one expects wherever trucks arrive for loading and unloading. Workers put in long days, and drivers accept long waits, so such transit points can be big employers, depending on the seasonal flow of goods. Zakho had a transient air.

"We go to Wargehe Delal," said Dubba.

"*Wargey . . . ?*"

"Wargehe Delal. It is the Delal Bridge."

A remaining arch of this once magnificent bridge spans the Little Khabur River, a tributary of the Tigris. It was an old edifice in a land of many such monuments.

"How would you build Wargehe Delal[17] without today's technology and equipment?" Dubba asked rhetorically. Huge stones had been wedged together to support foot and wagon traffic. We strolled at leisure around a tourist stop in a town without tourists. Dubba wore an expansive white shirt, as clean as white could be, over his pantaloons, with a simple black scarf, long enough to mop perspiration.

As we neared the Ibraheem Khaleel administration unit straddling the border, Dubba pointed to a fluttering Kurdish flag. "The red is for martyrs' blood, and that never ends. Our white is depicting freedom and peace. Green symbolizes lands, beauty you have seen. All bars are equal across banner."

I asked about the sun symbol mid-flag.

"It is to say wisdom. It is fire. We call it *Roj*. Here though, is an Iraq border under Kurdish government management. Our flag flies to say that."

Türkiye, painted across a high roof's frontispiece, marked the border crossing and announced the entry point into a new county.

"Mr. Rick, here we will leave you."

I'd had my hand held by safekeeping locals in a land of dangers, and was now leaving that casual care behind. In a matter of minutes I'd be testing the reentry workings of my Turkish visa. If found wanting, I'd be compromised. And even if I did get through, I still needed to find transportation

---

17 Wargehe Delal would, within a few years, become a name associated with a refugee camp providing housing for thousands of Yezidis who sought refuge from Islamic State jihadists, fleeing demands that they convert to extreme Islam and jettison their own faith.

once I got to the Turkish side of the border. I remembered what Ahmet had advised back in Van: "Find a taxi on the Iraq side of border, with Turkish license plates. They will be going back and might take you."

The four of us were walking toward the customs building when Huner pointed, "Taksi." Three drivers were haggling among themselves, and Hemin walked over, asking for a *taksi* heading to Turkey. "Where, Mr. Rick?"

I'd not thought this all the way through. Tatvan was my ultimate destination, with renewed hope of catching the once-missed ferry across Lake Van. I needed to get to a city in Turkey where I could catch a bus to Tatvan. I'd last looked at the map in Van, with the hotel staff; I knew the eastern route from the border up through Hakkari and Başkale was shortest, but that included the mountain passes where Kurdish rebels were fighting Turkish forces, so that option was off the table. I dug in my pack and unfolded the much-creased map. Hemin and Dubba peered on as Huner and I pressed it against the wall of a building.

"Sirnak," I said, as it was a prominent spot on the map, and a routing the Van hotel staff had shown me.

"Hmmm. Silopi. Cizre, Sirnak. Yes, that can be your route."

"Thanks, Dubba."

"You should be able to get a taksi to take you that far. Better still, ask for Siirt. It is further, yes, after Sirnak. If in a taksi, it is more pleasant ride. I think you should share."

"Share what?"

"Share taksi. Hang around, Mr. Rick. Wait for taksi to fill up with others who pay part of the fare. Then, you can afford to go further in that taksi."

Huner held the map against the wall, his hands and elbows bracing it against a breeze. From Siirt, there was a good road to Baykan and from there to Bitlis, and that should mean decent buses, or at least frequent ones. There were two routes from Bitlis to Tatvan. My departure from eastern Turkey by train into Iran was a few days away. I had no place to be until then.

"I will start with taksi to Sirnak, as that gets me across the border into Turkey. I will see if going beyond Sirnak to Siirt works." I mocked a shout: "*Taksi!*"

Hemin appeared with a taksi driver in tow. He, Dubba, and the driver spoke with rapid-fire words, and Dubba turned to me. "He is going to Cizre. And he says from there you can get bus to Sirnak. He will leave in two hours."

"I'm patient, but let's ask further," I suggested. "Sirnak is now where I want to get." We thanked the taksi driver and left him.

Hemin and I approached another driver, and Hemin asked if he was heading to Turkey.

"Yes, I am," he said in English. He was looking at me, having guessed whom the passenger was, and I could tell he was sizing me up. He was a youngish Turk, with stylish hair—dark, with hair cream to hold parts of it up and back. A white crewneck clung tight to his torso under a black jacket buttoned low. The collar rode high. He had pressed black slacks. His smirk broke into a grin of unusually bright teeth. I felt déjà vu. *I know this man, but from where?*

Happy to hear English, I was suddenly struck by how complicated all these negotiations would be without Hemin, Huner, and Dubba.

"Siirt?" I asked.

The man danced from foot to foot, his head teetering to the side opposite the stressed foot. It was a negotiation. I picked up his dance step, teetering in sync with him, and smiled. I still couldn't place his face.

"I can drive you to Siirt, but that is expensive. You OK with that?"

"No," I answered. "We can find others to share cost."

"Oh, yes, but I thought you might want to leave this morning instead of tomorrow night."

Checkmate.

Dubba spoke Kurdish, and he and the Turk went back and forth, with Hemin interjecting. I felt like a box of cereal hoping for a FedEx shipment, sitting around while they dickered about how best to deliver me.

Dubba went into English for my benefit. "If you wait one hour, maybe little longer, he should have another rider. Possibly two. He will say he's driving to Siirt, but likely only gets someone to Sirnak. You would pay rest all to him. On your own. You agree?"

"Cost?"

They spoke in Kurdish. The driver's smile glistened. Dubba conveyed the price to me, saying, "It is fair, I think. It should be less if others go in taksi with you—but don't hope that. Once he has you he has you. Expect to pay this amount regardless. It is how it works."

Huner brought me a bottle of cold water from the canteen and shook my hand while handing it to me. Hemin said, "Goodbye, Mr. Rick." Kaka's face rounded in friendship, the relaxed Dubba personality I'd seen for the majority of my trip replaced by that of a concerned friend. He knew my time in Iraq had been very good for me, but he could not know how touched I was by his kindness and help during my trip. I smiled, aiming to equal the sentiment that his face conveyed: rapport and respect, while alleviating any worries he held about my onward journey. Although Kaka was proficient in several languages, no words came.

We shook hands, and they left.

I turned around. My taksi driver was gone too.

I ran about, searching the taksi stands, as I'd not seen his actual car. I rushed to the café to see if he'd gone in there. I looked in a waiting area, where other passengers might be found.

There was a tap on my shoulder.

"Where'd you go?" the taxi driver demanded. His mannerisms sprang at me as though I'd seen them a hundred times.

"Where's your car?" I tried to balance his abruptness.

When we were in front of his green hatchback Honda, he let out a drawl: "This is *m-y* car. It's *t-h-e-e b-e-s-t* car."

"Fonzie." I said it under my breath. I knew I knew him. His self-assured smirk, his clothing, his talk, made him a dead ringer for the character from the American TV show from the 1970s, *Happy Days*.

"Give me your pack," the Fonz said as he opened the car's hatch. "I need you to put these cigarettes into your pack." In his trunk I saw dozens of cartons of contraband cigarettes, perhaps ten packets in each carton, wrapped in cellophane, with their American brand labels visible. "They will not check *you* as we go through border."

"You've gotta be kidding."

"No. I drive through here often. It is OK. They know me," he said nonchalantly. He had unzipped *my* backpack and was stuffing three long cartons of cigarettes into it all at once, looking over his shoulder away from me and toward the customs office.

"Look, Fonzie . . ."

"My name is . . ."

"Never mind. If you don't unpack those cartons, I will. And you'll lose this customer."

He stared at me. "There are more customers."

"Then find one to share my fare."

"You could be nicer."

"Keep the cigarettes out of my backpack." With that I reached into my pack and pulled them out one at a time. I threw them onto his trunk floor.

"They've got your fingerprints on them," he said.

I zipped my backpack and slung it over my shoulder. Immediately I thought of *Midnight Express*, a Hollywood movie I'd absorbed as shorthand for foreign travel gone badly.

We parted in a huff. I still felt we had a deal on the ride though, so I hovered close to his car, glugging bottled water. Twenty minutes later he came back with two businessmen, both with suit jackets on, one wearing a tie.

"They are going to Sirnak. One actually goes a little further, but not all the way to Siirt. Your price holds." To all of us he said, "We will leave in ten minutes and go through border."

We three passengers shook hands. The businessmen each placed a suitcase and an overnight bag in the trunk and went off, one to the washroom, one to get a coffee.

The moment they were out of sight, Fonzie said to me, "Stand there, right there." He positioned me as a shield between the customs office and his car. An accomplice. He lifted the hatch and opened the businessmen's cases. There was room in them, and he stuffed six cartons of cigarettes into each.

Closing the hatch, he said, "You sit up front with me. It is better."

It was right then that I should have left. Instead, I got in the passenger seat while he stood outside my door, holding it open. Before he closed it, he first wedged open the interior panel that held the window-winding knob and popped it off. Into that space he stuck more cartons, and then pressed the door panel's clips together again. When he closed the door, a bulge pressed against my right arm.

"I'm not sure I'll find a way to thank you, Fonzie."

While he and I sat in the car waiting for the businessmen, I noticed the long truck lineup. It would be hours of waiting. The two businessmen returned, and we were ready to go; Fonzie shifted out of first gear and into second. The four of us made toward another terminal: two businessmen, a lone traveler, and a smuggler.

The non-truck lineup progressed smoothly. When we were close enough to the first customs official, Fonzie moved quickly. "Put these behind your feet." He took three cartons of cigarettes from within his jacket and stuffed them under my seat and braced behind the calves of my legs. "Hold them tight."

When the taksi driver spoke, one of my favorite Fonz quotes was written all over his face: "Stupid, yes. Also dumb. But it is something I've gotta do."

He jumped out of the car with an air of irrevocable self-confidence, walking toward the official, jovial and carefree.

"What is going on?" asked one of the businessmen.

Thinking of the potential consequences, I said, "We may spend more time together than you planned."

"What do you mean?"

"Well . . . apparently he's friends with *this* border guard." And under my breath: "I hope so." I've often felt that in a dicey situation, sneaky is best. But the combination of sneaky and the Iraq–Turkey border made my situation increasingly stupid. Stupid makes me calm; I don't know why, maybe it replaces thinking. I tried that: thinking. Would telling these men what I knew lessen the risk of getting caught with contraband that had my fingerprints on it? I wasn't willing to take that risk. I could not imagine a good outcome if I sent the businessmen to look in their packs.

"You know something we don't?" the second man asked. I was inadvertently smuggling cigarettes out of Iraq; there were cartons at my feet, cartons beside my right elbow and, God knows, probably cartons in my pack. We were one misplaced comment away from getting caught.

"Nope," I said.

The border guard came around to the car's hatch, which was being opened by the Fonz. The guard asked, "Whose luggage are these?"

"Mine," said one of the well-dressed passengers.

"And that one is mine," said the other, sounding over-polite.

The guard closed the trunk. Simple as that. The Fonz jumped back in his seat, wearing a look of cocky entitlement that would probably get him out of jail long before the other three of us saw daylight. I waited for him to verbally slide me his "Aaaaeeeyyyy!"

Instead, the Fonz looked straight at me and said, "Next guard checks inside the car. Give me your cigarettes."

"*My . . . ? My . . . ?*"

"Quick. The trunk is cleared OK. I'll put these there." His hand fumbled beneath my legs, pulling out the cartons. He couldn't reach them all.

Hurriedly I handed him the remaining carton from under my feet, leaving more fingerprints. He shoved the goods inside his jacket and casually walked to the back of the car. There was a honk from the car behind, and Fonzie gave it no notice. He leaned into the trunk area, letting the packets tumble unseen from his jacket, and stuck the contraband under the two suitcases. He walked around the entire car and sat down in his driver's seat, blasé as usual.

He leaned over me and opened the glove compartment. Two cartons of cigarettes fell into my lap, though he was doing his best to gather them into the folds of his jacket. He repeated his shuffling trip to the car's trunk. When he returned, not a bead of sweat showed on his face. He looked at the two shocked passengers in the back seat, flashing his white teeth while saying nothing. In my head I could hear Fonzie's classic line: "You ain't nobody until you do what you want!"

Now he drove slowly up to the next official's booth. The guard came out and stood in front of the car, immediately moving to my side.

"Out."

I stood up with my pack in hand. The officer seemed nine feet tall—as far as I could tell his jackboots went up to my waist. He yanked the pack out of my hands and unzipped it. Finding nothing, he flipped open the glove compartment and rummaged about with his hand. He checked under my seat. "Get back in."

As we drove away, Fonzie turned to me. "Honest. I would have moved them from your bag if you'd let me hide them there. He would not have found them."

In an unfriendly imitation of the Fonz, I said, "Sit on it."

But we were not finished with the border. Fonzie pulled beside an unmistakably government building; square, featureless, efficient lines of stone and plaster that ran three stories high. Inside, the ceiling stared down from two floors up, above a counter wide enough so that those behind it were unreachable. Three officious-looking clerks leaned on this marble-topped fixture near the entryway. None of them were busy. Fonzie walked over to one, the three of us following in a silent conga line.

"What's this for?" I asked.

"It's protocol. They need to see your paperwork."

Fonzie handled everything, taking and passing over our passports. He jabbered away with the female official behind the counter. When my passport was returned to him, he passed it my way and said dismissively, "You are OK. For now. Wait outside if you wish."

I wished. Outside I walked around the compound, keeping the taksi in sight and waiting for more to happen. Half an hour later, I went back inside and saw only one of the businessmen standing there. He shrugged in my direction.

Outside again, at what was nearly an hour of waiting, the Fonz appeared and said, "It is not you. It is one man's paper. It's not complete. So they also are suspicious of other man. Both wear suits." It would be another half hour before the three of them returned. One more customs post awaited us, but it passed without incident. Our car drove away. We were in Turkey.

"Fonz, we should talk . . ." I began, bemused and angry.

"We are OK," he said. "You have no worries. Not now."

"Look . . ." I turned toward the two men in the back seat, one of whom was perspiring. This whole thing might have been more familiar to them, who knows, but it wasn't a type of business travel I was familiar with. Spy novels have this stuff, I thought. I widened my eyes and slowly cocked my head in a gesture asking them, "Any comments, guys?"

"We are through," said the man wiping sweat from his brow with a handkerchief.

The other parroted: "We are through."

I turned to Fonzie, who was for whatever silly reason nodding his head, and said, "We are through."

We cruised a multi-lane road through unlovely land full of truck lines, queues of cargo trailers, and pavement that collectively took the eye away from any rugged welcoming the hillsides wished to impart. In ten minutes we arrived in Silopi. I looked behind me to see which man might be getting out, but they both had confused looks on their faces. Fonzie pulled up to a pharmacy and bounced out of the car. He walked in the front door of the place carrying a handful of cigarette cartons from the trunk. When he came out he was pocketing cash.

We stopped again after another twenty miles on a double-lane road, just outside of Cizre, as the Fonz darted into a roadside general store carting more cigarettes. He was gone twenty minutes.

With nothing to do but wait, I took out a guidebook and had enough time to realize that near here, and to the south of Sirnak, was

Mount Cudi—or Cudi Dagh, or Mount Judi, or Qardu—which, based on the Qur'an, is thought to be Nûh's "place of descent": a third potential Mountain of the Ark location. Trying to put a positive spin on the last few hours of my life, I wondered how possible it would be to take this detour in the Noah story, since we were in the vicinity.

My revelry was short-lived.

Fonzie emerged from the store with bewilderment pasted on his face. He looked as though he'd gone inside to drop off the cigarettes and instead had sex with the merchant, but said nothing to us as he got back in the car.

After a few more deliveries, we found ourselves on the outskirts of Sirnak and dropped off one of the businessmen at a hotel. We were not much out of the main district of the town when the second man left us at an office building.

"Siirt, just you." Fonzie, who had by now delivered two or three dozen cartons of cigarettes, was less superficially jovial and more at ease. "One more stop." With that, we were at a roadside vendor. Cartons were removed from my door panel and taken inside the store for cash. Fonzie was back in a shot, counting the bills as he walked.

"You make much money at this?"

"Very profitable."

"Dangerous," I said.

"Oh yes. For you." He laughed at this; I didn't. "I drive border three days every week. It is my job. I don't transport cigarettes every time. I am careful. Border guards are friends. Sometimes."

"What if you are caught?"

"Yes. What if I am caught?" He thought a bit, with an unworried look. "I would no longer own taksi."

Changing the subject and recalling an earlier conversation, he said: "I know agent in Siirt, before main city. You can buy bus ticket from him to Tatvan. It is easy."

The day was warm as we entered Siirt, one hundred and twenty miles and a few hours after crossing the border. It was mid-afternoon under clear skies. The Fonz dropped me in front of a storefront jostling for the attention of sidewalk customers. He pointed to a sign that said "Ticket Agency" in Turkish and to the travel decals on the store's window. I had paid Fonzie in advance, so there was no more negotiation. As I got out of the car, he leaned over to shake my hand, suddenly fond of our escapade. "Thanks for your cigarette help." Then he flashed me a mouth-wide goodbye, honked, screeched his tires, and was gone.

The ticket agency was closed.

I knocked on the door several times, more loudly with each pounding. A woman came from the fruit stand next door, signaling she would phone someone.

Time passed, and two teenage boys appeared to assist me, looking as if they were on a school assignment for the absent owner. They did not speak English, and my Turkish was unhelpful. Unsure of what I wanted, they opened the agency. We consulted a map on their wall. Once "bus" and "Tatvan" were established, they conveyed "likely." The Fonz had told me what a bus ticket might cost, and I held that amount in my hand. Without negotiation, one of the lads took my cash—which instantly made me think I was overpaying. The other boy issued a ticket, all written in Turkish. The only word recognizable to me was 'Tatvan.' The one who'd taken my cash looked to the clock and mimicked the arms, the paper bills pointing to the minute hand. I deduced that the bus to Tatvan would be arriving soon. They walked me to the other side of the street and waited with me.

When they saw the bus coming, they flagged it down. The driver spoke sharply to them as I stepped up onto the bus stairs. It did not move. The driver shook his head as I showed him my ticket. He nodded, and then he shook his jowls, saying, "Full. No room." I again showed my ticket. He nodded. "Yes. Ticket. Full. No room." And it was true; there was not a seat to be had. The driver's comment was "Tomorrow."

My bus pulled away, leaving me on the curb.

Four Mountains of the Ark (hypothetical) are shown here. Three are literary locations for the landing of an Ark after the Great Flood: Nisir (Mt. Nimush) is from the Epic of Gilgamesh; Ararat is from the Torah and the Bible; Judi (Cudi) is from the Qur'an. A fourth presumptuous location, also depicted, is Mount Sabalan.

We went back to their business and found a city map. One stabbed at a circle that was numbered to a coded list, indicating the Otobüs Terminali, and said, "*Siirt Otogarı*." He pressed a finger gently to the jersey I wore, then onto the map. "Tatvan," he emphasized. Clearly, I must get to this bus depot and from there to Tatvan.

"Taxi?"

"No," he responded. It amused me that even those who didn't speak English understood "no."

"Where do I catch a bus to the bus station?" They did not understand my words but got the gist when I tried "Otobüs Terminali?" They walked me out of the shop, down the street a block to a bench with a bus stop sign. They indicated a bus should show . . . in a while. They went away, taking with them any hope I had of reimbursement. It is how it goes.

When a bus came, I called out "Otobüs Terminali?" The driver shook his head, closed the door, and drove off.

Fifteen minutes later, another bus came and this driver too shook his head, but before leaving he said something in rapid Turkish and gestured down the street.

I walked back to see if the teenagers were still in their shop. They were gone. Retracing my steps to a street corner, I saw a mother and little kids, one girl maybe ten, crossing toward me. Thinking the girl might learn English at school, I asked directions and they attempted answers. I got the gist that the bus connecting me with the Otobüs Terminali was at a different stop. I must go there—if only I could figure out which stop was the correct one.

In the middle of my exchange with the family, a growling motorcycle thundered up to us. A middle-aged man doffed his helmet, showing a hair crew-cut of military precision. He was astride a Harley Davidson that, at idle, was too loud to talk over, so he yelled.

"What do you want?"

I shouted. "The Otobüs Terminali, by bus. Or a taxi."

"No taxi. Not reliable. You want bus. Also not reliable, but . . ."

The family moved on. The motorcyclist placed his helmet across the handlebars. He turned off his engine and it rumbled still. Now even the traffic felt quiet. The man pounced, his voice still vibrating: "*Wha tha phuk are you doin here?*"

"Well . . ." My mind raced to find calming words. It was tough to distinguish if he was crazy or just rough around the edges. He seemed upset and big, not in that order. Trouble was mine for the having.

"You must be politician." He shook his head in disgust. "Don't look it. Or you are religious. Don't smell it. Or belong to an NGO. You here to change us?"

"Nope."

"You here to marry one of our women?"

"Just passing through . . ."

"No one just passes through here. There is no reason for a foreigner to give a shit about this place."

Since we seemed to be getting along, I asked about him.

"Air force pilot," he replied. "Jet fighter." He pointed away as though he'd parked one nearby. "You are from North America. I was in Labrador. Training for NATO flights."

He burst into a monologue involving Turkish politics, within which his armed forces were a major player. "There will be a coup, it is said," he began. "The Force, it has much political power. Forces are disgruntled." He talked of the growing public distrust of government, and also of the recent distrust of the armed forces. At first I was intrigued—a poli-sci lecture on the street corner in Turkey. Then I wondered if it was safe to even be seen in the general vicinity of a wild man talking so negatively about the government. He rolled on about the country's prime minister: "Erdoğan concentrates on winning European friends. Needs cross-investment Euros. For European support, first he must better treat Kurds and Armenians."

That would seem a good thing, I thought. The other side of that, the man said, was that "Erdoğan will make Turkey an Islamic state. Pious types restrict freedom of others." He made a threat: "Government will be stopped." In a country of coups, this seemed to me entirely plausible.[18]

Putting on his helmet, he did up the chinstrap. "If I had another helmet, I could take you to Otobüs Terminali. You would see why you shouldn't spend time here. You are nowhere."

Then came the simplest of explanations: "This bus stop is for neighborhood and you would need to make transfer. You would get lost. Actually, you are lost. You need cross-city bus. Walk down three blocks and stand at bus sign."

His Harley roaring again, the military man saluted me and rode away.

I walked over a few blocks, and when a bus came to the stop where I waited, my mention of Otobüs Terminali was greeted with a nod. I added "*Siirt Otogarı*" for clarification and was welcomed up the steps. Moving to the back of the bus, I sat among four kids and three men sharing the bench on a little rise with two side seats. They were friendly right away, one man asking in English, "Where do you go?"

"Bitlis. There to Baykan. Then Tatvan. By bus."

"Ah, fifteen minutes to Otobüs Terminali. Stay on this bus, even when I get off it."

It was the validation I needed. Dusk was approaching when he got off the bus. I looked to others who had overheard our exchange and one said, "Five minutes."

Otobüs Terminali, while airy and open, revolved around a darkened central corridor, wide and under a high roof. Merchants' stalls straddled both sides of the station. Under a sign that said Otobüs, I asked a woman

---

18 In 2011, 250 military officers were detained. Charges against them included conspiring against the government. The four highest-ranking officers resigned over an alleged plot and to protest the treatment of the armed forces command. Cowed, the once-dominant military authorities would no more hold sway. Half of Turkey's admirals went to prison, a contingent within the jailhouse population of four hundred retired or serving officers.

for a ticket to Tatvan, showing the one I'd bought earlier that had been declined. "It is not me," she said. "Maybe them."

"Them" were three young men in a stall bearing the sign "Vangölü Bus." I soon learned that Vedat, Dmar, and Hamra were a team: one acknowledged my existing ticket, another refused to give me a refund, and a third explained, "That bus has left: We have our bus in one hour. You need new ticket."

I bought one and waited. The hour came and went, and Vedat, tilting back in his chair, advised, "Maybe one more hour. It is big bus. Comfortable. Air conditioned."

Dmar asked about my travels, and when Hamra came by with tea, he brought four cups. "Sit down," he said. "Your ticket name is Rick." Then with an unexplained linguistic twist of his tongue he said, "Hi, Berk." And so it was that I joined them behind the counter.

Dmar stood and announced, "I'm getting dinner for us. And also for you, Berk."

Vedat's square eyes belied the truth behind this. "Big bus is not coming. Mechanical. But little bus, it will come. Just not now. We'll have meal."

"Not now?"

"Not now. Not soon. But tonight. Is good."

They spread a large towel over the concrete floor. Dmar returned with a paper box loaded with food. The four of us sat on the floor behind their sales counter.

"Is all delicious. Is all Turkish," said Dmar. As he handed me each serving he explained its name: *haşlama*, and *karurma*, a soup he called *mercimek*, and salad (*gorbasi*) and rice (*pirma*). Feeling I should have this information, he wrote the names down on a sheet of paper and gave it to me. We ate the hearty meal while sipping sweet tea. I learned they'd all been born in this town. None had traveled, despite working for a transportation company. All three were unmarried.

I went to use the bathroom and when I returned ten minutes later, I realized how dark and late it was.

"Bus is ready," said Vedat loudly to a group of nine passengers standing together in the wide aisle. Beside them was a traveler wearing a slouchy hat. I could not see his face. Vedat continued with "It is . . ." and his explanation spilled into the air. The locals nodded. Off they went, led by the man with the slouchy hat. I followed.

"*Tesseku aderim.*" I waved.

We walked to a concrete platform where one might presume the bus to Tatvan would have arrived and been prepared for departure. But that platform ended without any sign of a bus. We all looked around and realized we were in an acre-size lot with only a few buses, all parked for the night and shuttered. There were no overhead lights. The floppy hatted man walked on. We passed the empty buses and the yard opened wide. Not a running bus in sight. I kept close to the group. We left the station lot and moved onto a dark street. There were no lights to guide us, so I turned on my flashlight. "*Tesseku aderim,*" I heard.

All of us night travelers moved along a back street, sheep-like, following our slouchy-hatted leader, someone no one appeared to know. Halfway down that dirt street was an idling minibus with its parking lights on. The floppy hat man stood by the doorway, checking our tickets. I boarded last in the line, asking a hopeful, "Tatvan?"

The driver nodded and I made my way on board. All seats on the bus were taken. Only one option was left to me. I became the fourth person in the minibus's last row, with its three seats. Squishing onto the bench, I hugged my pack against my chest.

"It's midnight," a man said.

"Yes, it's midnight," said the slouchy hatted clerk as he closed the bus door and left us.

There was an argument between the driver and the man seated beside him, possibly about why a big bus scheduled to leave at 7 p.m. had become a minibus leaving at midnight. Whatever the particulars, it was carried out entirely in Turkish and appeared to be resolved, or at least temporarily put on hold, by the time we departed.

The driver, having let out a harangue that I took to mean he was innocent and full of testosterone, found the gas pedal. We shot our way along and up a hill and within fifteen minutes were driving through some kind of construction zone. There were detours and disruptions. A passenger smoked: the windows were closed.

The man beside me laid his head against the van's window wall, but when he fell asleep his head flipped to the side, flopped a bit forward and onto my shoulder, where it remained.

Our dolmuş veered around corners, the driver hell-bent on either picking up time or careening over the cliff. With only our headlights to guide us through the miles of dark dirt road, we sped ahead. I could see through clouds of cigarette smoke that the driver was engaged in animated conversation with both the man seated next to him and the man behind him on the same side. The driver's eyes, and his general sense of attention, were often elsewhere than the road, which resulted in corrective cornering that made the bus lurch in a worrying way.

If we went over the cliff, I thought as I looked around at my fellow travelers, I would be the last one out.

Streetlights appeared ahead and we stopped. Everyone disembarked from the bus. Although it was well after one in the morning, the place was waiting for us. There were stores selling clothing and food, as well as a mechanics shop. This transportation hub springing up out of nowhere was only a surprise to me. After all, thirsty and hungry passengers on a well-traveled road were not taken for granted, no matter what time of day it was. I returned from the toilets to find our minibus empty. A waving hand caught my attention and I went over to a low table where my fellow passengers sat on chairs, socializing, cups of hot tea in their hands.

I found a white plastic stool and sat among them, sipping tea from a half-filled cup offered to me. I thought, no one I know has any idea where I am. Next I thought, *I* don't have any idea where I am.

*　　*　　*

By the time our bus neared Tatvan, it was still pitch black outside, and only three passengers remained aboard. I had moved to sit behind the driver, who knew I was looking for a hotel, any hotel, in Tatvan. I had dozed off when the dolmuş came to a stop. Twice someone said "Tatvan hotel," but in my dream it was a spirit voice. One of the passengers shook me awake. I gathered my thoughts, and as I stepped down from the van, the driver pointed down a road that ended in darkness. "Hotel."

"Hotel?"

"Hotel. Walk. Two, maybe three blocks. It is there."

I had little choice but to hoist my pack and set off into the darkness.

A dimly lit old building emerged, as promised, and I walked up a wide stairway into a lobby. The foyer was broad, high ceilinged with fans swinging above an expanse likely furnished a hundred years ago. I could enjoy a day or three here. I imagined, in my sleep-addled daze, sitting in one of the high-backed wicker chairs playing backgammon. I knocked gently on the check-in counter. A man yawned his way from behind a wall, scrunching his eyes to clear them.

"Room?"

"Room."

He wanted cash, but not much, and handed me a key for a room on the second floor. The counter clock's display said 3:15 a.m.

At 6:30 a.m., I woke. The room around me was spacious, with two comfortable sitting chairs against a wall under slatted window blinds that protected me from whatever shone outside. There was enough light to reveal I'd fallen asleep lying on top of the bedspread, the blankets tucked in. I was up and in the shower, and not long after desperately seeking a coffee. I found the early fixings for a breakfast buffet on the lowest level, but nothing looked appealing. I returned to the lobby to check out, and asked about the ferry.

"Ferry," the clerk responded, writing down an evening departure of 4:30 p.m.

I walked the streets of Tatvan, finding a bakery where a man was just then pulling bread from ovens. He wore white clothing slathered in dough and crumbs. His hands looked toasted. I eyed a loaf so big it could feed a family. I felt a family's worth of hunger and bought it. Walking along the street, I tore off chunks of bread to eat until a woman whispered, "Tsk" in displeasure at my eating. In my hunger, I'd forgotten to respect Ramadan.

As I passed along the sidewalk where five men sat on tipped-over cargo boxes, I noticed they were playing a game using small tiles with numbers on their surfaces. Many tiles were face down, and others were held so that only each player could see his own numbers. One man motioned for me to join. I was eating and felt inappropriate, but he insisted and tipped over a wooden crate for me. So I sat down, and, realizing how distracting my bread's aroma must be, rolled the bag tight, tucking it behind my ankles. "It is for you. You only," the man who had bid me sit down said, and they went about their game.

I stayed with them until they were done playing, and then stumbled across a sign for an Internet café, so I walked up a set of narrow stairs that curved into a room with a few computers. I bought a Coke, paid for five minutes' access, and signed on. I emailed home the reassuring news: "Back in Turkey. Am safe. Heading to Iran."

Down again on the street, I noticed an alleyway and a shed under a STAR taxi sign, which rang a bell from my previous visit. I asked about Naim, who had driven me from Tatvan to Van weeks earlier. Within a minute he appeared, recognizing me right away.

"You are back? You want taxi to Van?"

"I will take the ferry this time. It's at 4:30. Will you show me your city?"

"We can go to Nemrut Daği," he said. "It is beautiful to view Lake Van from that high. Old volcano. There are two craters. One small, water is hot. One is big, water is cold water. Only ten kilometers from here to there. Six miles, that is."

"I would very much like to see that. And I wish to find a Turkey flag for my son Sean."

"Flag?"

"Yes, a full size one from your country. Better if it has been used."

"Meet me here later. I will drive you way by craters and then to the ferry. You say it leaves at 4:30?"

When I came back, it was 2:30. Naim handed me a Turkish flag that clearly had flown somewhere, its red faded. I didn't ask where he'd gotten it. It was dirty but beautiful—at least it would be seen that way. "Sean will love it," I said.

"A gift," said Naim. The ongoing and unsought generosity of people sat with me as a mark of their faith and self-confidence.

We began a drive through the city's streets, Naim telling me that I would love Nemrut. "I am proud to show you." We were maybe ten minutes on the way to Nemrut Daği when it struck me that the ferry schedule was, in my admittedly limited experience, unreliable and worth checking. Naim agreed. He pulled to the side of the road to make a call on his cell phone. "My dispatcher says it is 4:30 today," he reported. "Also that I should confirm with ferry company. Avoid ferry surprise."

He dialed the direct number of the ferry company, spoke in staccato Turkish, hung up, and roared the engine, tearing away from the roadside. "It leaving now. We go. Is only ferry today."

We raced across town and took shortcuts down side streets. Naim wove into the main thoroughfare, where there was no traffic light. I'm not sure why I feel that remote cities should somehow not have traffic jams, but some part of me feels they don't deserve the insult that comes with too many cars driving on roads built a century ago for horse carriages. Here, it was as though the sprawl of the automobile culture collided with a lakeside town that didn't want it. To honking disagreement, Naim nudged into the hectic flow of cars and through it. We burst onto the port lands and screeched to a halt in front of a building at the Tatvan İskelesi. "You'll need ticket."

We were in and out of the building and back in the car in under a minute, my ticket in hand. Naim sped to where the dock ended and the ship began. The ferry was loaded with cargo containers, and a forklift was shifting the last pallet on deck. The ferry's engines hummed. It was 3:00 p.m. I reached in my pocket to pay Naim for the ride.

He brushed it away. "No matter, Rick. You go now. Maybe run."

I ran down the walkway and jumped onboard, just as the ferry propellers engaged and churned the waters. A deckhand hauled a chain-link rope aboard. By the time I'd made my way to the upper deck, we were under way, aboard the industrial ferry named Tatvan.

Once we'd left port, and after my adrenaline subsided, the four-hour passage became a crossing of reflection, rather than the one of anticipation it would have been if I'd caught it two weeks earlier, when climbing Ararat was still in my future. I thought about my summit, and the improbability that I had managed to make it in and out of Iraq. The next night I would board the Trans-Asia Express from Van, Turkey, to Tehran, Iran. In this trip's sense, I would soon become "homeward bound."

In my period of reflection, it actually took some time before I noticed that there were no other passengers on board. A crewmember walked to the back of the boat once, where I sat, but after looking me over and seeing that I posed no threat, left me alone with my thoughts.

An hour later, another man came in my direction. He looked at me with officialdom's concern.

"I am captain." He took me to the bridge, picked up a pair of binoculars and pointed to the distance, knowing daylight would soon be gone. "Akdamar Island," he announced.

The crewmember brought me a glass of water, a treat he could not share, which he conveyed by zipping a thumb and finger across his lips to indicate daytime abstinence for Ramadan. I drank and passed it back, and glimpsed him, just before he cornered out of my sight, taking a sip of what was left.

Back outside on the deck, I felt the cold and wrapped a jacket around my shoulders. It was early evening and I thought about the Şahmaran Hotel in Van, grilled chicken and red wine mere hours away. I was hungry. The captain reappeared as if on cue and signaled me to follow him. I obeyed. He led me down an iron stairway of peeling paint, into an empty public seating area where purple chairs were welded to the deck.

There, on a white table, sat a bowl of rice with what looked to be yam, and chunks of what might be beef. He motioned that I should sit down and tapped the fork with his knuckle, indicating it was mine. I sat, picked up the fork, and looked up to see him leave. It was food shared from his dinner, hot and good. I ate it all.

Back on deck, it was as though the land lights around the lake were coming on in concert with the stars in the sky. The crewmember that had earlier brought me water came by to ask what I did in my home country.

I can't remember, or don't want to, is what I thought to myself, which was egotistical, bred from the feeling I had nothing to add to his life by sharing what interested him about mine. My life was as foreign to him as his was to me, and why should my line of curiosity overshadow his? It shouldn't have, but it did. We talked about him some more instead, and I learned he'd always lived in Tatvan; a man of thirty who had been a child soccer star, now with a boy of his own, who didn't like soccer.

Despite my having no nautical trade to offer or discuss, he took me back to the bridge. We were nearing the dockyards of Van. The captain told me what he was doing as though I'd become fluent in technical Turkish. He leaned out a window as he guided his massive craft against the sturdy timbers of the dock. With me leaning out the window at his left elbow, it felt as though he and I parked the boat together at Van İskelesi. Upon completion, he spat out the window, so I spat too. He smiled. Then we spat again, together this time, commemorating the docking ceremony. The things you learn.

Being the only foot passenger to walk off the ferry, I did so after watching the trucks shunt from shore to the boat as they prepared to haul the cargo trailers off the ship. They grunted up the drawbridge and away.

There was no taxi stand in sight, and the captain, watching from the bridge, signaled that I should walk further down the carriageway.

A hundred feet from where I stood, over on the other side of two sets of railway tracks, a dozen people sat around tables, drinking what looked to be coffee. Over and away, beside them, a few cars were parked in the darkness. On the distant southeastern shore, I spotted the hotel where I would be staying. I hoped for a taxi at the coffee spot, which from all appearances looked to be a station of sorts.

Climbing down to the tracks, I made my way across them, tripping on a rail in the process. I threw my pack up on the other platform and climbed out of the rail bed, scrambling onto the concrete terrace near the coffee place. A sizeable and jovial man at a table clapped in applause and signaled me over. "You have earned tea. Sit with us."

I was nobody to him and his companions, yet freshly grilled *köfte* was brought to our table right away and placed near me. The meat sizzled and my stomach whined in response.

"Eat. They are good," the burly man said. Before I could reach over, two of his friends helped themselves. He swatted their hands away, and they tittered in delight.

"I am looking for a taxi," I said.

"Sometimes this is a good place to look. Tonight, I am not sure."

"I need to get to a hotel."

"Where have you traveled from?" The question came from the table next to ours. I turned to see a bearded, aged man, his face half caught in the lamp's glare. I told him my story, beginning in Tatvan earlier that day.

The bearded man shifted in his seat, slowly, and rose to join our table. Reaching for the *köfte* with slender fingers, he chose a smaller one, leaving the last and largest for me. He shakily poured me some tea and said, "You must have longer story. How did you come to us in Van?"

I backed up, starting with the Van Gölü Express. When I got to the part about missing the ferry weeks ago, they all laughed. "It is!" one of the men exclaimed and another chorused him. "It is." The singularity of that expression summed it up.

"Well, certainly, 'It was,'" I echoed.

They were pleased to hear that I'd climbed Mount Ararat and then come back to Van, because, as the bearded man said, "Few people from West travel to Van. Fewer come back."

It went quiet. The ferry sat motionless. Inside, someone turned a light out. The burly man reached over to shake my hand. "My name is Muslim Giil. I will drive you to your hotel."

"You have a taxi?"

"No. But I have a car."

We trudged away, Muslim Giil and I, followed by the old man, back to his car, a Mercedes that looked as old as the man with us, and in a similar state of disrepair.

It would not start.

"It is," said Muslim Giil.

I took stock of my situation. I was sitting in a car that wouldn't start, with two men I'd known for under twenty minutes. We were at the far end of a lake port, where a ferry now sat empty and dark. All I could see of these men was by starlight.

Another turn of the key and all the Mercedes did was cough.

"It is," I said.

"It is," said the old man from behind me.

The Mercedes lurched forward on the third try. Muslim Giil fed it gas, and the tires suddenly caught dirt. We flew out of our parking pit and hurled down a lane. The driver did not want to ease up on the gas in case we stalled, and the muffler rattled when he double-clutched into third gear. He took his hand off the shift and pushed his flop of gray hair out of his eyes and back over his head. The man in the back seat snickered, "Again, it works."

Muslim Giil laughed.

I did not remember this area of Van from my previous visit and had no idea where we might be going. No one had asked where I might be staying, so I said, "Merit Şahmaran."

"Nice," said the old man.

But we were heading down dark back lanes.

"Where are we going?" I asked.

"Merit Şahmaran," Muslim Giil replied, as we suddenly sprang onto a highway I recognized as Van's main road.

"*Sapas dicam*," I said, expressing my appreciation and not a little relief.

They both replied, "*Sapas dicam*." The bearded man said, "*Sapas Dicam* is Kurdish for 'thank you.' We are Kurdish. Turkish is for thank you *Tesseku aderim*. You used Kurdish words for us. We like that."

Muslim Giil kept driving through increasingly familiar surroundings. Shifting into a lower gear, he stopped under the portico of the Şahmaran to let me out, leaving his car idling, just in case. We shook hands.

"*Sapas dicam*," I repeated.

"It is," he said.

Aysenur and Emre were on duty in the lobby. Emre said, "Welcome back. Dinner service is about to close. I will tell them to save you food."

"I'm starved!" I said. "I certainly can eat."

"You eat, Richard. Then tell us about Iraq."

EIGHTEEN

THE TRANS-ASIA EXPRESS

"You could almost say that the Cyrus Cylinder is a history of the Middle East in one object and it is a link to a past which we all share and to a key moment in history that has shaped the world around us."
—Neil MacGregor, Director of the British Museum, media comment

The morning light came late to my hotel room but stayed there. Despite that, I slept in, for the first time in what seemed like a while. Finally, I got up for coffee, honeycomb, and note-making before heading out to run errands.

I hitchhiked into Van and lunched in a corner café after an hour's walk up and down the city's high-step sidewalks. Van is a city of incessant activity, and after eating I sought out the slower pace of back streets and alleyways.

Mid-afternoon, back at the Şahmaran, I retrieved my stowed orange case, repacked, slept a bit, had a relaxed dinner, and checked out, all the time excited about the train journey to Iran that evening.

"Richard, it is good that you stay here three times in these weeks." Emre was making it easy to say goodbye. "Most people never visit Van even once. When will be next? One week?"

"I leave for Iran tonight," I replied. "You have made my stays relaxed."

"Van is relaxed for everyone. Unless you live here."

When Aysenur appeared, it was with quick steps and a sheaf of papers in hand, the manager's ensemble. "You have train tonight. Do not expect it to be on time. But plan that it might be. It does happen."

"Can you check?"

"No."

The Trans-Asia Express, a.k.a. the *Trans Asya Ekspresi*, begins in Ankara and makes its way to the Tatvan ferry, where its cargo of passengers disembarks and is ferried across Lake Van, where they board the Iranian-operated, Tehran-bound extension of this train. This is dicey. The Trans-Asia Express to Tehran departs Van only once a week.

Onboard the Iranian train, passengers cross the Turkey–Iran border and, after passport checks, on to Tehran. When all goes according to plan, this journey of 1,800 miles, from Istanbul to Tehran, takes two and a half days. But flexibility is an asset when making such plans.

"Richard, the Trans Asya Ekspresi to Iran, normally it is at 9:54 that it intends to leave," Aysenur reminded me. "You should be at Van Garı by 9:30 o'clock, but I would say 9:15. The train is never early, but you should be." He looked at the wall clock, indicating that it was time for me to get going.

Emre and Aysenur walked me out of the Merit Şahmaran and hailed a taxi for me. It was then that I should have asked him to tell the driver about my destination. I did not. I took that modest task upon myself when I settled in the back seat and we drove away.

"To the train station," I said.

I was heartened by his simple, taxi-driver-confident tone: "Yes. Train station." It was his city, after all.

When we pulled out of the hotel compound onto İpek Yolu, the traffic was light, but nearing the city proper, it became busy, and all of a sudden the driver took a side road. We plunged into low-lit neighborhoods and local roads, eventually emerging into the dock lands I'd arrived at the night before. We were back at Van İskelesi, where a fair number of people seemed to be waiting for the ferry to arrive. They were having barbecues with their families. Friday night was picnic night.

"Train station here?" I asked.

"Yes. Ferry comes here. Train comes here. Ferry meets train meets ferry. You get on." The taxi driver's encouragement continued. "It is where I think train station is. Am certain. I will carry your bag."

I recognized the lengthy concrete platform along both sides of the railway tracks, the tracks I'd crossed over upon my own arrival by ferry the previous evening. People milled about and kids played, everyone convivial. As the taxi driver pulled my pack, I asked again, "Train station? For sure?"

He nodded. "For sure." He even stopped and asked a man and woman, or at least his Turkish seemed to convey, and got affirmative nods. I asked in English, "Train?" They kept nodding.

The taxi driver drove away, leaving me looking out into the expanse of Lake Van, with the bow lights of the arriving Tatvan ferry two hours offshore.

In the next half hour, people left. They weren't waiting for anything. They were using the open space to cook and hang out with friends. I realized that once the ferry arrived this would be a truck traffic zone, and they were leaving before that happened.

Across the way from where I was standing was the only building big enough to function as a station; my happenstance rendezvous point the night before. It figured I was on the wrong side. I once more worked down to the tracks, this time hauling Big Bertha and myself over the rails, and climbed up onto the other platform.

"Rick!"

There sat Muslim Giil. It had been less than twenty-four hours since he'd taken me from here to my hotel.

"Tea?"

"Please."

I sat with him, a few men his age, and the bearded man who was with us the night before. With the ferry still far away, I asked Muslim Giil, more casually than I felt, "Did the train passengers make it onto the ferry in Tatvan?"

"No way to know," he said. "Train to Iran leaves Van when train leaves." It was that simple, but his next comment startled me. "If ferry left

296

early out of Tatvan, and train passengers missed it, they take bus to Van. Only way for them to meet Iran train before it leaves." He then asked what seemed to him an obvious question. "You waiting for someone on ferry?"

"No, I'm waiting to catch the train to Iran at this station."

"This no train station. Van Gari is train station. Train station across city."

"There are two train stations?"

"Just one." The urgency dawned on him before it hit me. "What time goes your train?"

"9:54."

He looked at his watch. "Is 9:44! You will not 9:54 be on train."

Alarmed, I said, "Is there a taxi?"

"No, but I have a car!" The two men with us laughed, bolted up from their chairs, and whooshed us away with their hands. "Hurry. Hurry."

We ran over the open ground, my heavy pack flopping uncontrollably until the two of us lifted and carried it. Muslim Giil tossed my pack into the backseat, both of us puffing and laughing.

Muslim Giil leaned in prayer before turning his key. It worked. He spurred the engine and we bolted across the lot and bounced onto the road. He sped away, turning on his lights when we approached a crowd of people milling about a corner store. He found an alley and we barreled along.

"Maybe," he said into the air.

"Maybe what?"

"Train to Iran. It is Iranian train. Maybe it waits for Turkey train passengers. If Turkey train missed ferry, then passengers may already be by bus at Van Gari. They may be boarding train as we drive."

"It is," I said, resolved to accept whatever the outcome was.

"It is." He smiled philosophically. He looked at his watch. "*It is* 9:52."

The Mercedes shot over an embankment, landing hard alongside the main road of Van. Away we went, station bound.

Muslim Giil braked directly in front of stairs leading into Van Gari. He was out of his car before I was and grabbed my bag. "Up the stairs."

Inside, people lounged about, slept on chairs, and ate food from shopping bags. No one looked to be in a hurry—a peaceful scene in railway stations everywhere, when the train is late.

Muslim Giil hurried to a counter and approached a clerk on my behalf. I hoisted my bags to where he was. He turned to me.

"You okay! Train delayed to Tatvan. Ferry waited. Passengers on ferry. Ferry late."

Outside the station doors, I saw a train, and the platform looked ready to accept passengers. Its whistle blew and shunted as the coaches picked up slack. Should I be rushing to get on this train? I wondered. No one else seemed to be in a rush to board. Were they even passengers?

"Wait here with my bag?" I pleaded. He nodded.

I ran. The train looked of a family with the Van Gölü Express's livery, but this train's signage instead read: Trans Asya Ekspresi. It was in motion, heading west. Wasn't that the wrong direction? A man came over and said, in Spanish-accented English, "This train is one for Iran. For you?" I nodded. He said. "And for me too. But it goes first to Tatvan ferry. Pickup of passengers from Istanbul and Ankara. Then comes to here with them aboard. That when you and me get on. Later from now."

The train's whistle blew again. With no passengers on board, it ventured away from the platform.

I wanted to thank Muslim Giil for his kindness, but he would not accept money. We walked out the station doors into the cool air. Down the street were carts of food, and he offered to get me "toast."

"*Sapas dicam*," I said, gratefully declining.

He bent his head of flowing gray hair and air kissed my left cheek. I did so in return.

"*Sapas dicam*," he replied, gripping my hand without any movement. I realized he was thanking me for the unexpected escapades. I must admit I choked up a little.

Then Muslim Giil drove away.

*   *   *

I took to the station's mood. I still felt a bit antsy, with no train in sight, but the logic of it all settled in as I waited.

The Spaniard stood beside me later. "To Tehran or to Iran?"

"Tehran for two nights. Then to London."

"Me. I spend three weeks in Iran."

"Just to travel?"

"Travel is everything. It is not 'just' anything."

He'd one-upped me in my own language.

"Luis," he said, tapping his chest.

"Rick."

We talked of our travels and home countries. He shared his crackers and cheese with me. We stood as we ate and talked, my back to the open station.

As we waited, I felt a movement behind me and turned to see two attractive Iranian women in their early twenties, both without head-scarves. They were watching us, listening in on our conversation. A man stood behind them.

"You are from where?" the older one finally asked, smiling.

The younger one said, "We are hungry for English. Will you speak with us?"

". . . Yes . . ." Who was I to decline this charming request?

"We have never heard English-speaking original," said the older.

"I am named Mona," came from the youngest.

"I am named Rick."

"Will you meet my parents?"

Of course.

Mona said of the woman with her, "Kamelia. She is my sister."

"This is Mother. Father." The introductions were done with point-ing and the males shaking hands, and self-conscious giggles. "Hamid is Kamelia's husband."

A young man came up to the group with soda drinks. "This is my brother Adel. He is going to university. We have short-term visas to Van to say goodbye to him. It will be two years before we see him again. He has study visa for USA."

The Spaniard stayed with us in the conversation.

Then the boarding call blared. The twenty-two hour journey to Tehran was about to begin.

Down the tracks came Trans Asya Ekspresi with narrow red and blue lines running the length of white-painted carriages.

On the platform, I wished Adel well in the United States, and encouraged him. "It is good for students to travel to another country. Our world's future depends on it." I left Mona's family to their goodbyes and tears of departure.

On boarding my sleeping car, I could hear the revelry of the passengers travelling together through Tatvan-to-ferry-to-train—that cacophony of languages and anticipation that made this hour a pleasant time for them.

I pushed my pack into compartment H, landing it on the floor in front of a man and woman.

"You'll want one of these," the man offered up. It was a glass of white wine.

The train jerked eastbound.

"Anthony. Actually, just Tony." We shook hands as his wife said, "Irene."

"Might that be an Aussie accent?"

"Melbourne," she said. "Retired and rambling."

Tony and Irene had sorted out their side of the room. I tossed my bag on a bed and accepted their wine. Next stops Kapıköy, Razi, Tabriz, and Tehran.

It was well after midnight as we passed the Turkey–Iran border and neared passport control. My anticipation of dealing with the formalities at Kapıköy had made for a restless attempt at sleep. Irene and Tony stayed awake as well, but no one spoke. Better tired than groggy in front of the border patrol.

At 3:00 a.m., the train pulled up short of any platform and stopped. Train officials walked down the corridors, ensuring that everyone was awake with passports open to Iranian visa permission. I'd gotten mine before leaving on the trip in anticipation of finding a way in.

We streamed off the train into a low-lit, dank room, square, its walls forty feet long. Two solitary windows were all we had to remind us of an outside world. The ninety or so train passengers formed two lines, one for men and one for women. A man told Tony there had been a third line five minutes ago, but the official manning it "broke fast for one hour."

There was no return route outside except through the customs turnstiles.

"The train won't leave without us," I said to Tony.

"You are saying we sit and get in line later?"

The answer came from Irene. "May as well."

Within a minute the two young Iranian women were over to visit, each in a knee-length smock over black jeans. Kamelia's husband was there with them. "We can explain what happens here," said Mona. "They will take you only one at one time. But one of you can wait in line for both of you." She said this to Tony and me. "You will need to wait on your own," she said to Irene. "We are here two hours. More maybe."

We explained our strategy, and I repeated my flippant comment.

"Do not think the train will not leave without you. It would," Kamelia warned.

Despite the long wait, customs was actually no hassle, and we crossed the border without incident. We were all remarkably fresh later that morning as the train slowed for a high trestle. A better view of this scene would have been from a hiker's trail below, looking up, yet from our train window it was still an impressive drop, one of the highest trestles in the world.

Mona and Kamelia, Iranian sisters and the author's fellow travellers, posing in front of the Trans Asya Ekspresi at Tabriz station, en route to Tehran.

I had taken lunch alone and later lounged in the roomette, reading with Irene and Tony. We'd passed through Tabriz, where we'd been able to disembark, walk about, and take photographs. Now, in front of us was five hundred miles of track without interruption. I snoozed. There was a soft tap at the door. Tony flung it open with his foot.

Mona stood in the doorway looking at me. "My father would like you to join us for dinner."

In the dining car, Father and Mother were waiting on one side of a table when we arrived. Mona slipped in to the window seat, and I sat beside her. Hamid and Kamelia were seated on the other side of the aisle, facing each other.

Our sextet silently concentrated on our menus to sort out dinner. I looked over at Hamid and Kamelia and my gaze went to a space outside the window, where the Caspian Sea lay one hundred miles away and out of sight.

This is a propitious spot, I thought, remembering something I'd thought about while resting earlier in the afternoon. The train's proximity at that moment was as close as I'd get to a contending (only remotely in contention) fourth Mountain of the Ark. We were in a distant region of the ancient land of Urartu. An old map I'd come across showed Lake Van at Urartu's center, with territory north into present-day Armenia and almost this far into Iran's northwest. The region was then known as the Kingdom of Van, sometimes interpreted as the Kingdom of Ararat.

In my pre-trip research, I had frequently been taken aback by how much work "*Ark*eologists" invested when attempting to prove their speculations. One impressive work-up was that of Robert Cornuke, who posited that the Ark's landing occurred far away from the region's namesake Mount Ararat, though still within Urartu. It fascinated me how ably individuals align rumors with desktop research and exaggerated claims of fact. Cornuke's quest caught my attention in part because one of his partners in the escapade was astronaut James Irwin's widow, who came to the conclusion that her husband had been searching on the wrong mountain—Ararat.

Cornuke's first choice for his mountain of the Ark was Mount Sabalan, sixty miles from where our train traveled. At 15,816 feet, Mount Sabalan is the third-highest mountain in Iran. In Cornuke's book, *The Lost Mountains of Noah*, based on reworking terminology, he postulated that Mount Sabalan was "the most compelling candidate for the final resting place of Noah's Ark." His back up choice was Iran's Mount Suleiman, where after a 2006 expedition he claimed to have the Ark within sight, an assertion that garnered Cornuke interviews on *Good Morning America* and CNN, along with Fox News. To make these claims feasible, he took the liberty of stretching both the known borders of ancient Urartu and the phrase "the mountains of Ararat" beyond their historical parameters to include his propounded mountains of the ark.

Though the case in support of Cornuke has been called "weak and unconvincing" and "misleading," I could not let go of the idea that, in addition to the three credible "Mountains of the Ark," there were modern storytellers who freely bent history and legend anew. It is highly debatable that Mount Sabalan (let alone Suleiman) would have been in the ancient land of Urartu, so what captured my interest, let alone Cornuke's? Perhaps it was the enduring ability of farfetched concoctions to draw us in, to remind us that, odd as some claims are, we can't look away.

The train jolted and brought me back from my window gazing. Mona said, "Rick. You daydream?"

Father spoke to me in Iranian, and I nodded to make him feel I understood. Hamid razzed, "You are being polite, Rick. He just told you he would order a nice Iranian *shaam* for you. That is dinner."

The meal was varied and delicious, and Father described the servings as Hamid and Mona took turns with the English renditions. It was lamb stew over rice with vegetables. They insisted I try the Iranian drink of runny yogurt called *doogh*.

Mona told me of her university studies. "It is now not easy for a woman to be in school like me, and I must have good grades. I wish to teach languages."

"Hamid, what of your plans?" He and Kamelia had been married for two years, with no children.

"I would like to study engineering. And to go to school in London. It is expensive and I have applied. It is my hope."

Tea arrived. The train swayed, making all of us rock sideways too. Mother, who did not seem near fifty years old, kept up the swaying motion, letting it evolve into a seated dance. She spoke and Mona turned to me. "Mother asks if you like Iranian music. Do you know it?"

"I imagine I would like it."

When the translations were complete, Mona said, "You will come to our train compartment. We have Iranian music there. Mother will teach you Iranian dance."

*   *   *

The top bunks were up in their couchette when we all arrived. I sat down with the three women while Hamid and Father took to the compartment across the aisle, door open; Mona sat next to me. Mother took out her cell phone and scrolled through her music files.

Over the phone's speaker came a folk song with a bite. Mother turned it louder, then rose, without a hint of self-consciousness, and began to dance. The floor space between the couchette's two bench seats was six feet by two, and we lifted our feet onto our respective seats to make more room, sitting cross-legged. Mother took the floor. She swayed gracefully, swirled slowly. Her face gleamed with Persian pride for the music, lifting her arms one at a time, curving them in and around one another as the song progressed.

Kamelia joined in as the music's tempo increased. Her dancing, in comparison, was rapid and felt more modern, even though it was clearly steeped in tradition and respectful to the folk story unfolding through the singer's voice.

Mona wove herself into a sway beside me. I picked up on her movements in our seated dance, trying to mimic her sense of rhythm.

There was a knock on the open door, and Hamid stood with his computer. "Rick, we have more choice. You will hear *today's* Iranian music."

Mother motioned for me to rise. Kamelia sat down, and Hamid lifted his feet so that the dance floor was open for Mother and me. There was enough room for me to follow her lead without touching, mindful of the cultural differences. I animated an air-twirl of her as one would in a jive or country and western dance. Mona rose, in what I took to be the Iranian equivalent of, "May I cut in?" We danced on the train to Tehran.

Hamid's computer continued to play modern songs and samples of older Iranian music. "Long ago, this was important," he said. *Switch.* "Now, this is." *Switch.* "But younger, like Mona, would listen to this." *Switch.* "Or this." *Switch.* "This is mine." *Switch.*

Hamid let the last song play with all the trappings of tradition, music I'd never heard before. I felt at once enchanted and culturally ignorant.

Hamid reset a song to play again. Mother sat, dancing, moving beautifully back and forth on the bench. She captivated me with her grace and drama. Mona sang along and Kamelia hummed, while Hamid snapped his fingers in time with the song, in an unusual way I'd never seen before. Two of his right-hand fingers at a time collided with two other fingers of the same hand, against his thigh. Then his left hand did a toss-up version of that with three fingers into the palm of the right hand. It was like an ancient instrument, basic yet mesmerizing.

I tried it myself, and my fumbling made them all poke fun at me. I reverted to the finger snapping I knew, the thumb and middle finger variety from common jazz, both hands on the go. It would not suffice. I had to learn to do it their way. Mona separated my fingers into pairs, the lower two against my knee. She forced their collision. It worked. Hamid's hands became a metronome. The four of us followed him in a band of hands, playing along with the Iranian song.

After I'd captured a video of this on my camera, I fell back into the rhythm. I sensed the elusive future of this country in its night train dancers—free-moving, inspired, independent.

We arrived at Tehran's Rah Ahan Railway station at three o'clock in the morning. The terminal was wide open for our late arrival, and we clambered out. I said my goodbyes to Tony and Irene as we shunted our bags off the train onto the concrete, and I scanned the next two cars, hoping to see Mona and her family. Hamid was on the platform, passing luggage off the train to the ground. Seven of their extended family had shown up. I joined the group, seeking out Mona. "I have come to say goodbye and to thank you."

"Oh, Rick, we were looking to find you. Our friends are here. Now a busy hello and busier farewell."

"Your family has been very kind to me."

"Women must wear hijab in Tehran," she said, tightening her own. "No more relaxed as on train." Her comment made me think that a

306

headscarf can make a Western woman mysterious, intriguing and unknowable—but of course that is a whimsical notion; here, the politically charged hijab does that for a nation, a custom of modesty for half the population, and a reminder of the frequent public seclusion of women, away from men. I find no enchantment in repression.

With the warmth of departing friends in her eyes, I felt a goodbye hug coming on. It didn't happen. She said, "We could hug you goodbye but it is wrong here. We cannot."

Kamelia stood beside her, adding more explanation. "If I carry my bag walking in front of you and I trip, you cannot help me back up. You are not my husband or brother or father. If you touched me, it would be trouble for me if official saw it to happen."

Hamid said, "I could help you, Kamelia. But please don't trip." While smiling in acceptance of what was, he burst into four-finger slapping on his wrist while humming an Iranian ditty, his farewell song.

"Thank you." I shook Father's hand. In his eyes was an understanding of time's oddness, gigantic changes of fortune, an acceptance of the present and hope for the future.

"Mother . . ." I called. She looked my way and I danced a little. The shuffle startled the family members who'd welcomed them home, and brought giggles from Mona and Kamelia. Mother's eyes shone.

Mona handed me a piece of paper. "This is my email. Hamid's is there too. He will send you finger-snapping video. You must send us yours."

And that is how we parted.

Inside the station, everyone made away as fast as they could clear luggage. I looked around for a driver I expected to meet me, despite the late hour, having made that arrangement through the hotel when I booked my room. I hoped he'd also be my guide while I was in Tehran. A disheveled young man came up to me, stretching his way out of a sleep he'd taken waiting for my ever-delayed train.

"I am Aref." Before I could respond, he said, "You are Rick."

"And you probably want to go home and sleep," I said.

His careless yawn widened, with no attempt at stifling. "I will take you to the Enghelab Hotel. You are there two nights, though one is slipping from you."

As we drove down Enghelab Avenue, he said, "Today is your day. You and Tehran. I will find you at breakfast. At seven. Is that okay?"

"Three hours sleep is all you'll have?" I asked.

"Is okay for you? Is okay for me."

Four hours later, as promised, Aref walked into the Enghelab Hotel's lobby and over to a staff member, asking after me. I'd barely helped myself to the breakfast buffet. A waiter poured coffee into my mug. Seeing Aref approach, I asked for a second cup.

Aref sat down. "Our coffee will not wake you up, Rick, but it won't let you sleep. Coffee in Iran is excellent."

"Good morning."

"If you like coffee, you should drink here this morning. Coffee houses, they are not popular with government. They are where people talk politics."

As we drove away from the Enghelab, Aref's thoughts ran out loud. "You are from America? Or Europe?" He did not want an answer. He was working out mentally what he should show me. "You want to see where the Shah lived, yes? Niavaran Palace. We can walk at the market to start. We will walk into the mountains at end of day."

When I'd awoken earlier, I found I'd left the curtains in my room open when I'd fallen asleep. The mountains north of the city made an impressive view. It surprised me how close they were, the size of them. I knew it was false, but I hadn't dissuaded myself from the notion of Persia as a giant expanse of desert. Tehran represents too much turmoil to be under the wing of such beautiful mountains, I'd thought. Their majesty became more evident when we got stuck in northbound traffic on Vali Asr.

The morning's great assault on my senses was not the smell of food or a sense of weather or even colorful attire. It was the intense din of cars and trucks. The city's architecture had conjured up an echo chamber. Tehran, city of noise.

The Grand Bazaar was visually hectic. No one moved slowly, and there was no loitering or meaningless gawking. Everyone went about their shopping, selling, or bartering in a purposeful way. Deals were concluded quickly. Spices were measured, packed, and wrapped, then exchanged for coins. If a bargain went sour midway in the bantering, the goods were smartly shelved without a grudge.

"Do not lose sight of me," Aref said, "or you maybe never get out of here." The maze had a rationale, but I could see myself disappearing in the labyrinth. The main stalls offered both perishable goods and expensive items, as many people used the market as a thoroughfare during their workday. The high volume of passersby was good for business. Off this main flow, and an aisle or two away, the rows of goods narrowed. Here you could find clothing or leather goods or mechanical parts; shoes, purses, wrenches. And everywhere, electronics in an abundance to rival what any advanced country would have on offer, underlying the strength of the black market economy, despite sanctions.

Tehran was a pedestrian no man's land. Not one face I saw looked pleased with the day.

Back in the car, driving through Imam Khomeini Square, Aref mused, "To know my city you must be driven by the Azadi Tower, and it is there." The giant arch, built in 1971 and 164 feet tall, rose from four stone strands angled to support a square pyramid-looking Islamic peak above eight thousand blocks of marble, all white. It commemorated a nicely rounded 2,500 years of existence. This marble monument was the tribute, a one-stop "Gateway to Iran." It went through a name change after the Iranian Revolution in 1979, becoming the "Freedom" marker, Azadi.

"Shajarian," Aref said when I asked about the music he was listening to. "Very popular but not with government. He sings against them. Does not like regime's sneer at people." "He" is Mohammad-Reza Shajarian. Hampered in attempts to perform in his own country, he has toured Europe with success. Challenging his homeland's ban on women singing in front of men, Shajarian used a performance in Turkey to invite his daughter on stage. Later, holding the *saghar*, a string instrument he made, he commented, "Part of our music has been silenced. Look at this instrument. It has four strings. If you remove one of them, it plays like that. To play properly, we need that sound, the voice of a woman."

Without discussion, Aref stopped the car in front of a building and got out. When I did too, he said, "National Museum of Iran. Go in."

I walked along the array of unprotected exhibits.

"Special," said Aref, indicating a well-protected area guarded by a security attendant.

I joined a queue, and waited in line until I was at the front and before me was the Cyrus Cylinder.

"It is a replica," I said. "Rather impressive."

"Not replica, Rick. It is Cyrus Cylinder."

"Well, that is actually in the British Museum. I'm going to see the original in London in a couple of days."

"Now, it is here," Aref said, to my astonishment. "It should always be here. It is Iran's. For time is on loan, as they say. From British Museum."

The Cyrus Cylinder was in Tehran for seven months. Surprisingly to me, I found myself alone with the storytelling cylinder, no one behind me in line. Dating from the time when Persian emperor Cyrus the Great overthrew Babylon, it has been called the first declaration of human rights.

To see this monumental and historic document, especially the original, made me gasp. I felt witness to its chiseled cuneiform words. Here was a statement that had withstood many attempts to destroy the vision of peace it espoused. The depth of art and readability in this original notably exceeded that of the replica I had at home, a gift from the Iranian Olympian.

The Cyrus Cylinder was a profound archeological find, documenting the emperor's enlightened approach to governing in the twenty-nine years beginning 559 BCE. The cylinder, made of baked clay, once secured in a building's structure so that all its sides showed, has been cracked by time and pitted by neglect, though the cuneiform is still readable today.

The British Museum's Neil MacGregor escorted the Cyrus Cylinder to Iran, calling it "one of the greatest declarations of the human aspiration," comparing it to America's Constitution and England's Magna Carta.

When we were finished, Aref and I walked toward the museum's exit, nearing a gift shop. In its window was a poster showing a beautiful writing pen with a facsimile reproduction of the Cyrus Cylinder as part of the design.

"Aref, do they sell that pen here?"

He spoke to the clerk and returned. "Never. They are unsure why pen's picture shows here, except it is a stunning poster . . . and display. Clerk says only two hundred pens were made."

"Where can I get one?"

"You want a poster?"

"*Aref . . .*"

"You can get *any*thing in Tehran."

We left right away. He drove to a market and we went to a store that sold pens. They'd never heard of the Cyrus pen, but sent us to a store that retailed luxury watches and goods. They could not find it in their portfolios. They suggested a store on a curved street corner at the floor level of a building festooned with flags. As soon as we arrived, my son Sean's penchant for flags distracted me, and I went off in search of Iran's, finding dozens of different flags from around the country to choose from.

Aref then took me to the unlikeliest tobacco and souvenir store at the building's base, and asked for the owner.

"Yes, he has heard of the pen," said Aref. "He will see if he can find one. He wants us to come back tomorrow."

"I fly out before sunrise."

Aref resumed what sounded like negotiations. He rebounded with a price.

"How does he know the price?"

"Rick, it is his price. He needs to know you will pay that or why bother with effort. Will you pay?"

I dithered.

"Tomorrow is same price," said an impatient Aref.

"Yes. I will pay."

We returned in an hour. I passed over two hundred dollars worth of Iranian rial and was asked for US currency instead, the seller adjusting the price to encourage me. Aref had told me to be prepared for this. I was. Black markets have their beneficial place for travelers. The man placed a varnished box in my hands. I opened it to find the thick pen exactly as it looked on the poster, as well as a numbered certificate of assured authenticity, with a few English spelling mistakes.

We worked our way north in Tehran, the day partly cloudy. The air hung stale and a bit moist in the city center. I mistook its stillness for a dryness I smelled but could not feel. I was thinking of fresh mountain air and the exhilaration of climbing on what Aref promised would be an invigorating day's-end hike. On the way, he talked like a tour guide with a few pre-plans in mind. "The last Shah was Mohammad Reza Pahlavi. You might know that. Before he was deposed, which happened with Iranian Revolution, the Imperial family was renowned for spiffy accommodations. You will see that now. It is Niavaran Palace."

The pavilion *was* impressive. It took design pretensions from a colonial mindset, made them extravagant, and plunked them into a lot of yard.

Aref asked, "Do you like libraries? You should see this one. It is *Farah Diba*."

"And *Farah Diba* means?"

"I am sorry to not explain. It is Exclusive Library of the Niavaran Palace. Private." He walked me toward a modern three-story building. Mostly books behind glass, kept away from grubby hands, filled the library's three floors. There was a railing on the third floor, opening to a square below. Custodians hung around the room's corners.

As we were walking down to the lower floors, I saw the caretakers above leave their second-floor posts through back doors. I stopped mid-staircase. "Aref, you keep going. I want one more look around up there."

With no one around, I went to a shelf and removed a book, taking it over to one of the Shah's couches. I imagined the Shah sitting there, as though we were going to talk about books, his nose in a different one.

Outside, Aref walked ahead of me, shaking his head at my misdemeanor. "You need a cola."

Aref made good on his promise that we'd have a short hike before dark. "We will go to the Alborz Mountains, to Darband," he said. We had walked a mile on a mountain path of fresh air, peaks above us and the city spread below, when Aref turned to me. "I am tired, Rick. And my little boy, he is awake if I go home now. So I will."

Nearing my hotel, he pointed half way down the side street, saying, "It is there you should have dinner. Food is good. It's only a fifteen-minute walk from where you stay."

Tired in my own way, I showered as soon as I hit the room. I lay on the floppy pillows and knew I had to resist their temptation. So I went to find dinner at Aref's recommended place. I arrived to find an empty restaurant, decorated as if nothing had changed around the country for a century. In a touch of modernity, photographs of former Supreme Leader Ayatollah Ruhollah Khomeini and his successor, Ali Khamenei, gazed down on me from the wall beside my table.

I toyed with my new Cyrus Cylinder pen, gripping around the inscription to comfortably write notes. I read the pamphlet that came with it, recognizing Cyrus the Great as "father of the Iranian nation." Inseparable from Cyrus building a sixth-century BCE empire linking a parcel of Greece to India and all the lands between to Libya and Egypt is the culinary cradle that resulted from trade in spices and techniques, herbs and talents. Persian cuisine is a history of flavors.

Some of the world's earliest wines came from Persia; Shiraz is linked to the Persian city of that name. When the evening's wine at the restaurant was poured, I was told, "This wine, it is the world in a glass." The food was delicious, and my last dinner in Iran turned out to be a leisurely one. The restaurant was still empty when I paid my check and returned to the hotel, feeling temporarily Iranian myself through a combination of atmosphere, emotions, and tastes, and very satisfied with Aref's recommendation.

NINETEEN

THE UNFINISHED QUEST

"We have often had to advance through error to truth."
—George Smith, *The Chaldean Account of Genesis*

Boarding a plane in Iran for England, I knew my trip was winding down, and there was only one stop left: a long-awaited appointment to cap off my time in the Middle East. Now, my flight from Tehran behind me, I found myself in a black cab traveling through the streets of London. A tourism associate had opened a one-off establishment adjacent to a reputable gentleman's club, wishing to attract foreign travelers with an open door policy: they'd let anyone in for a fee, contrary to the exclusiveness of the adjacent club. I paid the fee. The "club within a club" was located on the end curve of St. James's Square and shared an entrance and dining facilities (but not its rooms) with facilities that harkened back to the days of early British exploration. It was access to their historic library and lounge that had most interested me.

The porter looked upon my arrival as a mistake. My orange and gray rucksack may have been the first such tote to cross their threshold. My hiking boots and cord pants were not to his approval. Standards went out the door as I went in.

"Don't fret," I assured him, without elaboration on where I had come from in such scruffy attire. Respecting their protocols, I promised, "Next time you see me, I'll be scrubbed up."

He let me know I had a flight of stairs to climb—"two, actually"—above the club's facilities to where my registration would be accepted.

Heading out to find a reputable pair of slacks and a jacket from Selfridges or Marks & Spencer, I took a short cut through Bond Street and happened on a sale at a bespoke menswear store with a rack display. Feeling rather post-explorer, I found a tweed suit reminiscent of the early 1900s, one Janice would for certain dissuade me from wearing. I slipped on the jacket, and the store's manager came over to chat. The jacket fit, and when he asked my shirt's neck size I said 17¼, because once that had been accurate. He said, "There's no chance of that." I'd been off by nearly an inch, all due to pre-trip fitness and travel-induced weight loss. All the clothes I needed were there—a shirt, the suit, and even a pair of loafers, all reduced below half price, and thus into the sphere of my budget. I left suited and suitable for the British Museum, even if they found me a bit of a sartorial throwback.

When I returned to the club so attired, the porter did not recognize me. "Good evening, sir, how might I help you?"

Able now to walk about the "real club's" polished premises, I browsed the oak-shelved library, taking in paintings of naval engagements and shorelines and landscapes that were no longer holdings of the empire. To my delight, there was a map of Cyrus the Great's empire when Persia ruled a vast area, including North Africa and up to the Balkans.

From the bookshelves I pulled the *Encyclopedia of World Explorers,* hoping to find a section on the German-cum-Russian Friedrich Parrot and his first ascent of Mount Ararat.

I pressed a waiter button and ordered a sherry, as it seemed the thing to do. It was brought to me on a silver tray and left beside a reading table, where I'd scoured the book for an entry about Parrot's 1829 expedition. He was not mentioned. The adventurers documented for that time period reflected the greater geographical questions of the day, those that attracted funding and guided public support, particularly from the patrons of the London club on whose furniture I sat. Those included: 1829, Major Laing, a Scottish African explorer, *reaches the legendary city of Timbuktu*; 1831–1835, R. Fitzroy, a British seafarer and astronomer, *accompanied by the young Charles Darwin, explores Patagonia*; 1845, *Unsuccessful quest for the Northwest Passage* by the English Arctic explorer J. Franklin. The exploration of Mount Ararat was not rated among the great quests of the day.

I awoke the next morning. I was in London for two reasons. Later that morning I had a meeting scheduled with Dr. Jonathan Taylor, Assistant Keeper with the Middle East Department of the British Museum, set in place two months before I'd left home for Ararat. The second reason was that my wife, Janice, lived in the adorable town of Hale, and worked in nearby Manchester. I was to be on a northbound train later that day, unless I needed more time at the museum for research.

I walked down Pall Mall and over to Bloomsbury, well in time for the opening of the museum's doors. After taking a coffee in a shop across from the iron gates that led to the plaza, I walked through the courtyard, up the stairs and into the Great Court of the British Museum. I asked a security guard where I might find the good doctor, and was shown my name on a list of expected visitors.

A woman wearing a black skirt, white blouse, and glasses that made her look rather smart greeted me. "Mr. Antonson, we're pleased you are here. I understand from Dr. Taylor that you will have had quite a trip this past while. He's interested to hear about it."

She led me down a hallway paneled with wood and through a door that looked to be made of metal. We went into a hushed office area with a wooden table and six chairs set beneath a high ceiling. "This is the Arched Room," she informed me. "Dr. Taylor will be along soon."

What caught my attention were bookshelves on a second level above me. I sat down, rather in awe of the surroundings.

"Rick! I'm Jonathan. Glad to meet you. Tell me, where did you go? Not to Nineveh, please." He wore an open-collared shirt, no jacket, and light-gray denim pants—the rugged wear of a man daily engaged with antiquities. He carried four books under his left arm as we sat down.

I recounted the trip, in brief—brevity not being my strength.

Jonathan explained, "I have not been able to travel to Iraq, nor to Iran. Syria, yes."

I showed him the Cyrus Cylinder pen. "There will not be many of those about, even if you should find this one's been made as a knock-off," he observed. It was his business to know replicas and originals and he'd pegged that one properly—artifice, not art. As he cast a knowledgeable eye over the pen, I realized I'd brought a forgery into the home of ethical items. Sheepishly I reached for it.

He smiled and said, "I have time this morning, and we can talk. Tell me how best I can help you."

I wondered what lay undiscovered today at Nineveh. "It would be helpful to hear of any plans that may be—even informally, under consideration for further work at the Library of Nineveh ruins, and if so, when."

He was shaking his head before I finished. To his own disappointment, but with the learned sense of practicality, he assured me nothing was afoot.

In a 2004 report for the British Museum, Jeanette Fincke had written: "We do not know how many tablets are either still waiting in Nineveh to be discovered or have already perished and been lost forever." Her observation was that invaders, first in 612 BCE, and then ongoing, may have destroyed what they found in Nineveh or, in the spirit of looting and the spoils of war, carried away any number of cuneiform tablets.

Keeping in mind that the Nineveh site is large, any ongoing excavation opens new areas for misappropriation when authorities are not watching. The lack of a long-term plan for research has not helped. The ruins of Nineveh appear to have been more often ransacked over the centuries than they've been the subjects of methodical work.

Vandalism at the site has been ongoing for centuries, looters digging holes for access, disregarding care for items too large to haul away or too difficult to sell.

More innocently, yet no less disappointing for many visitors or even those posted in the region for work, irreplaceable souvenirs are easy to come by. Fincke commented that such finds "have since appeared in private collections or on the antiquities market." It seemed remarkable to me that comparatively few stray tablets have appeared from outside the official excavations.

The ancient gates of Nineveh are still visible today. Already, though, urban expansion of Mosul encroaches; modern needs for sewers and underground water pipes compete with preservationist pleas to leave the area untouched for further exploration.

I mentioned to Jonathan that I'd read that the earliest excavations of the 1800s were not as organized and documented as one might have wished for them to be. He replied, "That was a time before the discipline of archaeology was invented. The field of study evolved through such early work. Modern excavators of artifacts would have undertaken a systematic grid to mark their finds according to where they were located. That's a big part of interpreting what an object means. One might think such rigors of plotting the excavation may have moved the interpretation process along more quickly, but the opposite is true. Modern excavation is actually a much slower process, given the protocols." He added, "One could be more methodical in hope of a more cohesive understanding. It takes immense patience."

I said, "I wanted to be where George Smith first held the Flood Tablet in his hands. I'd like to know your take on that story."

He told me I was that very moment in the building where Smith made his 1872 discovery. "He probably read as fast as he could translate the cuneiform. It revealed the story of a flood, as I'm sure you know." I knew this but there was something about hearing it from him, at the British Museum, that was much more rewarding than coming across it in a book.

When the "discovery" was made, Smith, already thought of as eccentric by his colleagues, leaped with excitement. "He shouted and moved about frantically, animated in a way no one had seen him behave. In the hot thrill of the moment he tore off his clothes, undressing right in front of them."

It is a story with but one corroborator on record. Notwithstanding that, it enlivened the reputation of a reserved researcher.

The rare discovery didn't stop there. The public reception and the inherent controversy sparked by confronting biblical timelines garnered great newspaper coverage, particularly in the *Daily Telegraph*. The public wanted more of this claim of a flood story that predated Noah's. The newspaper's publisher decided to send Smith, an inexperienced traveler, to Mosul as a headline-grabbing escapade in search of a missing fragment from the tablet.

George Smith, the adventurer. Vybarr Cregan-Reid, author of *Discovering Gilgamesh*, wrote, "Had he not died so young, Smith could have gone on to become the Darwin of archaeology." Portrait © Simon Carr.

"Early in 1873, the *Telegraph* and George Smith embarked on a joint quest," Jonathan said. "The paper would cover his expenses if he'd go to Nineveh and explore further, seeking to find additional revelations, but the priority job was finding the missing fragment of the flood story. The *Telegraph* would have an exclusive on the initial reports."

A 1971 article in *Saudi Aramco World*, written by Robert S. Strother, pondered the odds faced by Smith: "It seemed flatly impossible that *his* special fragment of clay could have escaped destruction in the violence that produced such a tangle of rubble, but Smith had the eye of a hawk and an indelible mental image of what he sought."

Strother's article tells us what happened next. "Smith's great stroke of good luck, surely one of the most remarkable in the history of science, came on May 14, 1873. As usual, he had put the day's crop of cuneiform fragments in a sack and ridden back to the khan in Mosul where he and his horse were staying. Shortly after he sat down to examine them, he leaped out of his chair in joy. His million-to-one gamble had paid off. The fragment in his hand was the missing piece of the Deluge story, and it contained the 17 lost lines." He had succeeded, as he wrote later, in filling in "the only place where there was a serious gap in the story."

The newspaper's headline blared:

"THE DAILY TELEGRAPH" ASSYRIAN EXPEDITION
COMPLETE SUCCESS OF EXCAVATIONS
THE MISSING PORTION OF THE DELUGE
TABLET DISCOVERED.

More tablets, sequential with what was already at the British Museum, were found. Importantly, dates and details about Babylonia's ruling dynasties were portrayed in other fragments.

Smith gave way to the editors' demands, newspaper deadlines, and sales promotion, truncating his further research in Nineveh. He fed news headlines at home, and returned to England. The British Museum funded another journey in November of that same year. Smith's full report was eventually published in 1875 in his book *Assyrian Discoveries*.

Jonathan held out a copy of Smith's book for me to examine. "There are several books you should know about." He showed me Austen Layard's *Nineveh and Its Remains*, in an edition with a musty smell that made me want to hug it. He passed over another hardcover book, saying, "This is one you will be able to get easily as it is recent." I held *The Buried Book* by David Damrosch. Beside it lay a copy of Andrew George's translation of *The Epic of Gilgamesh*.

Jonathan got up. "I've to be upstairs for a brief meeting. I've just thought of two other books to retrieve while I'm up there. Spend time with these, and I'll be back presently."

In his absence, I went through the books from cover to cover in a glancing fashion, but with great interest and care, taking out my notebook and jotting down their publication details. I flipped through the pages of *The Buried Book*, reading about the broken tablet story culminating with a disheartening end to George Smith's work. Smith, media star and, in the minds of some, "the greatest of Assyriologists," made a final journey to Mosul at the behest of the British Museum trustees in 1876.

Ottoman officials wreaked havoc on his plans when he entered their jurisdiction, foisting delays on him. He did not near Nineveh until July, a season too hot for excavation work. Local officials were becoming skeptical of Britain's true ambitions—were the British seeking gold? Were they establishing stronger ties around the national government?

Smith knew he was entering an area restless with rumors and feuds, a region also plagued with health issues. He became sick with dysentery. Delirium took hold, and he was eventually forced to leave for England. The journey's first leg was a 350-mile crossing on horseback to Aleppo.

Sixty miles outside of Aleppo, in the village of Ikisji, Smith could no longer move and took refuge. Found there by an emissary of the British consul, he was transported by cart to Aleppo, where he died on August 19, 1876, at the age of thirty-six.

The books Jonathan provided shone a light on the merging of science and story, myth and history, clay-chipped records and oral traditions.

When he returned, I asked, "What portion of the Nineveh's library holdings do you think they moved to London?"

"We, too, would like to know the answer to your question."

In his book *Libraries in the Ancient World*, Lionel Casson wrote, "It has been estimated that Ashurbanipal's library contained about 1,500 titles; since many existed in multiple copies the total number of tablets is much greater." Fragments were tens of thousands.

Jonathan put the current times of war and conflict into context for me. "Without further exploration of the site, jointly with Iraq, we will not be able to confirm the extent of its holdings nor of their status."

I wondered if there would ever be more opportunity in my lifetime for professional archeologists and conservators to work through the ruins of the Library of Nineveh.

I assumed our meeting had come to an end. Instead, Jonathan asked me: "Would you like to see it?"

"See . . . ?"

"The Flood Tablet."

"Is that possible?"

"Come with me."

We were up the stairs in what felt like a blink. Down a hallway and around a corner, we came to a door, a back entrance. Jonathan opened it to a room where the morning visitors had not yet made their presence felt. He walked over to a display case and stood there, letting my own eyes find the treasure.

"*The Flood Tablet?*" I exclaimed.

"Yes, Rick, the Flood Tablet."

Later that morning, at Foyles bookstore on Charing Cross Road, I purchased a copy of *The Buried Book*. I learned that a replica copy of Layard's book was available through mail order. I was told where—down the street, around a corner, and four shops in—I might find a repro-duction copy of Smith's *Assyrian Discoveries,* which I did. Parceling the books into one bag, I went to a pub to celebrate. There was much food for thought.

With the satisfaction of the visit with Dr. Taylor in mind, I sipped a beer and envisioned a full circle of travels I'd almost completed. How-ever, that loop was still unfinished. The context for my attempt at under-standing the region of Mount Ararat and beyond would remain sorely lacking until I traveled to Armenia.

After lunch, during which I took care to avoid smudging the books, I boarded the 14:20 Virgin Train at London's Euston station, and arrived at Manchester's Piccadilly punctually at 16:49. The night before, once I was settled in at the club, Janice and I had talked on the phone for the first time in over a month. The Mayfield wine bar at Manchester's station holds court on the balcony, and I was set to meet her there for a long-awaited reunion before catching the National Rail train home to Hale at 18:17, arriving 18:49.

I'd reentered the world of schedules and precision.

TWENTY

MOTHER OF THE WORLD

"I do not believe there has ever been a massacre in the history of the world so general and thorough as that which is now being perpetrated in this region or that a more fiendish, diabolical scheme has ever been conceived by the mind of man . . ."
—Constantinople letter, from US Consul Leslie Davis to Henry Morgenthau, American ambassador to Turkey, July 24, 1915

Three years after my visit to the British Museum, I again saw the massif Ararat, this time while I was on a flight from Frankfurt, Germany, about to land in Yerevan, Armenia. My vantage point was our aircraft's southeast-facing window. In the distance was Lesser Ararat, and here, essentially at daylight's end and to my utter joy, was an *almost* full moon commanding the sky over the mountains.

I had the silly thought of pointing out to someone, anyone, onboard the plane, "I stood on top of that mountain," but I came to my senses and kept the thought to myself.

I remembered the five climbers who had stood there together in a single shared achievement. None of us would have completed the climb alone or without Kubi—at least I'd not have. Each one of the expedition members had shouldered me on—something I now understood: Goran's nudging the group to do its best; Charlie believing the ability to summit was as much in the mind as in the legs; Patricia reminding us of our commitment; Ian's confidence; Nico's selflessness enabling our success.

Out the plane's window and over Ararat, it was still two nights before the complete full moon, and the thought of such a sighting had not even crossed my mind when preparing for this trip. But the image visible from the plane's window was very close to the one I'd sought to capture (unsuccessfully so far). Other than the trinket I'd found at Ishak Pasha Palace, I'd not seen even a doctored image depicting that scene.

The north face of Ararat (we had climbed from the south) can be seen from Armenia's capital city, Yerevan, which is thirty-five miles away and less than twenty miles from the Armenia–Turkey border. The north is a more difficult ascent.

From Armenia, the term "forbidden mountain" took on a new connotation. Despite the efforts of US president Woodrow Wilson in 1920, all of Mount Ararat is now vested within Turkey, and to the eastern flank of Lesser Ararat, following the Tehran Convention of 1932 between Iran and Turkey. Today, a border fence erected by Turkey makes Ararat a difficult mountain for Armenians to touch, though it defines their daily lives. They call it *Masis*. It has also been called "Mother of the World."

My son Brent, forty-four, was teaching English in Iraq, and had flown up to meet me in Yerevan for a few days. He'd arrived two years after my own journey to Iraq. His responsibilities were split between Erbil and Sulimaniyah, and he had met Taha's family. I arrived at the hotel to find him drinking coffee in the lounge.

"Dad!" It was heartwarming to hear that—it had been over a year since we'd seen one another. We jumped into a hug that caused commotion among other patrons, the piano man, and the waiters.

"Where's the best place for Armenian food?" I asked, not needing a response. "Let me drop the bags upstairs and we'll go for dinner."

Five minutes later we were headed out onto the streets of downtown Yerevan. The billboard signs irked me; they were oversized and ubiquitous, and their intrusive placement disturbed the streetscape of charming architecture.

Brent advised, "Up a block is Tumanian, a roundabout way to where we're going, but it's a pretty walk. It's a stroll to the Opera House. We'll walk back through Republic Square."

"Did you see the moon?" I asked. "It'll be full in two nights. I have to find a photographer who can capture that."

Down a wide walkway was a joint Brent had been to the night before. Cold drinks arrived as we sat down. Brent recommended an Armenian *pide*; a cheese I didn't recognize, local salami, and tomatoes, which arrived folded into a sleeve of grilled bread. We took mouthfuls while catching up on family news, friends, our work. That morphed into talk of what we wanted to do in Armenia.

"Khor Virap," Brent said, tucking in to a second *pide*. "You must be thinking of going there." The photogenic monastery was partly restored, partly crumbling, a one-time place of imprisonment and the eventual site of a chapel. It is closely tied to the fact that Armenia became the world's first "Christian nation" about 1900 years ago.

"That site defines Armenia," I said.

"It's a country bordered by enemies," said Brent. "That's what defines Armenia."

"Maybe Ararat defines it?" I said.

"Armenia is a country with too much history and not enough geography," he trumped.

A man came by with little green apples and gave us a handful, then walked down the street to sit with friends at the next cafe. He'd left some at another table, and we watched people cut the apple and salt it before eating. We did likewise.

"I found an Avis agency this morning. I haven't driven behind a steering wheel in a year. Bring your credit card? I've got an Iraqi driver's license for my motorcycle and it should be good. Let's leave in the morning."

"Day after," I said. "I heard back from the man I mentioned, and the three of us are meeting up tomorrow." Through a colleague of my son Sean, I'd wangled an introduction to Tigran Zargaryan, head of the National Library of Armenia. He'd invited us to visit with him over lunch.

Descending the hotel's stairway to the lobby the next morning, we were met by a man with graying hair, thoughtful eyes, and a dignified posture. Tigran was wearing a jacket and tie, and we felt good we were too.

Offering an open hand, he said, "Welcome to Yerevan. I know where we should have lunch."

The waiter looked surprised at the arrival of Brent and me, but when he saw Tigran behind us, camaraderie broke out. Tigran told us, "You are my guests. He will serve us time-honored Armenian dishes. Armenians are very good with cooking."

"Tell me about your visit," he asked as we sat. Then he steered the conversation to a more substantive topic. "Many in the world media, politicians, people in general, ignore Armenia. They see it as a country to be shifted about. Not what America or Europe would call 'a player.'" Then, he went straight to the point: "What is it you seek here?"

"An understanding of Ararat's place in Armenian history, and to learn more about what occurred between Turkey and Armenia a hundred years ago."

"For Ararat, it is a mountain now in the wrong country. And that country has done much wrong to Armenia."

"The genocide . . ." I started. The obvious.

"That is single in its horror."

It felt early to be on this terrible topic, so I returned to the mountain. "Attempts to ascend Ararat from the north, through Armenia, were difficult and often not successful. I have read of Armenian climber Abovian, who was with Friedrich Parrot on the peak of Mount Ararat in 1829. While I'm here, I hope to learn more about him."

"Khachatur Abovian, yes. You should definitely understand our country's famous writer. That he also climbed the mountain is separate story—important, yes, but to the side. He wrote our first books in the modern Armenian language, using the Eastern Armenian dialect. *Wounds of Armenia.*"

"Wounds of Armenia?" asked Brent.

"It is the book for which he is best known. Though he is better known for disappearing."

"Disappearing?"

Tigran looked at Brent. "Abovian was your age when he vanished in 1848, having gone for a morning walk. No one knows where or why. He was never seen again."

"Enemies of his writing?" Brent asked.

"Abovian was not published when he was alive, not for the public. It was later that his work became widely available, so that does not seem a motive."

Tigran returned to Ararat. "Abovian was sent with Parrot in 1829 as a guide, though he hadn't been up the mountain himself. He could translate the language and provide introductions. Their expedition is famous for being among the last visitors to the village of Ahora, destroyed not long after in our worst natural disaster. From the summit of Ararat, Abovian brought back ice in a bottle, carrying it to Yerevan as Holy Water."

"Abovian also guided the geologist Hermann von Abich in 1845," I mentioned. "By then an experienced guide."

"Rick, you will have found the name Urarat," he said, changing the subject, "but"—turning to my son—"*you* may not have. In the Old Testament, we see Urarat as the name for this region, and for the mountains. It is indistinguishable from Ararat as a name, modified. When Latin filters the word, Urarat becomes Armenia. We are Urarat, Urartu, Ararat, Armenia."

As we took in a sweet-tasting dessert, Tigran broached the important topic. "We could talk about the atrocities you mentioned, if you wish. Better, though, would be for you to go up the hillside to see the memorial. Be thoughtful within the Genocide Museum."

Tigran took us to a taxi stand. As we waited he spoke. "We cannot—will never—forget Turkey was on purpose eliminating the Armenian

Secretary of State,
Washington.

858, July 16, 1 p m.

Confidential. Have you received my 841? Deportation of and excesses against peaceful Armenians is increasing and from harrowing reports of eye witnesses it appears that a campaign of race extermination is in progress under a pretext of reprisal against rebellion.

Protests as well as threats are unavailing and probably incite the Ottoman government to more drastic measures as they are determined to disclaim responsibility for their absolute disregard of capitulations and I believe nothing short of actual force which obviously United States are not in a position to exert would adequately meet the situation. Suggest you inform belligerent nations and mission boards of this.

AMERICAN AMBASSADOR,
Constantinople

Deciphered by

American Ambassador Morgenthau's telegram of July 16, 1915 was informed by recent unsettling events and anticipated the candor of Consul Davis's letter of July 24, 2015 (quoted in this chapter's epigraph).

people. Yet they will not acknowledge the terribleness. The Ottoman elite, German elite, they managed decisions aimed at killing Armenians. Today Germany, Canada, many other countries like France and Russia, recognize the atrocity. Not Turkey, though. Not yet."[19]

The taxi arrived, and Brent and I made our way to the site of memory.

A spire thrust into the sky to mark a holocaust. The memorial recalls—as best as one can—inexplicable tragedy. The museum itself is partially ensconced in the hillside, and we entered from above.

A young woman working for the museum asked if we needed information. Before we could respond, she moved us toward a display case. "This is from World War the First." Below the banner of "An Appeal to the American People" was the original letter, on White House stationery, under the signature of US president Woodrow Wilson. The girl encouraged that we look closer, saying, "You can hear with your eyes."

President Wilson addressed the magnitude of the dislocation, noting there were "more than 400,000" orphans and "more than 2,000,000 destitute survivors." His words confirmed his intentions: "Armenia is to be redeemed . . . So that at last this great people, struggling through night after night of terror . . . are now given a promise of safety, a promise of justice . . ."

Wilson accepted responsibility to oversee arbitration between Turkey and Armenia regarding four provinces, including Van. Mount Ararat was within the area under review. The resulting United States recommendation accorded Armenia a coastal section of the Black Sea and 40,000 square miles of land in the disputed provinces. Notwithstanding the evidence of the recent atrocities and the president's leadership, Congress stood aside and declined to support the mandate required to

19 In April of 2015, Pope Francis spoke at mass about "the first genocide of the 20th Century" having been inflicted upon the "Armenian people." A strong rebuke came from Turkish President Erdoğan against using the term. Prime Minister Davutoglu said Turkey does "share the pain" with Armenians, stating that many Turkish deaths also occurred during those conflicts. "Concealing or denying evil is like allowing a wound to keep bleeding without bandaging it," Pope Francis said.

AN APPEAL TO THE AMERICAN PEOPLE.

One year ago, in compliance with resolutions passed by the Senate and by the House of Representatives, I appointed days upon which the people of the United States might make such contributions as they felt disposed for the aid of the stricken Armenian and Syrian peoples.

American diplomatic and consular representatives and other American residents recently returned from Western Asia, assure me that many thousands of lives were saved from starvation by the gifts of the American people last winter. They also bring full assurance of the continued effective distribution of relief and report that the suffering and death from exposure and starvation will inevitably be very much greater this winter than last unless the survivors can be helped by further contributions from America.

Reports indicate that of orphans alone there are more than 400,000, besides women and other dependent children, reaching a total of more than 2,000,000 destitute survivors. The situation is so distressing as to make a special appeal to the sympathies of all.

In view of the urgent need I call again upon the people of the United States to make such further contributions as they feel disposed, in their sympathy and generosity for the aid of these suffering peoples. Contributions may be made through the American Red Cross, Washington, D. C. or direct to the American Committee for Armenian and Syrian Relief, Cleveland H. Dodge, treasurer, One Madison Avenue, New York City.

29 October, 1917.

Woodrow Wilson

US President Woodrow Wilson's letter appealing for donations to assist the Armenian people was a follow-up to a proclamation in which he stated the need was: "in view of the misery, wretchedness and hardships, which these people are suffering."

enforce this decision. Despite initial Turkish conciliation, the boundaries were later altered, when in 1920 Turkish and Soviet military maneuvers reduced Armenia to a landlocked satellite country in the USSR.

As we were leaving, the attendant said, "It is a ceaseless pain."

Partway through the following morning we kept our plan to visit Khor Virap. We drove out of town on Admiral Isakov Avenue, Brent behind the wheel and me inspecting a foldout map that I'd given up trying to refold correctly.

"It can't be more than half an hour," he said, although at that point neither of us realized I'd misguided us onto the M-5 when we should have chosen the M-15.

Much later, having missed two logical turnoffs with the hope that an adjustment road would show up ahead, we took an exit and pointed the car southward into the plains and down unmarked roads not on my

"Orphan City," Alexandropol in northern Armenia, coped with the ongoing waves of desperate Armenian orphans forced to leave Turkey. The migration continued beyond 1915 into the early 1920s, reaching a peak of 22,000 children. Image courtesy of the Near East Relief Historical Society, Near East Foundation collection, Rockefeller Archive Center.

map. Using Ararat as a compass mark, we knew the general direction. Or thought we did. The mountain wasn't moving, but it didn't always seem to align with the map.

There was no rush. The farmlands were pleasant and we had lots to talk about, until we noticed we could no longer see Ararat. Traffic dwindled until it was just a tractor and us. When an equipment merchant's sign said groceries were available, we pulled over.

Returning to the car with potato chips and chocolate bars, two soft drinks, and directions, Brent said, "Stay on this road another mile, turn left, which would be east. We drive on the paved road. Stop at the stop sign. Another mile or so later there's a dirt road. It actually connects another mile on to a pretty good road, which will eventually take us to where the map markings show Pokr Vedi on H11. That's how we get to Khor Virap."

Two more stops for redirections, a thorough scouting of the farmlands and small community clusters, and forty-five minutes later, we were down to a half tank of gas as we arrived at Khor Virap.

The mountain backdrop looked "modern" in contrast to the seasoned brown of the monastery's protective walls and its slim, cathedral-like tower. We walked up to the brow of the hill, where Khor Virap's mezzanine affords a stunning view of Mount Ararat.

This is a vital place for Armenians to pilgrimage, a hub of religious belief. The Armenian Church's patron saint, Gregory the Illuminator, was imprisoned here for fourteen years around 300 CE, when he was known as Grigor Lusavorich, an instigator in the eyes of established rulers. We could see the Armenian-Turkish border fence off in the distance, far closer to the monastery than to Ararat.

The day had turned sunny and the place was crowded. In the mass of families toting digital cameras I found a lonely man. He sat silently on a chair and had a small display of printed pictures propped beside him. Slouched at the shoulders, he was unshaven and wore an unwashed jacket. His pants were threading at the cuffs, hanging over scuffed shoes. Nestled in his lap, held by his right hand, was a Polaroid camera. With that museum piece in his grip, he was decades out of sync, anachronistic, and appeared irrelevant to what was going on.

A young man and woman approached the man, wanting their photograph taken. They handed him their Nikon. He declined, pointing to the work he offered. It dawned on the young man and woman that they'd like a printed picture. They passed him money, and he set up the two of them, with Ararat in the background. Within a minute he handed them the printed picture, then sat back down to his post.

"Dad. Come here." Brent beckoned from the stair beneath the monastery's tower. He motioned me up and through a church doorway. The gothic chapel sat under the dome of the Holy Mother of God church. A baptism was being conducted as we entered. The family cradled their child for a blessing. Another set of grandparents and family members waited nearby in a processional queue. Candles, aided by an electric bulb, provided the light that the dusty stained-glass windows kept out. The ambiance, which reminded me of standing in a holy cave of sorts, was mysterious.

In the time since my summit of Ararat, I'd begun writing a travel narrative. Thinking that right now might be a chance to source a missing image, I whispered, "The Polaroid man looks like he's been here forever. Think he's got a photograph of a full moon over Mount Ararat?"

"Let's go ask him," said Brent. People mumbled "Shhh" with an Armenian accent. We hurried outside, the daylight stopping us for an eye-adjusting moment.

The photographer was hunched over, unmoving and unoccupied. He looked up slowly, as though he sensed our shadows.

"*Vwi govoretye pa-Ruski*?" Brent asked. "Do you speak Russian?" The two languages widely spoken in the area are Russian and Armenian.

"*Da*." The old man smiled, keeping his lips together as though opening them would make him vulnerable. "*Pachimoo vwi govoritye po-Ruski*?" he asked, wanting to know why Brent spoke to him in Russian.

Brent explained he'd lived in Russia for a year, teaching English. He gauged the man. "Do you have a photograph of Mount Ararat with the full moon?"

It was a long shot. Lacking equipment and skills ourselves, we knew that only a craftsman could capture such an image in the quality I sought. The man's eyes lit up as he conveyed in Russian, "Yes. But not with this!" He held up his camera. We could see the markings of *Svetozor*, the former USSR's assembler of Polaroid units. "I am for many years a professional."

"Tell him I want to buy his photograph of Mount Ararat with the moon."

The man responded while looking at me, as my son explained. "He has a photograph. Just one. He says it is stunning. It is at his home."

"Can he go and get it?" I was suddenly anxious.

The response brought complexity. "His name is Vage. He needs permission from the priest to leave here."

"Vage. How much for the photograph?" I asked.

There was a hurl of Russian phonetics between the two of them.

"Dad, you've got to do right by him. I think that he does not want enough money from you."

The photographer wanted what amounted to less than ten dollars in American money. It was pennies on the dollar that a Western photographer would charge for publication rights. I put a down payment in his hands.

The man packed up his wares and we followed him into an on-site residence. A partially clothed deacon, barely old enough to be out of seminary, stopped us short and told us to leave. The old man handed him the Polaroid and went away with us.

"Tell him I want to use his photograph in a book."

When that was translated for Vage, I heard back, "I also told him we will pay what the priest says is a fair price."

Vage sprang straight into the chapel. We were three feet behind. The second baptism was under way, the priest bestowing blessings in hushed tones. Vage made straight for him.

"He's going to stop the service! What have we done?"

Vage veered through the baptismal ceremony, threading between the parents, the wrapped child and the priest, darting into a door beyond. He returned with a senior priest and we stepped outside under the portico.

Vage, Brent, and the priest spoke to one another in Russian. Once I spoke the priest asked, "You speak English?"

"Vage has a photograph of a full moon over Mount Ararat," I said, now able to participate directly. "If it is good, I wish to pay him for rights to use it in a book. He agrees, but wants too little money."

The priest and Vage conversed in Armenian. The priest mentioned a new amount to us. "It is a price that he will accept. It is not for you to say otherwise."

Brent reminded me, "We've not seen the photograph."

"Father, here's what we wish to do in front of you," I said.

I had earlier decided on a suitable amount. I'd apportioned bills in my pockets out of sight of the photographer. I took one hand's worth of Armenian dram and passed that to the photographer, a proper topping up of the down payment I'd given him, assuaging my conscience. The total exceeded the priest's stipulated price by a respectful amount. It was still modest in my view, given the potential end use of the photograph. Vage fanned the bills and looked pleased. I took an equivalent amount from my other pocket and handed those drams to the priest. "This is for the church—a donation in Vage's name. All of it is for the full rights to his photograph." The four of us shared one firm handshake after another, followed by a chorus of "*Spacibo.*"

"Now let's go see if this photograph is any good," Brent said.

I hopped in the front seat of Vage's dented Lada. He let his car ease down the hill and chug to life in a Russian-engineered jump-start. In one movement he rolled and lit a homemade cigarette, drew in the flame, and puffed heartily. Looking behind me, I saw Brent slip the smoke-free rental vehicle out of the parking lot and onto the road behind us, the nicotine addict in him jealous of our smoke-filled car.

Vage's car stopped at a locked gate. I was already coughing from the smoke but needed this friend, so did not complain. He tapped his cell phone, trying to reach a guard. Failing at this, frustration slipped from his lips and he leapt out of the car. Hustling down the roadway and around the lowered barricade, he burst into the guard shack and returned, dangling keys. He unlocked the gate and, once our car was through, relocked the bolt. We drove away with the keys, the guard shouting behind us.

We headed towards the village of Pokr Vedi, miles away. Our cars pulled over near a ditch where expired truck parts rested like dinosaur bones. I expected to wait while Vage retrieved the photograph. Brent was out of his car, offering his lit smoke to Vage.

"*Spacibo*," said Vage, crossing the street to a yard with a high wooden fence. He unlocked and foot-pushed the gate open, stepping over a timber threshold. He twitched his head to indicate that we should follow him.

I stepped through the gate and back in time as I heard the translation. "He says, 'You are the first people I have had visit my home in twenty years.'"

In his backyard was an acre of leftover car parts and chicken shacks and used farm implements. Vage turned around to face us with a self-conscious happiness. His smile revealed teeth held together by gold

"Photo Vage," as we nicknamed the engaging photographer, with the author.

fillings. "*Eta moy toilet,*" he said, pointing. In the yard, a porcelain tub supported by metal claws at the base looked pristine and functional, and nearby was an outhouse.

Entering the three-room house, I was told that "coffee is coming" and "you'll want to sit in that room."

Vage stood to his full height for the first time, the curve of his back disappearing in the confines of his home. The kitchen was nicely kept, the dishes put away, and the countertop wiped clean. A small fridge sat on a wooden box, a broken clasp wedged in to hold it closed.

"*Kotayk,*" said Vage, passing me a cold can of beer. The taste was tart and strong, though not heavy.

We were in a room organized like a lived-in work studio. Every wall or open space had a purpose. He invited us to take a couch covered in neat bedding, tucked in. The floors were part wood and part buffed cement, all smooth and swept.

As I sat on the couch, my elbow hit the television set. Vage turned on a static connection, twisting the rabbit ears. Over the next hour that we were there, the pictures were never once clear, nor was I ever sure what we were watching.

"*Pirvay, oo nas bodit nemnovo vodki,*" he announced to us and I heard, "You and him are about to bond with vodka and coffee." The fridge door opened and bottles rattled. Vage reappeared with shot glasses. He set them on the wooden arm of the couch.

He carried a propane tank from the other room. Precariously balanced on top of it was a hotplate serviced by a gas hose taped to the tank's nozzle, which he turned open. It hissed. Vage flicked a match off a strip of sandpaper and lit it.

"Just in time," I breathed. He set the coffee pot to boil atop the makeshift stove, and then poured the fridge-cooled vodka from a bottle labeled Imperial.

This called for a Russian word: "*Na strovya!*"

"*Na strovya,*" I returned. "To health."

Across from us, and under his bed, were hundreds of books, in bundles of three or five, each group tied with burlap string and stacked. There was no room left under the bed; all of it was jammed with stored books, nearly fifty cubic feet of them.

Vage explained his lifestyle with an endearing barrage of misplaced consonants and random vowels, or so it sounded to me. *"Knigi vazhni dlya menya. Oni moya zhizni."* The explanation was relayed back as, "Books are important to me."

There was no lost rhythm in Vage's speaking. He spoke through Brent's voice as the comments were redirected to me: "My life is photography, but my knowledge is books."

Vage brought a chair in from the other room and sat on it, tending the propane stove as one might add kindling to a wood fire. My two companions looked at home in the surroundings, a reminder to me that Brent can live on the thin edge of nothing—and that appeared to be just about what Vage possessed. It was my underestimation.

Along the wall was a well-made bookshelf, at least six feet wide and spanning from floor to ceiling, behind locked glass doors. Vage stood and brought down four binders. They were photo albums. He placed them on the floor beside the propane tank and opened the first one.

Vage flipped through page after page of his photo collection, showing commercial work and many extraordinarily attractive women, as Brent narrated. "He was a professional photographer. He photographed many beautiful women. His wife left him." After a pause came Vage's candor. "I was young. I was handsome."

We all smiled. There were dozens of such pages. Then a spread fell open with a newspaper clipping showing half a dozen photographs of a dapper man, dark haired, with a nicely formed nose and a mischievous smile beneath unquestioning eyes.

"That's him," said Brent.

"How old are you?" I asked Vage. There was a smiling debate between the two of them that I could not understand. If there was a bet on the table, I'd have put cash behind what I whispered to Brent: "Going on seventy?"

"He's fifty-seven," came the answer.

Brent returned from the outhouse to find Vage and me sipping more vodka. I held out my mug, and Vage poured.

"Did you use the bathtub?" I asked.

"No, but I left the water running for you."

We laughed and Vage, not knowing why, joined us. They each took a cigarette and lit it off the ones they were already smoking.

"Could we see the photograph of Mount Ararat?" I asked.

Photo Vage, as he'd become to us out of a reference for the professional work we'd just seen, returned all but one of the binders to the shelving. The instant cameraman had revealed himself as a talented advertising executive, a sophisticated photographer, a self-trained academic, a voracious reader, and, even with all I now knew about him, still very much a mystery.

He sat down on his chair. There was one binder he'd propped behind the propane tank that he'd not replaced in the main shelf and had been ambivalent about revealing its contents. Now he opened it.

Every photograph was of art magazine caliber, and they featured a woman. Vage looked at me and said of his wife, "She was beautiful, yes? Now she lives in Russia. Moscow, I think. We are not together. Not for many years."

He turned a page showing pictures of a young girl growing through childhood and into her teens. He looked into my eyes and said, "My daughter. Only child. Lives far away." With that, the binder was closed. He rose and placed it on his bed.

Vage walked back to a shelf of CDs and chose one.

I was told, "We must go to another town. A friend has a photography store. That friend will give us a copy of the photograph on this CD."

*   *   *

I'd driven with Vage to Marmarashen, northbound on the main highway to Yerevan, in his smoke-filled Lada. We stopped ten minutes off that highway on a street of narrow stores. Vage, clutching the CD, asked us to wait while he went to a photography shop, six feet wide at best.

Our morning trip had lasted into late afternoon, and dinner hour was nearing. We walked back and forth on a sidewalk, never out of sight of the storefront Vage had entered. At last he came out, alone. He handed me a CD. The deal was done. He grinned, happy to have taken this trip with us. We were about to part when Brent said, "Dad, we still haven't seen the photograph! You've no idea if it works for you."

Vage took us to a room of photo-printing supplies and a large computer screen on the desk. His friend took the disc Vage had given me and inserted it in the slot, bringing up the image.

I was swept with gratitude.

A clear, brilliantly composed photograph appeared on the screen. The panoramic shot captured a magnificent view of both Mount Ararat and Lesser Ararat. And above that splendor hovered an almost full moon.

"Thank you, Vage. Thank you for everything! *Spacibo*."

Evening crept up on us. Dusk fell as we drove back to Yerevan. The trip would be over in the morning with our flights out of Armenia.

We let a side road take us up a hillside. Once there, we stood with an unobstructed view of Mount Ararat. Masis was away and high, though from our perch we had the illusion of being eye-even with its peak as we looked across the Ararat Valley. At long last, this is the way it happened for me: a completely round sphere hung in a motionless moment, free of cloud. There was a full moon over Mount Ararat.

"That mountain symbolizes more death than any other landmark on earth," Brent said.

"And hope . . . if you consider the ark stories."

He grinned at me. "Can you really imagine those foothills under flood?"

I thought, but didn't say, that maybe Black Sea waves *had* lapped toward this world seven thousand years ago, spawning a legacy of fact and fable. Instead I said, "Anyone who lived through that would have quite the story to tell."

Brent closed our conversation. "And every survivor would remember it differently."

Photo Vage's photograph of a full moon over Mount Ararat, with Lesser Ararat to the east. © Photo Vage, Armenia

I am assured at any rate
Man's practically inexterminate.
Someday I must go into that.
There's always been an Ararat
Where someone someone else begat
To start the world all over at.

—Robert Frost
A-Wishing Well

AFTERWORD: BEGIN AGAIN

As my own journeys to Ararat in 2010 and Armenia in 2013 retreat into "a montage of moments," I remember that I was shown the best of welcomes in some of the most troubled places. Those I met were at the forefront of cultural democracy and will need "reconstruction tourism" to help with the creation of economic well-being, when the time is right. They will not let our geo-curiosity rest at home; they wish us to come and visit with them.

Travels near Ararat and beyond will always be amid temporary détentes. What was, isn't; what is, won't be. There is no lasting resolution for the future, unless peoples forget their pasts. That's not going to happen, least of all in this region of the world.

To this day, Greater Kurdistan remains a sorrow, not a nation. It is said, "The Kurds have no friends but the mountains." The Kurds have spent three hundred years running against history's headwinds. The "Kurdish Question" becomes harder to ignore when the Peshmerga fight alongside coalition forces to hamper and destroy ISIS (*Daesh*). Will the coming decade see a nation of Kurdistan, in some form, rise from the turmoil in Syria, Iraq, Iran, and Turkey? If so, will it be accomplished by dismembering portions of one or more of these countries? Would creation of such a new nation attempt to include Mount Ararat? How would that sit with Armenians, even those of Kurdish heritage?

This human-headed winged bull was bulldozed by militant extremists during an intentional assault on the historic remains at the North West Palace of Ashurnasirpal (King, reigning 883—859 BCE), at Nimrud, March 5, 2015. UNESCO Director General Irina Bokova condemned "in the strongest possible manner the destruction of the archaeological site of Nimrud in Iraq . . . nothing is safe from the cultural cleansing underway in the country."

Turmoil in this region may lessen, but it will not cease. In Henry Kissinger's book *World Order,* his summation is this: "In our own time, the Middle East seems destined to experiment with all of its historical experiences simultaneously—empire, holy war, foreign domination, a sectarian war of all against all—before it arrives (if it ever does) at a settled concept of international order."

Ararat and the Ark will remain entwined as namesakes; science is an explainer but not an excuser—legends have remarkable tenacity. As this book went to press in 2016, there had been no independent scientific validation, for example, of the "discoveries" from the highly publicized 2010

349

Chinese–Turkish expedition to Mount Ararat that made news headlines around the world. One example ran in the *Daily Mail*, Australia:

"WE'VE FOUND NOAH'S ARK!" . . .
CLAIM EVANGELICAL EXPLORERS ON MISSION TO SNOW-CAPPED ARARAT
(BUT BRITISH SCIENTISTS SAY, "SHOW US YOUR EVIDENCE")

Similar announcements had been made by the Hong Kong–Turkey group in 2007, 2008, and 2009, purporting to have proof of Noah's Ark on Mount Ararat. What differed in the 2010 media blitz was the release of video footage showing expedition members in a cave above the twelve-thousand-foot level on Ararat and within a wooded-walled room, claiming to be inside the missing Ark.

The lead organization on these search achievements is Noah's Ark Ministries International (NAMI), based in Hong Kong, along with its Turkish mountaineering partner Armet Ertugrul (Paraşut). That turns out to be the same Paraşut I'd tried to contact on my trip to Ararat, with the intention of climbing to his reputed ice cave.

NAMI's publicity included a screening of *Noah's Ark Discovery* on National Geographic Television, one of television's top-ten archaeological programs viewed that year. In response to cynicism about their declarations, a 2010 *Christian Science Monitor* article by Stephen Kurczy stated: "There is no plausible explanation for what they found other than it is the fabled biblical boat."

However, given the lack of reputable third-party corroboration of any of the evidence they—or anyone else making similar claims—have presented, all claims are found wanting. NAMI, and its enabling Turkish partner Paraşut, risk earning a place on the roster of tricksters like Ronald Wyatt, who once rode a roar of self-promotion around the discredited Durupinar site not far from Mount Ararat.

There are those, however, who provide context through ongoing scholarship, and who harken back to Leonard Woolley's words: "Beneath much that is artificial or incredible there lurks something of fact." As oceanographer Robert Ballard told an interviewer, "It's foolish to think you will ever find a ship. But can you find people who were living? Can you find their villages that are underwater now? And the answer is yes."

I maybe most agree with Irving Finkel, who once observed, "I don't think the ark existed—but a lot of people do. It doesn't really matter. The Biblical version is a thing of itself and it has a vitality forever."

My odyssey's encounters have left lifelong friendships. I've spent evenings with Taha and Gulie and Andam in their home. Their family in Iraq is safe, despite the dangers. Others, like my Iranian train dance partners, have remained email pen-pals. Those I climbed Mount Ararat with are always up for correspondence and periodic exchanges about leaving on another grand quest together. Whether that adventure actually happens is not important. I will send a copy of this book to Photo Vage, so he can see his lovely photograph of a full moon over Mount Ararat adorning the back cover of this book.

My eyes were thoroughly examined by a doctor upon my return, and whatever visual disruption occurred descending from the summit of Ararat was—like so much in that region, except for the mountain itself—temporary.

A TIMELINE

BCE = Before Common Era, CE = Common Era, secular terms replacing the Gregorian calendar's BC (Before Christ) and AD (Anno Domini—In the Year of Our Lord).

The Origin (with its debatable dates)

13.82 billion years ago	In the beginning . . . The Big Bang. Singularity. Start of the universe.
4.54 billion years ago	Earth forms (according to radiometric age dating).
600,000 to 1 million years ago	Phanerozoic evolution of complex life: multicellular to human.
500,000 to 200,000 years ago	Evolution of *Homo sapiens* onward to today.

BCE

c. 15,000	Height of most recent glaciation.
c. 12,000 –10,000	Earliest date for traditional "Creationist" view of earth's formation, with humankind in attendance.
c. 6000	First settlements in area that became ancient Nineveh (today Mosul).
c. 5600	**Epic high water. A great deluge. The Black Sea Flood** (argued speculation). Mediterranean Sea

	waters rising through the Sea of Marmara burst through the Bosporus isthmus to flood freshwater lesser Black Sea and form saltwater Black Sea.
c. 5000–3500	Additional settlements take place in region that eventually becomes Mesopotamia.
	Initial community of Erbil begins, one continuously inhabited to the present.
4004	Creation of the Earth, according to literal interpretation of Bible, worked up using the generational "begets," by Rev. James Ussher (in 1650).
c. 3300–3100	Cuneiform script developed.
c. 3100	Mesopotamia emerges more formally as a region.
c. 2700–2500	Gilgamesh (King of Uruk) lived (according to Babylonian written records, he may have lived closer to 2100 BCE).
c. 2000–1800	**Flood Tablet** written down (earliest known); **Epic of Gilgamesh**, including Chapter XI, containing the flood story; **hero is Utnapishtim**.
c. 1900	The prophet Abraham (Ibrahim, Abram) leaves Mesopotamia for Canaan.
c. 1900–1700	**Ark Tablet** written down (earliest known); Babylonian flood story; **hero is Atrahasis**. Prior to Ark Tablet, revealed in 2014, the earliest written version of this story was from 1635 BCE.
c. 1000	Mesopotamia begins period of Assyrian then Persian dominance.
c. 860	"Kingdom of Urartu" and "Mountains of Urartu" referenced (Urartu became Urarat, then Ararat—and, in the Latin, Armenia); Anatolia, today in Turkey, was largely included; Urartu was also known as the Van Kingdom.

c. 650	Neo-Assyrian king Ashurbanipal (reigning 668–627 BCE) constructs new palace and builds library at Nineveh.
c. 612	Over 30,000 fragments of cuneiform tablets buried in library at Nineveh, under assault from Medes. Assyria falls to the Babylonian Empire.
c. 600	Ancient Armenian Kingdom emerges.
c. 597	Babylonian destruction of Jerusalem. The Babylonian Exile of Jewish people begins, perhaps facilitating their introduction to the Babylonian Flood Story and other narratives; Jewish exile lasts sixty years (two to three generations).
c. 590	Mount Ararat ceases to be under the Kingdom of Urartu.
c. 550	First Persian Empire (Achaemenid) founded by Cyrus the Great.
c. 539	Cyrus the Great overthrows Babylon. Cyrus Cylinder is written/created.
c. 537	Jews freed by Cyrus as part of his abolishment of slavery and granting religious freedom; Jews able to return and rebuild Jerusalem; the writing of Hebrew texts begins.
c. 538–332	**Noah's Ark** story written down (earliest known): Book of Genesis of the Hebrew Torah (or the Pentateuch), eventually becoming part of the Christian Old Testament in the Bible; **hero is Noah**.
c. 275	Berossos (writer, astronomer, and priest; of the Chaldean people who controlled Babylonia from 625 to 539 BCE); references the flood narrative and ark in the remnant excerpts found from his *History of Babylonia*.
c. 190	Greater Armenia evolves.

Common Era (CE)

0 to 300 CE	Ongoing developments of Judaism and Christianity. Ongoing, interrelated writings, and evolution of differences in faith and documents.
301–14 CE	Armenia adopts Christianity as state religion.
428	Kingdom of Armenia ends.
570	Birth of Islam's founder, Muhammad, in Mecca.
c. 632	**Nûh's Ark** story written down (earliest known). Qur'an (Koran) revealed to Muhammad, including the story of the great flood; **hero is Nûh.**
1271	*Travels of Marco Polo*, reference to the Ark being on Mount Ararat.
1299	Establishment of the Ottoman Turkish Empire.
1453	Constantinople's name changed to Istanbul. Straddles Bosporus Strait; territory on the west side of the city seen as Europe; territory on the east side of the city seen as Asia.
1647	Adam Olerius (German) wrote of seeing wooden remains of the Ark on Ararat.
1829	Dr. Friedrich Parrot (German), first official ascent of Mount Ararat.
1835	Henry Creswicke Rawlinson, British envoy in Baghdad, began deciphering the Cuneiform alphabet.
1840	Most recent volcanic activity of Mount Ararat (earthquake/destruction of Ahora monastery).
1845	Austen Henry Layard (British envoy) begins excavating Assyrian ruins at Nineveh with Hormuzd Rassam.
1845	Herman Abich (German), ascent of Mount Ararat.
1850	Colonel Khodzko (Russian), ascent of Mount Ararat.
1853	Hormuzd Rassam (Assyrian), Layard's successor as envoy for the British Museum, excavated the Library of Nineveh.

1856	Major Robert Stuart (British), ascent of Mount Ararat.
1868	Douglas Freshfield (American) comes within a thousand feet of reaching the peak of Mount Ararat.
1872	George Smith (British) rediscovers the *Epic of Gilgamesh* by translating the "Flood Tablet" while working at the British Museum.
1876	Sir James Bryce (British), ascent of Mount Ararat.
1888	E. de Markoff (Russian) claims to have found wood from the Ark during his successful August summit.
1908	"Young Turks" become an influential party in Turkey under the banner of the Committee for Union and Progress.
1914	World War I begins. Mount Ararat is under Armenia's jurisdiction.
1914–18	Mount Ararat situated in disputed Turkey/Russia jurisdiction.
1915	"Red Sunday," April 24. Beginning of the Armenian genocide and Turkish civil war. Estimated deaths: Armenians 500,000 to 1 million; Kurds 30,000; Turks in the tens of thousands.
1916	Lieutenant W. Roskovitsky (Russian) makes widely reported flyover of Mount Ararat and claims "sighting" the ruins "of a boat." Mount Ararat under Ottoman Empire's jurisdiction.
1918	World War I ends.
1918	First Kurdish petition for an independent Kurdistan country; Mount Ararat possibly in Kurdish lands; petition unsuccessful.
1920	Treaty of Sèvres: considers an independent Kurdistan, though the city of Van, for example, would not be part of it.

1920	British mandate over Iraq and French mandate over Syria granted by the League of Nations
1923	Birth of the Republic of Turkey.
1923	Treaty of Lausanne: revokes pledge to create an independent Kurdistan, and establishes the modern borders of Turkey, Syria, Iraq, Bulgaria, Egypt and Sudan.
1932	Iraq independence declared.
1935	Persia is renamed Iran.
1939–1945	World War II.
1945	Eryl and Violet Cummings begin decades-long collecting of all known Noah's Ark research, establishing the Cummings Archives, later aligning with the Institute for Creation Research.
1948	Reşit Sarihan (Turkish) claims to discover Ark formation on his farmland near Mahşar, eighteen miles from Mount Ararat.
	The Convention on the Prevention and Punishment of the Crime of Genocide (the Genocide Convention) is adopted by the United Nations General Assembly.
1951	Oliver Crosby (American) forced back from summit of Mount Ararat.
1952	Fernand Navarra (French) summits Mount Ararat.
1954	John Libi (American), ascent of Mount Ararat (again in 1969).
1955	Publication of Navarra's *The Forbidden Mountain*.
1959	Lieutenant A. Kurtis (Turkish), flyover and photo imaging of Ark structure near Mahşar.
1960	Captain Durupinar (Turkish), military photo specialist, reviews Kurtis images, then co-leads an expedition to Mahşar; the area becomes known as the "Durupinar site."

1960	*Life* magazine (USA) publishes a purported image of Noah's Ark near Ararat at Mahşar (Durupinar site).
1963	*The Anatolian Smile*, a film about the Armenian diaspora.
1970	Kurdistan's status as a semi-autonomous state recognized within Iraq but not enacted in law.
	Publication of Violet Cummings's *Noah's Ark: Fact or Fable?* The Cummings Archives give rise to the term "Arkaeology."
1972	John Warwick Montgomery publishes *The Quest for Noah's Ark*, a comprehensive overview of available research, relying heavily on the Cummings Archives and recounting his own ascent in 1970.
1973, 1982, 1983, 1984	Astronaut Col. James Irwin (American), expeditions to Mount Ararat.
1978	Abdullach Öcalan founds rebel PKK (Kurdish Workers' Party) in Turkey, seeking Kurdish independence.
1979	Islamic Revolution in Iran.
1980	Iraq invades Iran.
1982	Publication of Violet Cummings's *Has Anybody Really Seen Noah's Ark?*
1988	Earthquake in Armenia, December 7.
	Iraq–Iran war ends.
1990–99	Mount Ararat "closed" to expeditions.
1990	First USA-led "Iraq War" begins.
1992	Formal establishment of the Kurdistan Regional Government as a semi-autonomous regional state.
1993	Russian Academy of Sciences expedition to the Black Sea, drilling sediment cores.
1997	Australian court case: geologist Dr. Ian Plimer vs. creationist organization Ark Search.

A TIMELINE

1998	Publication of Ryan and Pitman's hypothesis about a Bosporus flood into the Black Sea: *Noah's Flood: The New Scientific Discoveries about the Event that Changed the World*.
1999	PKK's Abdullah Öcalan imprisoned by Turkey's government.
	Robert Ballard (American), "discoverer of the Titanic," mounts National Geographic expedition in search of a possible Great Flood and Black Sea relationship.
2001	Noah's Ark National Park established at Durupinar site, near Uzengili (previously known as Mahşar), by Turkish government.
2002	Durupinar site (Mahşar) claims made by Ronald Wyatt (American) are labeled bogus by former associates and under scrutiny by international media.
2002	Film *Ararat*, written and directed by Atom Egoyan, starring Arsinée Khanjian.
2003	Second USA-led "Iraq War" begins.
2003	Recep Tayyip Erdoğan elected president of Turkey; re-elected 2007, 2011.
2004	Film *Women of Mount Ararat*, directed by Erwann Briand.
2005	Kurdistan (Northern Iraq) with own parliament extends semi-autonomous boundaries
2009	Publication of study (in *Quaternary Science Reviews*) by Liviu Giosan, disputing magnitude of Black Sea rise of water levels post last ice age.
2010	Chinese/Turkish team ascends Mount Ararat, claims discovery of Ark.
2011	Earthquake near Van.
2013	PKK and Turkish government agree to a ceasefire.

Ban on using the Kurdish language is somewhat relaxed to allow the use of W, Q, and Z in personal names.

2014   *Noah*, film starring Russell Crowe, Emma Watson, Anthony Hopkins.

Ark Tablet revealed; publication of *The Ark Before Noah: Decoding the Story of the Flood*, by Irving Finkel.

2015   BBC/Blink Films documentary on replica of round ark: *The Real Noah's Ark*.

Release of the film *1915*, Alec Mouhibian and Garin K. Hovannisian, co-writers/directors.

Play *Women of Ararat*, by Judith Boyajian, performed in Watertown, Massachusetts.

ISIS destroys antiquities at Nimrud.

Pope Francis acknowledges the Armenian genocide as "the first genocide of the 20th century."

PKK and Turkey government 2013 ceasefire is canceled.

October, Erdoğan returned to power with majority in Turkey election.

2016   January, EU foreign affairs chief called for an "immediate ceasefire" in Turkey's Kurdish region where PKK militants and the Turkish army remain in conflict.

February, Kurdistan Security Council announced the arrest of an ISIS "cell" in Erbil, Iraq.

February, Azerbaijan warned of a military option to resolve "the smoldering conflict with Armenia."

February, President Erdoğan threatened Turkey will "open the gates," allowing hundreds of thousands of Syrian refugees through his country and into Europe.

APPENDIX

I take this opportunity to share a few remnants of research.

A residuum: Genealogical charts created from ancient Hebrew texts imply an actual building schedule of 75 to 120 years for Noah's Ark. According to the early math, Noah was (on the speculative calendar) not yet 500 years old when word came down from on high, initiating project timelines including design, sourcing materials, erection, gathering animals, and stowing provisions. Inferred by such extrapolations, Noah would have been 600 years old when floodwaters set his Ark adrift.

While there are no recorded directions to Noah (or Nûh or Utnapishtim or Atrahasis) about building on budget, today's full-sized replicas of Noah's Ark often face financial woes and missed deadlines. Whether motivated by dreams, religion, architectural challenge, or the curiosity of construction, such endeavors give insight into what a replicated Ark might look like. Each differs in appearance, while keeping with the general schematics of common Biblical reference.

In Hong Kong, two billionaire brothers built a full-scale ark in front of the Tsing Ma Bridge and on Ma Wan Channel as the cornerstone for their Noah's Ark theme park, which opened in 2009.

With modern construction equipment and investment of over one million US dollars, Johan's Ark (or Ark van Noach) took three years to complete. It opened to the public in 2012 in Dordrecht, the Netherlands. Johan Huibers conceived it after a nightmare in which a massive flood washed his home country away.

Nearing completion is a full-sized replica as part of Ark Encounters, a themed attraction affiliated with a new Creation Museum in Kentucky. Tagged as the "Hidden Ark," a separate destination attraction is planned for the Miami area.

Visiting one of these, as I did in Hong Kong, brings to mind the challenges of housing what one published estimate put as over 1.5 million species (let alone the invertebrates): "A cow weighs about half a ton; so, for the clean cattle alone, we're talking three and a half tons. Ditto for camels, perhaps three-quarters of a ton for sheep, and half ton for goats. Add in all the marsupials, bison, rhinoceroses, elephants, reptiles, amphibians, birds, and so on, and we quickly exceed sixteen-hundred tons for animals alone." That weight total was absent their feed (or what one presumes a daily throwing overboard of mounting excrement).

In 2014, a scaled-down model in the round design of a coracle was constructed in India, following the Ark Tablet's four-thousand-year-old "blueprint." It leaked.

The concept of preserving existence of life following an earth-destroying catastrophe seldom avoids inferring the story of Noah's Ark. The (inactive) NASA Lunar Ark project contemplates the moon having an outpost as a "sanctuary for civilization." Originators call for "creation of a space age Noah's ark." Separately, the Frozen Ark Project, by the Zoological Society of London with the University of Nottingham, "aims to preserve the DNA and living cells of endangered species to retain the genetic knowledge for the future." And in remote northern Norway, the Svalbard Global Seed Vault is a "secure seed bank to preserve a wide variety of plant seeds that are duplicate samples, or 'spare' copies, of seeds held in gene banks worldwide."

Radically more efficient are efforts to ensure humanity's ability to survive a scourge, bringing the "Ark" connotation new meaning. The Smithsonian Institution and partners have the Global Genome Initiative, which includes 200,000 samples of "tissue extracted from a living thing somewhere in the world" in the Natural History Museum's collection. The goal is five million vials with "DNA that holds the key to each species' unique identity," creating the "largest museum–based biorepository."

ACKNOWLEDGEMENTS

Books are hybrid creations, brought about with the ideas and collaboration—sometimes unwitting—from many interested and caring individuals. This work benefited from the early guidance of mentor and editor John Eerkes-Medrano, who passed away suddenly and with parts of this manuscript-in-progress on his desk. Dania Sheldon has been permissions editor and a believer in where this book was going, helping with many images that were difficult to source and being a trusted sounding board on matters of content and approach. Cory Allyn of Skyhorse Publishing has been the book's editor, patiently shaping and nudging it toward publication, always insightful, often inspiring—ever remindful of the eventual reader's needs and expectations. Those three have their fingerprints on this work, and I am indebted to each.

I have learned much and gained greatly from those who read the manuscript in part or in whole during various stages, and among these are Darren Johner, Karen von Muehldorfer, Jon Hutchison, Jess Ketchum, Dean Peter Elliott, Scott Wayne, and Paula Salloum. Some of those mentioned in the book took a helpful look at sections involving their names and those include Dr. Jonathan Taylor, Tigran Zargaryan, Taha, and Andam Jabbar. My expedition mates (Ian Moffat, Goran Jovanovic, Patricia Ristich, Charles Crockatt, and Nicholas (Nico) Vanderstoop) were each offered the opportunity to review the chapters about our time together for their comfort and corroboration. I was in touch with Zafer, wanting to know about his planned drilling at the Durupinar site, and initially he was open to sharing an update but then went silent, repeatedly so. At a crucial stage in this book's development I met pale-ontologist Dr. Susan Turner, of Australia, who proved to be a wealth of advice, as has been Theresa Jackson, International Studies Department, University of North Carolina, Wilmington. I did my best to meet the heightened expectations that came for the book from each of those indi-viduals, and where it falls short, the responsibility rests with the author alone.

I thank Garry Marchant, one of a rare breed who've made a success-ful lifelong career of travel-related writing, published around the globe, for his foreword to this book.

Eric Leinberger is an extraordinary mapmaker, and I thank him for creating each map herein to tell a story. Simon Carr's Ark Comparison Chart and individual portraits are impressive additions. Photographer Don Waite patiently ensured all images were converted into workable quality for publication. This is the third book of mine these three have accented with their professionalism, and I thank them.

I'm grateful to my agent Robert Mackwood, principal of Seventh Avenue Literary Agency, who brought about my relationship with Sky-horse Publishing for this and two earlier books, as well as one in the future.

There's the "Antonson focus group" as well: my brother, Brian, and sons, Brent and Sean, with whom I bounce around endless questions or avenues I'm exploring—about everything from the book's title to writ-ing challenges to various iterations of the maps, always receiving crisp responses and judgment; I'd not want to embark on a writing project without them. My wife Janice fashioned a wonderful writing space for me in Australia (and until she read an early draft of the manuscript, did not know how long it took me to find someone to read Taha's letter . . .); her encouragement on all things book-related has been pivotal to its eventual completion.

Any errors, omissions, or conflicts of hypotheses are my own respon-sibility—let them encourage others toward more research.

ABOUT THE AUTHOR

The author amid the ruins of Ishak Pasha Palace. Portrait © Simon Carr.

Rick Antonson is the author of *To Timbuktu for a Haircut: A Journey Through West Africa* and *Route 66 Still Kicks: Driving America's Main Street*. He is co-author of *Slumach's Gold: In Search of a Legend*, the story behind the Pitt Lake lost gold mine featured in Discovery Channel and Animal Planet's television series *Curse of the Frozen Gold*. He has served as president and CEO of Tourism Vancouver; chair of the board for the Destination Marketing Association International, based in Washington, DC; deputy chair for the Pacific Asia Tourism Association, based in Bangkok, Thailand; and president of Pacific Coast Public Television Association, aligned with PBS affiliate KCTS in Seattle. He has traveled extensively with his wife, Janice. In five trips over a dozen years, Rick and his sons Brent (author, *Of Russia: A Year Inside*) and Sean have circumnavigated the northern hemisphere by train. He recently hiked the Kokoda Track in Papua New Guinea. Rick has spoken internationally about the concept of Cathedral Thinking. He holds an Honorary Doctorate of Laws from Capilano University, Vancouver. Rick and his wife make their homes in Vancouver, Canada, and in Cairns, Australia. www.rickantonson.com

SOURCES AND RECOMMENDED READING

Balsiger, Dave, and Charles E. Sellier, Jr. *In Search of Noah's Ark*. Los Angeles: Sun Classic Books, 1976.

Bell, Brian and Melissa Shales, Editors. *Turkey, Insight Guide*. London, 2009.

Berlitz, Charles. *The Lost Ship of Noah: In Search of the Ark at Ararat*. New York: G. P. Putnam's Sons, 1987.

Bonomi, Joseph. *Nineveh and its Palaces: The Discoveries of Botta and Layard, Applied to the Elucidation of Holy Writ*. London: Third Edition, H. G. Bohn1857; Elibron Classics reprint, 1999.

Carrington, Richard. *A Million Years of Man*. New York: World Press, 1963.

Casson, Lionel. *Libraries in the Ancient World*. New Haven: Yale University Press, 2001.

Cline, Eric H. *From Eden to Exile; Unraveling Mysteries of the Bible*. Washington: National Geographic, 2007.

Corbin, B. J., ed. *The Explorers of Ararat: And the Search for Noah's Ark*. Long Beach: GCI Books, 1999.

Cornuke, Robert, and David Halbrook. *In Search of the Lost Mountains of Noah: The Discovery of the Real Mts. of Ararat*. Nashville: Broadman & Homan Publishers, 2001.

Cummings, Violet. *Has Anybody Really Seen Noah's Ark?* San Diego: Creation-Life Publishers, 1982.

_____. *Noah's Ark: Fact or Fable?* San Diego: Creation-Science Research Center, 1972.

Damrosch, David. *The Buried Book: The Loss and Rediscovery of the Great Epic of Gilgamesh*. New York: Henry Holt and Company, 2007.

Dobbs, Kildare. *Away from Home: Canadian Writers in Exotic Places*. Toronto: Deneau Publishers, 1985.

Fagan, Brian M. *Return to Babylon; Travelers, Archaeologists, and Monuments in Mesopotamia* (Revised Edition). Boulder, CO: University Press of Colorado, 2007.

Finkel, Irving. *The Ark Before Noah: Decoding the Story of the Flood*. London: Hodder & Stoughton, 2014.

Finkel, Irving, and Jonathan Taylor. *Cuneiform*. London: British Museum Press, 2015.

Frost, Robert. *In the Clearing*. New York: Holt, Rinehart and Winston, 1962.

Hovhannisyan, Nikolay. *The Armenian Genocide*. Yerevan, Armenia: Republic of Armenia, National Academy of Sciences Institute of Oriental Studies, 2002.

Hovhannisian, Sen. *Armenia Ararat*. Yerevan, Armenia: Publishing House NAHAPET, 2008.

Irwin, James B. and Monte Unger. *More than an Ark on Ararat*. Nashville: Broadman Press, 1985.

Jwaideh, Wadie. *The Kurdish National Movement, Its Origins and Development*. New York: Syracuse University Press, 2003.

Kanner, Rebecca. *Sinners and The Sea; The Untold Story of Noah's Wife*. New York: Howard Books, Simon & Shuster, Inc., 2013.

Keller, Werner. *The Bible as History; Digging up the Bible*. La Vergne, TN: BN Publishing, 2008.

Khachikyan, Armen. *History of Armenia*. Yerevan, Armenia: Edit Print, 2010.

Kissinger, Henry. *World Order*. New York: Penguin, 2014.

Hazleton, Lesley. *The First Muslim; The Story of Muhammad*. London: Atlantic Books, 2013.

La Haye, Tim, and John Morris. *The Ark on Ararat*. New York: Thomas Nelson, 1976.

Larsen, Mogens Trolle. *The Conquest of Assyria; Excavations in an Antique Land 1840–1860*. London: Routledge, 1996.

Layard, Austen Henry. *Discoveries in the Ruins of Nineveh and Babylon with Travels in Armenia, Kurdistan and the Desert*. London: John Murray, 1853. Reprint. London: Elibron Classics, 2005.

_____. *Nineveh and its Remains*. London: John Murray, 1882. Reprint. Guilford, CT: The Lyons Press, 2001.

Lemkin, Raphael. *Raphael Lemkin's Dossier on the Armenian Genocide*. Glendale, CA: Center for Armenian Remembrance, 2008.

Lightman, Alan. *The Accidental Universe; The World You Thought You Knew*. New York: Vintage Books, 2013.

Maine, David. *The Preservationist*. New York: St Martin's Press, 2004.

Mandeville, John. *The Travels of Sir John Mandeville; The Fantastic 14th-Century Account of a Journey to the East*. Mineola, NY: Dover Publications, Inc. 2006. First published, London, Macmillan and Co., Limited, 1900.

Melikian, Danielle. *Armenia, From Centuries to Eternity*. Yerevan, Armenia: Vahagn Melikian Family, 2011.

Mitchell, Stephen, trans. *Gilgamesh*. London: Profile Books, 2004.

Montgomery, John Warwick. *The Quest for Noah's Ark*. Minneapolis: Dimension Books, 1974.

Navai, Ramita. *City of Lies: Love, Sex, Death and the Search for Truth in Tehran*. London: Weidenfeld & Nicolson, 2014.

Navarra, Fernand. *The Forbidden Mountain*. London: MacDonald & Co., 1956.

_____. *Noah's Ark: I Touched It*. Plainfield, NJ: Logos International, 1974.

Parrot, André. *The Flood and Noah's Ark*. London: SCM Press, 1955.

Parrot, Friedrich, and W. D. Cooley. *Journey to Ararat (1859)*. New York: Harper & Brothers, 1859.

Plimer, Ian. *Telling Lies for God: Reason vs. Creationism*. Sydney: Random House Australia, 1994.

Robertson, Geoffrey. *An Inconvenient Genocide: Who Now Remembers the Armenians?* Sydney: Random House Australia, 2014.

Ryan, William, and Walter Pitman. *Noah's Flood: The New Scientific Discoveries about the Event that Changed the World.* New York: Simon & Schuster, 1998.

Salter, James. *Solo Faces.* Boston: Little, Brown and Company, 1979.

Shockey, Don. *Agri-Dagh (Mount Ararat): The Painful Mountain.* Ringgold, GA: TEACH Services, 2006.

Thomas, Lisa, Editorial Director. *Strange But True.* Washington: National Geographic Society, 2015.

Thorne, T. K. *Noah's Wife, 5500 BCE.* Springville, AL: Blackburn Fork Publishing, 2009.

Trip, Charles. *A History of Iraq.* Cambridge: Cambridge University Press, 2007.

Wells, Carveth. *Kapoot: The Narrative of a Journey from Leningrad to Mount Ararat in Search of Noah's Ark.* New York: National Travel Club, 1933.

Westerman, Frank. *Ararat: In Search of the Mythical Mountain.* London: Random House, 2010.

Wilson, Ian. *Before the Flood: The Biblical Flood as a Real Event and How it Changed the Course of Civilization.* New York: St. Martin's Griffin, 2004.

In the Internet-enabled world, desktop research has become akin to a nearly untraceable game of hopscotch wherein one seeks background information and jumps from offered source to related topics and on to appealing side notes, all without ever returning, or tracking, the educational journey. I am one who has done that and garnered many insights and ideas and corroborated concepts which are reflected in this book, though the exact sources are so many that it would require pages of website listings to account for them, so they are not shown. However, on any topic of interest from this book, one can be assured of exceptional sources for both the matters identified and contrarian views, debates, and counterpoints, all enjoyably provided through any search mechanism.

CREDITS AND PERMISSIONS

Images

All maps © Eric Leinberger and Rick Antonson

page xiv: 19th-century line drawing of Mt Ararat. From Alexander Mac-Donald, *The Land of Ararat; or, Up the Roof of the World: By a Special Correspondent*, published 1893. Courtesy of the British Library.

Foreword, page xviii: Photograph of Khor Virap courtesy of Andrew S. Behesnilian.

Chapter 1: The Forbidden Mountain

page 9: Photograph of Mount Ararat and lesser Ararat © and courtesy of Wojciech Ogrodowczyk.

page 17: Cuneiform tablet recording the allocation of beer. ©The Trustees of the British Museum. All rights reserved.

page 19: The Flood Tablet. ©The Trustees of the British Museum. All rights reserved.

Chapter 3: Whirling Dervish

page 48: Whirling dervishes photograph courtesy of Wikimedia Commons, photographer Schorle.

Chapter 4: The Van Gölü Express

page 62: Courtyard of the palace of Sargon II: Hero, called "Gilgamesh", taming a lion. Ca. 710 BCE. Limestone. 4.5 x 1.88 x 0.22 m. AO19861. Photo: Thierry Ollivier. Musée du Louvre, Paris, France.

page 66: Image of Friedrich Parrot courtesy of the Manuscripts and Rare Books Department of the Tartu University Library, Estonia.

Chapter 5: Women of Ararat

page 82: Kurdish woman fighter. Photograph reproduced by permission of Flickr member BijiKurdistan.

page 83: Kurdish woman fighter with dove. Photograph reproduced by permission of Flickr member BijiKurdistan.

Chapter 6: Turkish Honeycomb

page 91: The Ark Tablet. Photograph copyright Guardian News & Media Ltd. 2015. Reproduced with permission.

page 92: Photograph of modern-day coracle courtesy of Sreeraj PS.

page 93: Photograph of the round ark replica © Kuni Takahashi. Used with permission.

Chapter 7: Taking Tea with Van Cats

page 103: Painting of Noah's ark, by Simon de Myle (fl. 1570), "Noah's Ark on Mount Ararat"; oil on panel; private collection in southern France. Image courtesy of Wikimedia Commons.

Chapter 14: The Lost Ship of Noah

page 204: Photograph of Ishak Pasha Palace courtesy of Wikimedia Commons, photographer Attaliev.

page 207: Photograph of Durupınar courtesy of John Dawson, www.lakedistrictwalks.com.

Chapter 16: The Buried Book

page 246: Illustration: Reconstruction of the north-eastern facade of Sennacherib's (681 BCE) palace (Kouyunijik). Assyrian. From Austen Layard Discoveries in the Ruins of Nineveh and Babylon, London, 1853. / Universal History Archive/UIG / Bridgeman Images.

371

Chapter 18: The Trans-Asia Express

page 311: Photograph of the Cyrus Cylinder. ©The Trustees of the British Museum. All rights reserved.

Chapter 20: Mother of the World

page 330: Ambassador Morgenthau's telegram courtesy of the National Archives and Records Administration of the United States.

page 332: President Wilson's letter of appeal to the American people. Photograph courtesy of the Mathers Museum of World Cultures, Indiana University.

page 333: Armenian orphans at the gates of Alexandropol. Photograph courtesy of the Near East Relief Historical Society, Near East Foundation collection, Rockefeller Archive Center.

Trip Images

Goran Jovanovic's photographs appear on pages 135, 136, 137, 144, 153, 163, 171, 178, 180, 191 and 196. Kubi took the one on page 157, and Brent Antonson's photograph is on page 338. The photograph on page 345 is by Photo Vage, photovage@hotmail.com. All others are from the author. Image on page 24 sourced through Taha Jabbar.

Texts

Translations of the Bible, unless otherwise indicated, are from the King James Version, reproduced in the United Kingdom with the permission of Cambridge University Press.

The following translations are from the Holy Bible, New International Version®, NIV®. Copyright © 1973, 1978, 1984, 2011 by Biblica, Inc.™ Used by permission of Zondervan. All rights reserved worldwide. www.zondervan.com. The "NIV" and "New International Version" are trademarks registered in the United States Patent and Trademark Office by Biblica, Inc.™: pages 182–183, the quotation beginning "So Noah came out . . .," which is from Genesis 8:18–22; page 196, the quotation beginning "Never again will the waters . . .," which is from

372

Genesis 9:15; page 211, the quotation beginning "The sons of Noah . . .," which is from Genesis 9:18–19.

Translations of the Koran (Qur'an) are from *The Koran*, trans. N. J. Dawood, 4th rev. ed. (London: Penguin, 1974). Reproduced with permission.

Translations of the Epic of Gilgamesh are reprinted with the permission of Profile Books (UK) and of Simon & Schuster, Inc., from *Gilgamesh* by Stephen Mitchell. Copyright © 2004 by Stephen Mitchell. All rights reserved.

page xv: Cuneiform characters courtesy of Joe McCormack at virtualsecrets.com.

page xv: Arabic text is from the Qur'an, 11:44.

page xv: Hebrew text of Genesis 8:4 is from the Westminster Leningrad Codex, provided without restriction by the J. Alan Groves Center for Advanced Biblical Research.

Chapter 1: The Forbidden Mountain

Epigraph, page 1: From Oliver S. Crosby, "Demavend and Ararat, 1951," courtesy of the American Alpine Club Journal, published in 1954.

page 8: "God paid mind . . ." Reprinted from the Tanakh: The Holy Scriptures. Copyright 1985 by the Jewish Publication Society, Philadelphia.

page 14: footnote 4, quotation reproduced by permission of Douglas Todd.

Chapter 2: The Bosporus Strait

Epigraph, page 28: From Jenna Millman, Bryan Taylor, and Lauren Effron, "Evidence Noah's Biblical Flood Happened, Says Robert Ballard," courtesy of ABC News.

page 35: "then burst all the well-springs . . ." Reprinted from the Tanakh: The Holy Scriptures. Copyright 1985 by the Jewish Publication Society, Philadelphia.

Chapter 6: Turkish Honeycomb

page 84: Epigraph. From "Irving Finkel: Reader of the Lost Ark," by Tom Chivers. © Telegraph Media Group Limited 2014.

page 93: Excerpt from *The Ark Before Noah*, by Irving Finkel, 2014, Hodder & Stoughton, London, courtesy of Hachette Books Ireland.

page 95: Excerpts from D. Longuinoff, "Ascension de l'Ararat," published in the *Bulletin de la Societe de Geographie* for 1851. Extrait du *"Bulletin de la Société de Géographie"* (Paris), 4ème série, Tome I, 1851.

Chapter 11: Final Ascent

Epigraph, page 166: From Bryce, James. *Transcaucasia and Ararat, Being Notes of a Vacation Tour in the Autumn*. (Original work published 1896) Reprint. London: Forgotten Books, 2013.

page 182: "The cornea doesn't get as much oxygen . . ." is quoted from Jennifer Byrne, "'Extreme sport' patients present specific set of visual needs," *Primary Care Optometry News*, September 2003.

Chapter 12: Walking Bones

Epigraph, page 184: From H.W. Tillman, *Two Mountains and a River*, 1949, Cambridge University Press.

Chapter 18: The Trans-Asia Express

Epigraph, page 294: From British Museum, "The British Museum lends the Cyrus Cylinder to the National Museum of Iran," press release, September 10, 2010. http://www.britishmuseum.org/about_us/news_and_press/press_releases/2010/cyrus_cylinder_loan.aspx.

page 311: From Neil MacGregor's TED talk "2600 Years of History in One Object," presented at TED2012. Quoted with the permission of TED. The transcript of the entire talk is available at https://www.ted.com/talks/neil_macgregor_2600_years_of_history_in_one_object/transcript?language=en.

pages 320–321: Excerpts from Robert S. Strother, "The Great Good Luck of Mr. Smith," *Saudi Aramco World* 22.1 (1971). Courtesy of *Saudi Aramco World.*

Chapter 20: Mother of the World

Epigraph, page 325: The letter from Leslie Davis to Henry Morgenthau is in the public domain, as it was written as part of Davis's official duties for the United States government. It is held in the US Department of State archives. NA/RG59/867.4016/269. *United States Official Records on The Armenian Genocide* 1915–1917. Compiled with an Introduction by Ara Sarafian, London, 2004, pp. 461–462.

Afterword: Begin Again

page 349: From Henry Kissinger, *World Order*, Penguin, 2014. Reproduced with permission of Penguin USA and Penguin UK.

INDEX

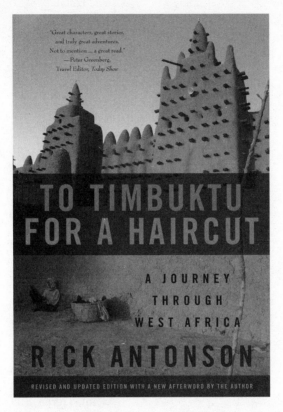

"In the magical-travel-names department, Timbuktu undoubtedly holds the trump card—Marrakesh, Kathmandu, or Zanzibar are mere runners-up—but Rick Antonson's trek to the fabled desert city proves that dreamtime destinations are found in our minds just as much as on our maps."

—Tony Wheeler, co-founder of Lonely Planet
and author of *Bad Lands: A Tourist on the Axis of Evil*

"Great characters, great stories, and truly great adventures. Not to mention . . . a great read."

—Peter Greenberg, Travel Editor, *CBS News*

"The remarkable combination of Rick Antonson exploring the ancient mysteries of Timbuktu matched with the rich culture of Mali that he captures so well . . . makes a page-turner from start to finish. Rick's underlying story confirms my own experience in that amazing land."

—Jerry W. Bird, editor, *Africa Travel Magazine*

Timbuktu's most famous landmarks are three mosques. This minaret has been often remudded since its creation hundreds of years ago. The mosques have been cited as "unique earthen architecture."

Touch a Map of the World

WHEN I WAS A BOY, EVERY OCCASION MY FATHER left the house was important. I and my older brother would pester him: "Where are you going, Daddy? Where? To work? To church? To the store?" And in the vernacular of the day, or perhaps with a flippancy meant to silence us, he would say what I believed to be the truth: "I'm going to Timbuktu to get my hair cut."

So began my own feeble notions of travel. With the irrefutable logic of a child, I understood that one day I, too, must go to Timbuktu and get my hair cut. After all, how far could it be?

Fifty years later, a world away, I walked a path among mud homes as old as time, baked by a dry heat that choked my breathing. It was impossible to tell the sand from the dust unless you stood on it. A young boy was setting up a chair with a missing leg in front of his parents' house. Sand piled by the doorway, nudged there by desert winds that pushed relentlessly through these village streets. His left foot suddenly slipped over the edge of the path's centre ditch. The slip almost caused him to fall into the shallow sewer. He noticed me as he regained his balance, and I stopped and looked into his eyes. We were only a metre apart. The youngster, maybe five years old, stared down my greeting. His eyes widened in a glare of determination. He crossed his dusty arms and clasped each defiant shoulder with a scraped hand. Sand and drool encrusted his lips in loose granules. The rose colour of his tongue showed and he did not smile. I felt like the first white man he'd ever seen, and not a welcome visitor. His face proclaimed his proud independence. He knew that whatever had lured me to travel there was hollow. But he did not know that I was looking for a shop where I could get my hair cut.

It was my wife's idea. I had time available for being away the coming January, all of it, and Janice didn't. For half a year we'd talked about my taking a solo journey. But her interest began to fade when the topic of "What *I'll* do" reared its head. We were in Prague to hear the International Olympic Committee's decision naming the host destination for the 2010 Olympic Winter Games. My colleagues and I had launched Canada's Vancouver-Whistler bid six years earlier and were now part of the Canadian delegation. Janice and I arrived in the Czech Republic two days in advance, near midnight. In search of a late dinner, we walked on the cobblestones of the Charles Bridge, looking into the dark waters that flowed beneath. The roadway led us to an open but near-empty restaurant, where our lives were unexpectedly changed within minutes. While waiting for our grilled chicken over pasta we talked about *the bid* and then anything but *the bid.*

My wont at such times was to compile a mental list of projects I could accomplish within a month. Friends had suggested everything from a long walk to a short sailing voyage; my family advised a month's vow of silence in a Tibetan monastery. It must change you, people said; you'll come back better for the time away. Whatever you do, don't stay home and do chores.

Our wine arrived before the meal, and without any preamble, I said to Janice, somewhat desperately, "It's only six months away. I've got to pick something to do and start getting ready!"

Her eyes clouded. A pause stilled the air. Exasperated, she finally said across the table: "Why don't you just go to Timbuktu."

Stunned by the perfection of her suggestion, my head jerked. I could feel my lungs fill with oxygen. "Brilliant," I said. My heart took stag leaps. "Absolutely brilliant." We looked at one another. Janice sipped her red wine, unsure of what she had wrought.

"I'm going to Timbuktu," I committed, so profound was the image. "Just as soon as I find out where it is."

Touch a map of the world. Move your hand to Africa. Press a finger to unfamiliar West African names like Benin, Togo, Burkina Faso. Look north, above Ouagadougou, to the nation of Mali, and there, near the River Niger, find the most ethereal of names, Timbuktu.

It is easier to point out countries of terror and despair, of dictators and abusers. The facts of sub-Saharan Africa are awful, the past mired in exaggerations, the future one of faint hope. Perhaps we understand Africa only marginally better than those who, in the not too distant past, hid their geographic ignorance by filling in the uncharted voids on their maps with sketches of fantastic monsters.

To exploration-mad societies like France and England in the eighteenth and nineteenth centuries, Timbuktu lay at the unknown edges of cartography. Its sheer unassailability challenged even their most intrepid travellers. It acquired such an aura that even today many people believe Timbuktu is fictitious. It is assuredly not.

Our globe's most exotically named travel destination is rooted in the language of Berber, though it has been distorted to the point that only myth explains its genesis. I've found it commonly written as *Timbuctoo*, *Tombooctoo* or *Tombuctou*, *Tombouktou*, and less often *Tumbyktu*, *Tembuch*, *Tombuto*, *Timkitoo* or *Tambuta*, as well as the word used here: *Timbuktu*. The most frequently used label is the French, *Tombouctou*, which one finds on Mali maps and postcards.

In Tuareg folklore, the place began with an old woman who looked after the nomads' well when the men went trading or hunting. Tuareg Imashagan, desert people, first set camp in Timbuktu around A.D. 1000. Their well, *tin* in Berber lingo, provided water that was free of the illnesses they contracted nearer the River Niger, where they grazed camels and cattle on the burgo grass, and it became their preferred spot. As summer annually gave way to autumn's temperate rains, these nomads moved on and left their goods in care of the old woman, commonly referred to as *Bouctou*, which translates as "woman with the large navel." It was her well, and thus her name, that became renowned. The linking of proprietress and place formed "TinBouctou." *Timbuktu*, one of the world's finest names, is "the well of the lady with the big belly button."